Case Grammar Applied

Summer Institute of Linguistics and
The University of Texas at Arlington
Publications in Linguistics

Publication 127

Publications in Linguistics is a series published jointly by the Summer Institute of Linguistics and the University of Texas at Arlington. The series is a venue for works covering a broad range of topics in linguistics, especially the analytical treatment of minority languages from all parts of the world. While most volumes are authored by members of the Institute, suitable works by others will also form part of the series.

Series Editor

Mildred L. Larson
Summer Instituteof Linguistics

Volume Editors

Marilyn Mayers
Bonnie Brown

Production Staff

Eugene Loos, Managing Editor
Laurie Nelson, Production Manager, Compositor
Hazel Shorey, Graphic Arts

Case Grammar Applied

Walter A. Cook, S.J.

A Publication of
The Summer Institute of Linguistics
and
The University of Texas at Arlington

©1998 by the Summer Institute of Linguistics, Inc.
Library of Congress Catalog No: 97-62075
ISBN: 1-55671-046-1
ISSN: 1040-0850

Printed in the United States of America
All Rights Reserved

08 07 06 05 04 03 02 01 00 99   10 9 8 7 6 5 4 3 2 1

Copies of this and other publications of the Summer Institute of Linguistics may be obtained from

International Academic Bookstore
Summer Institute of Linguistics
7500 W. Camp Wisdom Rd.
Dallas, TX 75236-5699

Voice: 972-708-7404
Fax: 972-708-7433
Email: academic_books@sil.org
Internet: http://www.sil.org

Contents

Preface xi

1 Case Grammar Theory 1

1.1–1.3 Case Grammar goals
1.1. Case structure 1
1.2. Case lexicon 2
1.3. Case systems 3

1.4–1.6 Logical structure
1.4. The proposition 5
1.5. Predicate 7
1.6. Argument 9

1.7–1.9 Case roles.
1.7. The nature of case roles 10
1.8. Case inventory 12
1.9. Subject choice hierarchy 18

1.10–1.12 Case frames
1.10. Preliminaries to case assignment 20
1.11. Case tactics 24
1.12. The revised Case Grammar matrix 25

1.13–1.15 Derivation
1.13. Existence of related predicates. 28
1.14. Bidirectional derivation 29
1.15. Lexical decomposition 31

1.16–1.19 Covert case roles
1.16. Deletable roles 38
1.17. Coreferential roles 40
1.18. Lexicalized roles 41
1.19. Where is the Theme? 43

1.20–1.22 Methodology
1.20. Text analysis procedures 45
1.21. Conceptual graphs 46
1.22. Case Grammar and conceptual graphs 51

1.23. Conclusion. 52

2 The Basic Domain 55

2.1–2.2 Basic State verbs
2.1. State with single Os 57
2.2. State with double Os. 66

2.3–2.4 Basic Process verbs
2.3. Process with single O 69
2.4 Process with double O 77

2.5–2.9 Basic Action verbs
2.5. Action with A=O coreference. 78
2.6. Action with O-lexicalized. 81
2.7. Action with both roles overt 82
2.8. Action with double O 88
2.9. Action with double Agent 89

3 The Experiential Domain 91

3.1–3.3 State Experiential verbs
3.1. Experiential state with E-subject 93
3.2. Experiential state with Os subject 105
3.3. Experiential state with double Os 112

3.4–3.5 Process Experiential verbs
3.4. Experiential process with E-subject. 113
3.5. Experiential process with O-subject 115

3.6–3.9 Action Experiential verbs
3.6. With A=E coreference 119
3.7. With A=O coreference 121
3.8. With O-lexicalized 122
3.9. With all roles overt. 122

4 The Benefactive Domain 127

4.1–4.2 State Benefactive verbs
4.1. State with B-subject 129
4.2. State with Os subject 133

4.3–4.4 Process Benefactive verbs
4.3. Process with B-subject 135
4.4. Process with O subject 136

4.5–4.7 Action Benefactive verbs
4.5. Action with A=B coreference 137
4.6. Action with O-lexicalized 138
4.7. Action with all roles overt 139

5 The Locative Domain 143

5.1–5.2 State Locative verbs
5.1. With O-subject (Os,L). 146
5.2. State with L-subject (L,Os) 156

5.3–5.4 Process Locative verbs
5.3. Process with O-subject (O,L). 159
5.4. With L-subject (L,O) 162

5.5–5.10 Action Locative verbs
5.5. Action with A=O coreference (A,*O,L /A=O). 165
5.6. Action with A=L coreference (A=L,O) 170
5.7. Action with O-lexicalized (A,*O,L) 170
5.8. Action with L-lexicalized (A,O,*L /L-lex) 173
5.9. Action with all roles overt (A,O,L) 174
5.10. Double Agent verbs 181

6 The Modality 183
6.1 Auxiliaries as main verbs 183
6.2. Neutralization of the perfect. 184

6.3–6.5 Tense and aspect

6.3. Nonprogressive tenses (States and events) 186
6.4. Progressive tenses (Events only) 190
6.5. Habitual tenses (Events only) 193

6.6–6.11 Modal verbs

6.6. Epistemic modals. 198
6.7. Root modals 201
6.8. Ability modal 203
6.9. Epistemic modals with tense. 204
6.10. Root modals with tense 205
6.11. Ability modal with tense. 207

6.12–6.13 Negation

6.12. Negation of propositions. 208
6.13. Negation with modals 208

6.14–6.19 Logical structure

6.14. Performative layer 211
6.15. Tense-Aspect-Modal layer 212
6.16. Propositional layer 213
6.17. Noun phrase modification 214
6.18. Parsing with Case Grammar 214
6.19. Knowledge representation 219

7 Verb Ontology 221

7.1–7.3 The Basic domain

7.1. Class 1: Basic State. 223
7.2. Class 2: Basic Process. 225
7.3. Class 3: Basic Action 226

7.4–7.6 The Experiential domain

7.4. Class 4: State Experiential. 229
7.5 Class 5: Process Experiential 231
7.6. Class 6: Action Experiential 232

7.7–7.9 The Benefactive domain

7.7. Class 7: State Benefactive 234
7.8. Class 8: Process Benefactive 235
7.9. Class 9: Action Benefactive 236

7.10–7.12 The Locative domain

7.10. Class 10: State Locative 238
7.11 Class 11: Process Locatives 240
7.12. Class 12: Action Locative 241

7.13. Conclusion 244

Alphabetical Lexicon 247

Case Lexicon 253

References 261

Index 267

Preface

In a recent work, *Case Grammar Theory* (1989), I attempted to present the history of Case Grammar in terms of the various models proposed within case theory. These models included Charles Fillmore (1968, 1971, 1977), Wallace Chafe (1970), John Anderson (1971), the thematic relations of Jeffrey Gruber (1976), and Ray Jackendoff (1972, 1976, 1990), and the applications within tagmemics as developed by John Platt (1971), Austin Hale (1974), Robert Longacre (1976), and Kenneth and Evelyn Pike (1977). Each of these models was examined with respect to their (1) deep structure, (2) list of cases used, (3) organization into case frames, (4) derivational systems, and (5) covert case roles. This work concluded with the exposition of the Case Grammar Matrix Model, using the better insights of the models described.

The Case Grammar Model has been recommended for use in natural language processing by leading computational linguists. Terry Winograd, in *Language as a Cognitive Process,* states, "Case structure can be used as a way of representing the underlying structure of sentences, and can be filled in by whatever computations can be made to work" (1983:323). John Sowa, in *Conceptual Structures,* adds, "Case grammar had a strong influence on Artificial Intelligence because it provided a convenient set of labels for conceptual relations" (1984:223), useful in Sowa's conceptual graphs. James Allen, in *Natural Language Understanding,* adds, "Significant generalizations can be made concerning how noun phrases are semantically related to verbs and adjectives in a sentence. The most influential work for computational approaches has been Case Grammar and its successors and modifications" (1987:196).

The present work, *Case Grammar Applied,* is devoted to the application of the Case Grammar Matrix Model to English text analysis. Terry Winograd, while stating the usefulness of Case Grammar in computational systems that deal with a limited domain, regrets that "there has never been a large scale satisfactory coverage of English verbs" (1983:324). The value of Case Grammar in text analysis remains merely speculative unless researchers can provide a comprehensive analysis of the meaning of verbs in actual contexts. The object of the present work is to present Case Grammar analysis in depth, referring to illustrations in the Case Grammar literature and to many examples developed over the past twenty years, especially from the analysis of some five thousand clauses in Ernest Hemingway's *The Old Man and the Sea.*

Chapter 1 deals with the revised Case Grammar Matrix Model, including broader definitions of the cases and the comparison of localist systems such as Thematic Relations and nonlocalist systems such as the Matrix Model. The relation between Case Grammar and conceptual graphs is also explained.

Chapter 2 deals with the Basic domain that includes all State, Process, and Action verbs which use only the Agent and Object cases. This domain excludes all verbs which require an Experiencer, a Benefactive, or a Locative case in their descriptions.

Chapter 3 deals with the Experiential domain, the domain of sensation, emotion, cognition, and communication. It describes State, Process, and Action verbs which include an Experiencer case.

Chapter 4 deals with the Benefactive domain, the domain of possession and transfer of property, and describes State, Process, and Action verbs which include a Benefactive case.

Chapter 5 deals with the Locative domain, the domain of physical location and movement, and describes State, Process, and Action verbs that include a Locative case.

Chapter 6, "The Modality," deals with other elements involved in the logical representation of sentences, including tense, aspect, modals, performatives, and negatives, showing how these elements may be included in the logical structure, and ending with a sample sentence parse using Case Grammar.

Chapter 7, "Verb Ontology," summarizes the analysis of the more than 500 examples in chapters 2 through 5 and demonstrates the verbal hierarchy expressed by the twelve cells of the Case Grammar Matrix, organized by verbal domain, verb type, and argument structure. Each of the verb types is described together with its conceptual graph, its frequency of occurrence, its subtypes, and its defining characteristics.

The appendix to the text contains an alphabetical lexicon, listing all of the verbs in the examples together with their case frames, and a case lexicon, with the verbs sorted by case frame together with references for each verb to the pages where the use of the verb is exemplified.

Acknowledgement is due to all those students who, in Case Grammar seminars at Georgetown University over twenty years, contributed to the analysis and discussion of the clauses in the Hemingway text. As with students always, they inevitably taught me while I was teaching them.

1
Case Grammar Theory

1.1–1.3 Case Grammar goals

Case Grammar is a semantic valence system that describes the logical form of a sentence in terms of a central predicate and a series of case-labelled arguments. Case Grammar does not deal with surface cases such as nominative and accusative; it deals with the meaning behind these cases. Case Grammar is not a grammar, it deals only with the semantic level of a grammar, and within semantics it deals only with the inner structure of a single clause. It does not deal directly with tense, mood, aspect, or negation. It does not deal directly with the interconnection of clauses. As a semantic interpretation system that is universal across languages, it is not tied to the syntax of any particular language.

Case Grammar has two goals. One deals with the semantic level of a grammar, the other deals with the formation of the lexicon. For the grammar, Case Grammar provides a method for sentence semantics which describes the meaning underlying each simple sentence; for the lexicon, Case Grammar provides a method for further defining each sense of each verb in terms of semantic cases.

1.1. Case structure

The first step in semantic analysis is to extract the predicate (verb or predicate adjective) which is the key to the logical structure. The second step is to determine the number of arguments required by the predicate

1

which is extracted. The third step is to assign case labels to the arguments required by that predicate. The predicate can then be defined in terms of its full complement of case roles.

Long before the advent of Case Grammar, logicians were describing simple sentences in terms of predicate and arguments. Predicates were defined as one-place (monadic), two-place (dyadic), or three-place (triadic) predicates. Sentences (1)–(3) illustrate the logical notation for monadic, dyadic, and triadic predicates. The predicate is placed in initial position, followed by the required arguments, in order, enclosed in parentheses.

(1)   The old man /died.   one-place
      DIE (man)

(2)   John /enjoyed /the show.   two-place
      ENJOY (John, show)

(3)   Bill /told /Mary /the story.   three-place
      TELL (Bill, Mary, story)

Case Grammar is built upon this essential predicate-argument structure. It simply adds case role labels to indicate the relation of each noun to the central predicate. The verb and nouns in the structure are CONCEPTS, the case role labels indicate RELATIONS. Charles Fillmore, and other case grammarians, have simply added labels to a pre-existent logical structure.

1.2. Case lexicon

The case lexicon gathers the case labels of each verb into a CASE FRAME. This case frame then becomes part of the lexical entry for each distinct sense of each verb. The case frame is not the complete lexical entry. The verb entry should also contain syntactic features and semantic features relative to the verb's core meaning.

Syntactic features. These features stipulate the category of the verb as [+V]. To this category are added subcategorization features, based on the syntactic context in which the verb occurs. By means of these contextual features, verbs are distinguished as transitive [+__NP] and intransitive [__], depending upon the presence or absence of an NP complement. This subcategorization includes "the range of complements which a given item permits" (Radford 1988:339). Although Chomskean linguistics (1965) provided many context free features for the noun category, such as [+common], [+count], [+animate], and [+human], no context-free features were provided for verbs. Lexical predicates were further specified by selectional features, which listed the types of subject and object that could occur with a given predicate. For example, a transitive verb which required an animate subject and an inanimate object was classed as [+NPan ___NPin]. The complete description of a verb contained three features [+V, +___NP, +NPan___NPin]. The first feature states the bare [+V] category, the next two features were contextual and defined the verb not in intrinsic terms, but in terms of surrounding categories.

Semantic features. The case frame, with its logical relations made explicit, is a valuable addition to the lexicon which creates a verb typology including verb type, verb domain, and verb adicity (the number of arguments required by the meaning of the verb). The information in this case frame classification is supplemented by the semantic features inherent in the verb. It provides a different perspective on lexical items, groups verbs together in new ways, and can be linked to specific syntactic correlates for each verb. By implication, the case frame provides context-free features for the verb. The feature [+stative] is implied in the static versus dynamic distinction in the case frame; the feature [+active] is implied in the presence or absence of Agent in the frame. The combination of these features isolates three verb types and defines State verbs [+stative, −active], Process verbs [−stative, −active], and Action verbs [−stative, + active].

Given a lexical entry that includes the category, subcategorization, selectional features, and case frame, how are the syntactic elements linked to the semantic case elements? Case roles represent semantic structure, and subcategorization represents syntactic structure. In a Fillmore type Case Grammar, linking is performed by the subject choice hierarchy (see §1.9). The cases are listed in the frame according to preferred subject choice.

1.3. Case systems

Case roles form a paradigmatic system of contrasts used in the description of verbs. The case system may be nonlocal, local, or mixed. Local and nonlocal systems are mutually translatable, that is, a local case system is easily converted into a nonlocal system.

Nonlocal systems. Fillmore's original Case Grammar (1968) uses a non-local case system. The principal cases were Agent, Instrument, Dative, Object, Factitive, and Locative. Fillmore's original model considered all locative expressions, whether stative or directional to be in complementary distribution. Chafe's case inventory (1970) included Agent, Patient (Object), Experiencer (Dative), Benefactive, and Locative. Instrument and Complement (Factitive) cases were also considered, but not available as subject choices. Cook's case inventory (1979, 1989) included Agent, Experiencer, Benefactive, Object, and Locative. Following Fillmore and Chafe, Cook's Locative case included physical location and direction (Source, Path, and Goal).

Fillmore's nonlocal Case Grammar has the advantage of being more highly descriptive with a clearer notion of domain. Verbs that require only the Agent and Object cases form a Basic domain. The other three cases are domain markers, separating verbs into Experiential (psychological predicates), Benefactive (possessive predicates), and Locative (physical location predicates). But it loses the distinction between Location, Source, Path, and Goal.

Local case systems. Anderson's localist Case Grammar (1971) used four cases, nominative (Object), ergative (Agent), locative, and ablative (Source). The Locative case was used as both allative (Goal) and locative (Location), producing reductively a five case system with Agent, Object, Location, Source, and Goal. The nominative (Object) was considered to be obligatory to every predication. Jackendoff's Thematic Relations (1972), following Gruber (1976) used a five case system with Agent, Theme (Object), Location, Source, and Goal. Jackendoff and Gruber also considered the Object to be obligatory to every predication. The distinctive feature of local case systems is that physical location is used as the prime analogate for verbal description. Local cases (Location, Source, and Goal) are used concretely for physical location, and abstractly for the Experiential and Benefactive domains.

Localist Case Grammar has the advantage of unifying the use of Source and Goal prepositions across domains. The disadvantage is, that unless concrete and abstract location are distinguished, the case frames tend to be non-distinctive and few in number. However, local case systems are easily translated into non-local case systems. Agent is Agent and Theme is Object. Verbal descriptions that use only these two cases should be identical. When local cases are used concretely, local systems have the advantage of distinguishing Location, Source, Path, and Goal. When used abstractly, the local cases can be translated into Experiential and Benefactive domains.

Mixed systems. A more recent trend has been to combine local and nonlocal systems to gain the advantages of both systems. Jackendoff (1987:394) proposes a Thematic tier (local) and an Action tier (nonlocal). Somers (1987:206) proposes a grid with local cases (Local, Source, Path, Goal) in one dimension and nonlocal cases (Active, Objective, Dative, Locative, Temporal) in the other. The local dimension has the advantage of unifying the use of prepositions and distinguishing stative and directional locative elements. The nonlocal dimension has the advantage of distinguishing Experiential (psychological), Benefactive (possessive), and Basic domains.

1.4–1.6 Logical structure

In knowledge representation, it is useless to speak of predicate-argument structure without first answering the question: predicate-argument structure of what? Knowledge is represented in terms of propositions. But propositions are represented in syntax by clauses, not sentences. Therefore the text must be reduced to clauses before the semantic analysis begins. This requires on the part of the analyst, or the syntactic parser, enough knowledge of syntax to reduce all texts to a sequence of KERNEL SENTENCES by undoing the effects of all known transformations. Only then can an analysis in terms of predicate-argument structure be applied to each single clause in any given text. The semantic structure underlying any proposition is a predicate-argument structure. To understand this predicate-argument structure it is necessary to understand (1) what is a proposition, (2) what is a predicate, and (3) what is an argument. This predicate-argument structure may be enhanced by case labels indicating the relation of the arguments to the predicate.

1.4. The proposition

Semantic representation is based upon the analysis of propositions. A proposition is a statement in which something is predicated of a subject. Syntactically, the clause is the basic unit of information, no matter how clauses are arranged in sentences. A clause is defined as a string of words containing one and only one predicate. Each clause in its underlying structure is reduced to a kernel sentence.

Kernel sentences. Kernel sentences are defined as simple complete statements, active and affirmative (Chomsky 1957). Each clause in the text is a kernel sentence, and case frames are applied only to kernel sentences. In Chomksy's 1957 model, all sentences were derived from kernel sentences by transformations. Kernel sentences were derived by phrase structure rules.

Simple is opposed to complex and compound. Complex sentences consisting of an independent and a subordinate clause are broken into two clauses. Many subordinate clauses are used to fill a case role, usually the Object role, in the main verb. Compound sentences, consisting of two or more independent clauses, are broken into individual clauses. Case Grammar does not deal with the conjoining process.

Complete is opposed to elliptical. If the sentence fragment contains a main verb or its auxiliary, it may be analyzed as a full clause, but first all syntactic deletions must be restored to reveal the kernel sentence. If the main predicate is missing, the sentence fragment is given no case frame.

Statement is opposed to questions and commands. Case Grammar has no device for differentiating statements, questions, and commands. Case frames are not applied directly to questions and commands, but to the statements which underlie the questions and commands.

Active is opposed to passive. Passive sentences in Case Grammar do not receive a separate analysis. The case frame for a true passive sentence is the case frame for the corresponding active sentence.

Affirmative is opposed to negative. In Case Grammar affirmative and negative sentences are represented by the same case frame. Sentence negation may be represented by a negative operator external to the basic proposition.

Text reduction.   Since semantic representation is in terms of the logical structure underlying propositions, and propositions are represented by clauses, texts must be reduced to clauses. This reduction is necessary to collapse certain syntactic distinctions that are not relevant to logical structure. The analyst must be able to reduce the text to kernel sentences by undoing the effects of such transformations as embedding, conjoining, deletion, passive, and negative. It is this kernel structure that is the basis for the predicate-argument structure. Text reduction is illustrated in the following sentence.

(4) He was an old man who fished alone in a skiff in the Gulf Stream
     and he had gone eighty-four days now without taking a fish.

     a. He was an old man
         = he /was /an old man
     b. who fished alone in a skiff in the Gulf Stream
         = he /fished /alone /in a skiff /in the Gulf Stream
     c. and he had gone eighty-four days now
         = he /had gone /84 days /now
     d. without taking a fish.
         = he /had not caught /a fish

There are other transformations that must be undone to reveal the underlying kernel structure. Among these are focussing devices like
extraposition and there-insertion, and embedding transformations like
subject raising and Equi NP-deletion. Sentences in the text that use these
devices must be reduced to simple kernel sentences.

(5) It is true that John loves Mary.   extraposition
     = That John loves Mary /is true.

(6) There were birds singing in the garden.   there-insertion
     = Birds /were singing /in the garden.

(7) John seems to me to be sick.   subject-raising
     = John is sick /seems /to me.

(8) Paul wants to leave.   Equi deletion
     = Paul /wants /Paul leave.

    Predicate-argument structure is "built around a central verb" (Chafe
1970:10). The conceptual universe is made up of verbs which describe
states or events, and nouns which describe things. "Of these two, the
verb will be assumed to be central and the noun peripheral" (Chafe
1970:96). Anderson adds, "verbs are central relationally: they govern the
case functions contracted by nouns. Nouns are primary referentially"
(1971:31, footnote 1).

1.5. Predicate

    What constitutes a predicate? I had always assumed, perhaps naively,
that logicians, linguists after 1965, and especially case grammarians,

recognized predicate adjectives as predicates. Adjectives are predicated of subjects in any NP + be + adjective structure.

Therefore, I was somewhat surprised to find that Gruber (1976), followed by Jackendoff in all writings up to 1990, claimed that adjectives were arguments. It was easy to see how this conclusion was reached in Gruber's rather strict localist system. The Theme is defined as "the Object in motion or being located" (Jackendoff 1987:377). Since the Theme is always in motion or being located, then Location, Source, or Goal occur in every predication. Since the NP in the NP + be + adjective structure is the Theme, the adjective must be the Location. Predicate adjectives then become arguments of the predicate be, interpreted as be at, rather than predicates. In the Gruber-Jackendoff lexicon, no adjectives appear as predicates. The logical difference between Fillmore and Gruber is shown in the following example.

(9)   The milk is sour.
       Fillmore: BE SOUR (milk)
       Gruber: BE AT (milk, sour)

Predicate adjectives. The predicate element in predicate-argument structure may be a lexical verb or a predicate adjective. This position originates with Lakoff (1970, appendix A) in which the arguments for verbs and adjectives as members of the predicate supercategory are attributed to Lakoff and Postal. "We will try to present a case for the plausibility of the assertion that adjectives and verbs are members of a single lexical category (which we will call VERB) and that they differ only by a single syntactic feature (which we shall call ADJECTIVAL)" (Lakoff 1970:115, appendix A).

In a subsequent article, "On Stative Adjectives and Verbs in English" (1966), Lakoff summarizes his position. "A close study of English syntax would reveal that adjectives and verbs are treated identically with respect to a considerable number of transformational rules and have a large number of lexical properties in common...Such facts would constitute strong evidence for the assertion that what traditional grammarians called adjectives and verbs are really members of the same major grammatical category" (1966:15).

This position, that verbs and adjectives both act as predicates, is explicitly adopted by most of the case grammarians. Fillmore states, "I am adhering in this discussion to the Postal-Lakoff doctrine, which I find thoroughly convincing, that adjectives constitute a subset of verbs" (1968:27, footnote 36). Chafe says, "I shall take the position that every sentence which is of interest to us is built around a predicative element...for example, in the sentence *the clothes are dry* there is a predicative element involving the meaning *(be) dry*...Henceforth I shall refer to predicative elements as verbs" (1970:96). Anderson (1971:38) adds, "I am assuming (with the more Aristotelean of the Arabic grammarians) that 'verbs' and 'adjectives' are categorically identical...In particular we shall find 'verbs' and 'adjectives' with parallel combinatorial possibilities with respect to cases, and entering into (intrinsically) suppletive sets." Harold Somers (1982:239) says, "Following what Fillmore (1968) calls the Postal-Lakoff doctrine (Lakoff, 1970), though the notion dates back to Sapir (1921:117), we shall use the umbrella term 'verb' to mean both a member of the traditional syntactic class verb and a construct involving elements belonging to other syntactic classes, particularly for example adjectives," and later "Sentences containing State verbs, as the name suggests, indicate the state or condition of the primary argument, typically the surface subject of the verb. They often consist of the predicative use of an adjective...which may be in the form of a past participle" (1982:242). In the present work, the term VERB is to be interpreted as logical predicate; when the syntactic class verb is intended, it will be referred to as a lexical verb.

1.6. Argument

What is an argument? In predicate calculus, arguments are elements required by the predicate, usually expressed in the predication as nouns or prepositional phrases. In syntax, arguments seem to correspond with elements like subjects and verbal complements, excluding adverbial adjuncts. In Case Grammar, Fillmore distinguishes proposition and modality. The proposition consists of a "tenseless set of relationships involving verbs and nouns (and embedded sentences, if there are any), separated from what might be called the modality constituent" (1968:23). Within this proposition, the verb is the predicate and the nouns are arguments related to that predicate by a universal set of case roles. The modality consists of "such modalities on the sentence as a whole as negation, tense, mood, and aspect" (1968:23). This modality also includes most adverbial adjuncts. Case Grammar adds labels to logical arguments. In sentence (10) the first argument is identified as an Agent who does the eating, the second argument is identified as an Object (Theme), the thing that gets eaten.

(10)   Adam /ate /the apple.
　　　Logic: EAT (Adam, apple)
　　　Case: EAT (Agent, Object)

What do case labels add to arguments? In logical notation, arguments are distinguished by position. The first argument is the logical subject, and the second (and third, if any) arguments are logical objects. But this designation does not reveal any similarities for the cross-classification of predicates. Case labels relate predicates to each other by determining the verb adicity, the verb type, and the semantic domain to which each verb belongs.

For example, the verb *put* is listed in the case lexicon as an A-O-L verb. The verb *put* is then a triadic predicate, since it is described in terms of three labels; the verb belongs to the verb type Action, since one of the roles is an Agent; and the verb belongs to the domain of physical location and motion, since it contains a Locative case. This verb is classified as a three-place Action Locative verb with an A-O-L case frame. Under this classification, the verb *put* is like all triadic predicates in requiring three arguments. This verb inherits all the properties of Action verbs and belongs in the same semantic space as other locative verbs. All of this cross-classification follows from the case labelling of the arguments.

1.7–1.9 Case roles

The essentials of Case Grammar, according to Fillmore, are a list of cases, the representation of structure in terms of a case frame, and a subject choice hierarchy. Within the context of Case Grammar one must consider (1) the nature of case roles, (2) the list of cases, and (3) the subject choice hierarchy for arranging cases within case frames.

1.7. The nature of case roles

What are case roles? In the underlying predicate-argument structure, case roles are the relations that arguments bear to their predicate. Case roles are relations, not categories. Fillmore (1968:24) originally described cases like Agent and Dative in terms of features like [+animate], but later he clearly distinguished case relations from the features of nouns that fill those cases. Fillmore states, "I no longer confuse selection restrictions to animates with true case-like notions" (1971b:42), and later "this part of the initial formulation of the (Case Grammar) proposal was wrong" (1975:6), and finally, "I am now more careful about keeping relational notions (cases) and categorial notions (animate) distinct" (1977:65).

John Sowa, in *Conceptual Structures* (1984), presents a model which includes Case Grammar, semantic networks, and the logic of Charles Peirce. According to Sowa, "Fillmore's *Case Grammar* (1968) had a strong influence on Artificial Intelligence because it provided a convenient set of labels for conceptual relations" (1984:223). These relations, or cases, form a case frame, represented by canonical graphs. Case Grammar represents the meaning of a sentence in terms of a central predicate (verb, adjective) and a series of case-labelled arguments (nominal, adverbial) required by the meaning of that predicate. Conceptual graphs represent Case Grammar in a box and circle notation. The boxes enclose CONCEPTS, defined as "basic units for representing knowledge" (1984:39). These include the major categories noun, verb, adjective, and adverb. The circles enclose RELATIONS, defined as "the roles that each concept plays" (1984:79). These relations are the cases of Case Grammar. Sowa believes that "conceptual graphs are a universal, language-independent deep structure" (1984:38). The same is said of Case Grammar.

(11)   Adam /ate /the apple.
       Case: EAT (Agent, Object)
       Graph: [ADAM]←(AGNT)←[EAT]→(OBJ)→[APPLE]

Predicate logic represents the verb *eat* as a two-place predicate requiring two and only two arguments. Case Grammar adds the generalization that the two required arguments are an Agent, who does the eating, and an Object, which is eaten. Conceptual graphs represent the same information as the Case Grammar analysis, but more clearly distinguishes the concepts, verb and nouns which are enclosed in boxes, from the relations, Agent and Object which are enclosed in circles. The direction of the arrows in the graph indicate that the verb is central and the source of the case relations, Agent and Object.

Fillmore introduced Case Grammar as "a conception of base structure in which case relationships are primitive terms of the theory" (1968:2). In a case labelled predicate-argument structure, cases mark the relations that arguments bear to their predicate. At the level of abstraction at which case labels are applied to predicate-argument structure, case relations are the only primitives of the theory. Cases, which are relations, cannot undergo decomposition, and they are a necessary and sufficient system for the classification of semantic structures. Predicates, which are concepts, may undergo decomposition, and the atomic elements in the underlying structure may receive case labels. But this deeper structure is easily reduced to a case frame for the original decomposed predicate by McCawley's predicate-raising rule, described in *Prelexical Syntax* (Georgetown

University Round Table 1971:21). After predicate raising, tree pruning rules will apply to the structure. (See §1.15 Lexical decomposition.)

1.8. Case inventory

Fillmore (1975:7) claims that the basic questions about the list of cases remain unanswered: (1) What is the correct list of cases? (2) how are they defined? and (3) how do we know, in principle, when the list of cases is complete?

What is the correct list of cases? There is no correct list of cases; individual linguists have their own preferred list of cases. How are they defined? If cases mark the relation of arguments to a verb, then cases must be defined in terms of the verb. How do we know when the list is complete? Only by extensive text analysis, testing a list of cases against the verb structures found in the text.

Whatever the list of cases chosen, Fillmore (1975:5) suggests that this list must be small in number, adequate for the description of all the verbs of a language, and universal across languages. The small number of cases is generally interpreted as ten or less. Adequacy means the case list is necessary and sufficient for verb classification. Universal means the same list must apply to all languages, not just English.

The Case Grammar Matrix Model proposes five cases: Agent, Experiencer, Benefactive, Object (Theme), Locative. These case roles are relations, not categories. They do not have defining features, they merely express the relation of the argument to the predicate.

Case roles are part of the meaning of the predicate in the lexicon, before they are applied to any particular noun phrase in syntax. Among these cases, Agent and Object are primary cases, used in the description of every verb. Experiencer, Benefactive, and Locative are secondary cases, marking specific domains in the lexicon.

Agent (A). Agent may be considered as a HYPERCASE which includes animate Agents, Instruments, natural forces, whatever is capable of producing the action required by the verb. An Agent is an adequate cause of the action. The use of case roles like Agent creates a system of argument types. This system "implies that the Agent arguments of two different verbs have something in common" (Van Riemsdijk and Williams 1986:241). What these Agent roles have in common is that they are the subject of an Action verb. Cases are relational and are read onto the noun from the verb. As Wallace Chafe observed, "if we are confronted with a surface structure such as *the chair laughed* and forced to give it a meaning of some kind, what we do is interpret *chair* as if it were abnormally animate, as dictated by the verb. What we do **not** do is to interpret *laugh* in an abnormal way as if it were a different kind of activity, performed by inanimate objects" (Chafe 1970:97). The alternative to an Agentive hypercase is an extension of the case inventory to include such cases as Agent, Instrument, Force, Cause. This extension of the inventory causes a proliferation of verb types in the lexicon, and loses the generalization that all action verbs have something in common. Economy in the lexicon is the principal reason for a unified Agent case. Should the sentences in (12) receive one case frame or many? If case relations spring from the verb, and the verb in the lexicon is marked as an Agent-Object verb, then the subjects of all four sentences should be listed as Agents.

(12) a. John /broke /the window.
      b. The wind /broke /the window.
      c. The hammer /broke /the window.
      d. A rock /broke /the window.

According to Chafe "the ability of a noun to occur as an Agent depends on its semantic specification as a thing which has the power to do something, a thing which has a force of its own, which is self-motivated" (1970:109), and he adds, "there seem to be some nouns (such as *heat, wind*), however, which are not animate but which may nevertheless occur as Agents" (1970:109). And in discussing sentence (12d) he states, "it seems to me at least likely that this noun is an Agent...The noun *rock* is not intrinsically potent and is not therefore normally eligible to occur within an Agent noun, but it may be that any such noun can be given a derivative potency" (1970:155).

Object (O). The definition of the Object (or Theme) case depends upon whether the analyst believes in the obligatory-O hypothesis which claims that the Object (or Theme) role occurs in the description of every verb. In this hypothesis, Object becomes a hypercase including such variants as Patient, Affected, Complement, Neutral, and Factitive. If the obligatory-O hypothesis is accepted, its variants then are considered in complementary distribution and the various meanings are interpreted according to the verb entry. An Object or Theme which is obligatory forces a deeper analysis of the structure.

Jeffrey Gruber, in his *Studies in Lexical Relations* (1965, reprinted 1976) states: "The theme also has the significance of being an obligatory element of every sentence. It appears to be the focus of the construction syntactically and semantically" (1976:38). Ray Jackendoff endorses this position in *Semantic Interpretation in Generative Grammar* (1972). "The fundamental notion in Gruber's analysis is the Theme of a sentence. The centrality of the Theme accounts for the term Thematic Relations...In every sentence there is a noun phrase functioning as Theme" (1972:29). John Anderson in *The Grammar of Case* (1971) also believes in an obligatory Theme. "I am suggesting that nom (nominative or Theme) is the notionally most neutral case...I shall also be proposing that nom is the only obligatory case" (1971:37), and later, in speaking of the unique status of nom, he states, "this uniqueness is characterized in terms of the unique status of nom as a case element that is universally present in the clause" (1971:50).

Charles Fillmore, in *The Case for Case* (1968), stops short of declaring the Object case to be obligatory in every clause. According to Fillmore the Object is "the semantically most neutral case, the case of anything representable by a noun whose role in the Action or State identified by the verb is identified by the semantic interpretation of the verb itself" (1968:25). In a later work, *Some Problems for Case Grammar* (1971b) he states, "the Object case is that of the entity which moves or which undergoes change, and I still use it as a wastebasket" (1971b:42). But even if the Object case is not obligatory, its meaning is determined by the semantic interpretation of the verb itself.

The implication of the universal O-hypothesis is that many different meanings will be assigned the Object label, and that these meanings will be in complementary distribution within the system. Thus, Object may be an item described, a moving entity, an entity that is affected or created by an activity, or even neutral. In this framework the Object must be some kind of HYPERCASE which would include Patient, Undergoer, Affected, and other terms. The first consideration would be Gruber's preoccupation with "What is the Theme?" (1976:45). It must be there in every clause. The advantage of the obligatory-O hypothesis is that it is a generalization that unifies the case system by preventing the proliferation of cases. It also forces the analyst to look for covert roles, contained in the semantics of the verb but not always present in surface structure. Some roles are deletable, some are coreferential, some lexicalized into the verb. The obligatory-O hypothesis forces the analyst to look more deeply into semantic structure. The disadvantage is that, at this level of abstraction, many semantic distinctions within the Object "basket case" are overlooked, as illustrated in sentences (13)–(15).

(13) John /painted /the chair.   A,O
      Affected Object, exists before the action.

(14) Harry /built /the house.   A,O
      Created Object, does not exist before the action.

(15) Mary /read /the book.   A,O
      Neutral Object, neither created nor affected.

But in the context of a Case Grammar analysis, are these distinctions really necessary? The choice is up to the analyst. It is certainly possible to remain at a level of abstraction which concentrates upon the number of places, the verb type, and verbal domain to describe predicates. To retain this generalization, the sentences (13)–(15) would be classified as Agent-Object verbs, and the precise meaning of the Object case would be determined "by the semantic interpretation of the verb itself" (Fillmore 1968:25). The different meanings of the Object role would permit the introduction of subclasses within the class of Agent-Object verbs.

Experiencer (E). Experiencer is the case required by an Experiential verb. An Experiencer is a person experiencing sensation, emotion, or cognition. With verbs of communication, the Experiencer is the hearer. Experiential verbs constitute a special domain, which, within the lexicon, isolates all the inner psychological experiences of mankind into a single verbal category. Any verb with Experiencer in its description belongs to this Experiential domain. Experiential verbs include State Experiential (E,Os) such as *like* in sentence (16), Process Experiential (E,O) such as *enjoy* in sentence (17), and Action Experiential (A,E,O), such as *tell* in sentence (18).

(16) Tim /likes /ice cream.   E,Os
      E   V   Os

(17) Helen /was enjoying /the play.   E,O
      E   V   O

(18) Hilda /told /John /a story.   A,E,O
      A   V   E   O

Benefactive (B). Benefactive is the case required by a benefactive verb. With State verbs, Benefactive is the possessor of an Object. With Event verbs, whether they are Process or Action, Benefactive is the

nonagentive party in the transfer of property. Benefactive verbs consti-
tute a special domain dealing with possession and transfer of property.
Any verb which has Benefactive in its description belongs to this domain.
The Benefactive may be positive or negative, that is, the Benefactor may
gain or lose in the transfer of property. The Benefactive domain includes
State Benefactive (B,Os) such as *have* in sentence (19), Process Benefac-
tive (B,O) such as *inherit* in sentence (20), and Action Benefactive
(A,B,O) such as *give* in sentence (21).

(19) Donald /has /a watch.   B,Os
       B   V   Os

(20) Mathilda /inherited /a fortune.   B,O
       B   V   O

(21) Frank /gave /Susan /some flowers.   A,B,O
       A   V   B   O

Locative (L). Locative is the case required by a locative verb. Locative is restricted to physical location in space. The definition of the
Locative case depends upon whether the analyst believes in the complementary distribution of all Locative elements under a single Locative
label. According to the unified Locative hypothesis, all stative locatives,
such as Location, Orient, Extend, and all directional locatives, such as
Source, Goal, Path, or Transit point, are in complementary distribution
and are all simply called Locative. The locative case is stative when used
with a stative verb, and directional when used with a Process or Action
verb.

Charles Fillmore, in *The Case for Case* (1968), opts for a unified locative. "The list of cases includes L, but nothing corresponding to what
might be called directional. There is a certain amount of evidence that
locational and directional elements do not contrast, but are superficial
differences determined either by the constituent structure or by the character of the associated verb" (1968:25). As evidence he cites the use of
the pro-word *there.* "The phrases *to the store* (Goal) and *at the store* (Location) are variants of the same entity, determined by the movement or
nonmovement character of the associated verb" (1968:25). In sentence
(22) the L-phrase denotes stative location, but in sentences (23)–(24) the
L-phrase is directional.

(22) The book /is (located) /on the table.   Os,L
        Os   V   L

(23) The ship /went /to Africa.   O,L
       O   V   L

(24) Students /brought /their lunch /to school.   A,O,L
        A   V   O   L

This analysis does not exclude the multiple expression of Locative. With stative locatives, many phrases may be used to express a single Location, as in sentence (25). Fillmore notes, "it is clear that we have in this sentence one place specification, so on the semantic level the one-instance-per-clause principle is not violated" (1971b:51).

(25) He /was sitting /under a tree /in the park /on a bench.   Os,L
       Os V   L1   L2   L3

With directional locatives Fillmore states, "a sentence with the Path designated can contain an unlimited number of Path expressions, as long as these are understood as indicating successive stretches of the same path" (1971b:51), as illustrated in sentence (26).

(26) He   /walked /down the hill /across the bridge.   A=O,L
       A=O   V   L-Path   L-Path

      /through the pasture /to the chapel.
       L-Transit   L-Goal

The advantage of the unified Locative case is that it is a generalization that clearly defines Locative as the domain of physical location and motion. All case frames that contain a Locative will be within that physical domain. Nothing more is necessary in a labelled predicate-argument structure. The disadvantage is that since all Locatives are considered to be in complementary distribution, the distinction between Source, Goal, Path, Transit point, Location, Orient, and Extend is lost. These distinctions are very useful for recognizing various elements as Locative. Where necessary for the semantic analysis these distinctions can be marked as Source Locative, Goal Locative, or Path Locative, but again, the case analysis is not a complete semantic description, and the type of locative is often deduced from "the semantic interpretation of the verb" or recognized by the type of preposition.

Modal cases. Modal cases are cases that do not enter directly into the classification of verbs, and include such cases as: Time, Manner,

Instrument, Cause, Result, Purpose, outer Locative, and outer Benefactive. Fillmore (1968:23) states that "certain cases will be directly related to the modality constituent, as others are related to the proposition itself." Modal cases are principally adverbial adjuncts. They do not enter into the subcategorization of a verb, and they are not subject to selection restrictions. The failure to distinguish modal from proposition cases results in the proliferation of case labels, such as manner, means, medium, instrument, purpose.

Locatives may be propositional or modal. Fillmore (1968:28, footnote 34) states that the distinction of inner (inside the VP) and outer (outside the VP) locatives corresponds to his distinction of propositional locatives (belonging to the Proposition) and modal locatives (belonging to the Modality). Locatives within the Proposition label arguments essential to the meaning of the verb; locatives within the modality label adjuncts possible with virtually any verb. Fillmore illustrates the difference in sentences (27) and (28).

(27)   John /keeps /the car /in the garage.   A,O,L
       A   V   O   L

(28)   John /washes /his car /in the garage.   A,O
       A   V   O   L-modal

The verb *keep* in sentence (27) is a three-place predicate meaning *cause to remain in a place,* with the Locative an essential part of the verb's meaning. The verb *wash* in sentence (28) is a two-place predicate requiring only the Agent who does the washing and the Object washed. The Locative is not part of the meaning of the verb, and is therefore considered an adjunct.

Benefactives may also be propositional or modal. In State verbs expressing possession (or lack of it) the Benefactive expresses the essential possessor. In Process verbs the Benefactive expresses the essential person acquiring or losing possession. In Action verbs, the Benefactive expresses the nonAgentive party in the transfer of property. On the other hand, Benefactives with *for,* meaning *for the sake of,* are modal and may occur with virtually any Action predicate.

1.9. Subject choice hierarchy

Fillmore considered the subject choice hierarchy as one of the essentials of a Case Grammar theory. Case-labelled predicate-argument structures must be related to syntactic structures by some linking device.

One option is to specify the linking of each case to its argument, which is not economical. Another option is to link the elements of the case frame with the subcategorization frame by coindexing, as in Jackendoff (1976). Fillmore's option is to establish a subject choice hierarchy in which the cases are ranked within the case frame according to their likelihood to be chosen as subject. This hierarchy is determined on the basis of frequency, and constitutes a generalization of what are the more likely subject choices within the grammar.

Charles Fillmore, in *The Case for Case* (1968) arranged his case frames with the verb in initial position followed by the cases in hierarchical order. The basic cases in the model were Agent-Instrument-Dative-Object-Locative, given in that hierarchical order. In order to match the case frame with the subcategorization syntactic feature, linking was accomplished not by coindexing but by the subject choice hierarchy. The highest ranking case in the frame was chosen as subject, the next highest as direct object if the verb was transitive.

In *The Case for Case* Fillmore suggests: "For most combinations of cases there is a preferred or unmarked subject choice; for some there is no actual choice—the subject is uniquely determined. In general, the unmarked subject choice seems to follow the following rule: If there is an A, it becomes the subject; otherwise, if there is an I, it becomes the subject; otherwise the subject is O" (1968:33). In *Some Problems for Case Grammar* Fillmore writes, "The cases exist in a hierarchy, and this hierarchy serves to guide the operations of certain syntactic process, in particular that of subject selection. It figures in subject selection by determining which noun phrase is to become the subject of the sentence in the unmarked instance. That case in a sentence which, according to the hierarchy of cases, outranks the others is the one which has the noun phrase it is associated with selected as subject of the sentence" (1971b:37). Normal subject choice follows the subject choice hierarchy. These are the unmarked subject selections.

Rank shift. There are also nonnormal subject choices. These are the marked options, and the choice of subject must be registered in the lexicon. In nonnormal selection, the subject is uniquely determined by the verb. On nonnormal choice of subject Fillmore states: "Certain predicators have their own lexically determined subject choices...a grammar must therefore provide some way of re-ranking the cases for particular sentences" (1971b:37). This can be accomplished if we "move some initially non-leftmost element into the leftmost position in the list of cases" (1971b:37). Accordingly, in the present work, nonnormal subject selection is represented by changing the order of cases within the case frame, as in sentences (29)–(30).

(29)   The toys /are /in the box.   Os,L
         Os   V   L

(30)   The box /contains /the toys.   L,Os
         L   V   Os

Wallace Chafe (1970) also introduces a case hierarchy for subject selection. "Postsemantic subjects are established...on the basis of the semantic relations Agent, Patient, and so on" (1970:243). "An Agent or Experiencer noun takes priority in becoming the subject...a Beneficiary noun has the next priority...otherwise a Patient noun becomes the subject" (1970:244). The hierarchy here is Agent/Experiencer, Beneficiary, Patient, and then presumably Locative. Using this subject choice hierarchy, Chafe needs no coindexing to indicate the subject choice.

1.10–1.12 Case frames

Once the list of cases is determined, verbs may be classified according to their case frames. A case frame is a configuration of one to three cases that are required by the meaning of the verb. Case frames are listed in the lexicon as part of the meaning of the verb.

1.10. Preliminaries to case assignment

Assigning case role labels to a logical structure may seem to be totally arbitrary, and in fact, there is no universal agreement on the number of case role labels, or the way in which they are defined. This task is simplified if the labelling of arguments is deferred until other questions are answered, such as (1) how many arguments are required by the verb? (2) what verb type is in the structure? and (3) to what semantic domain does the verb belong? Once these three basic questions are answered, the assignment of role labels is simplified.

Verb adicity.   Adicity (Rappaport and Levin 1988:7) is the number of arguments required by a predicate. The term is a generalization from mon-adic, dy-adic, tri-adic referring to one-place, two-place, and three-place predicates. Before arguments can be named, it is necessary to know how many arguments are in the structure, that is, how many labels will be needed.

For any given verb, how many arguments are needed? One way of discerning the number of arguments is to refer to the subcategorization feature of the verb. The required arguments are the subject and all necessary complements of the verb. If the verb *give* requires both a direct and an indirect object, then the verb is a three-place predicate. Another test is to place the verb in a context, using indefinite pronouns for the argument. If the verb *give* in context yields *Somebody gives something to somebody else,* then the verb is a three-place predicate.

Verb type. The notion of verb type evolved slowly within linguistics. It is not found in early Chomskean models (1957, 1965). It probably begins with Lakoff's article on "Stative Adjectives and Verbs" (1966), in which he demonstrates that most adjectives are States, but there are some stative verbs, and most verbs are Actions, but there are some action adjectives. States do not take the progressive or the imperative; Actions take both the progressive and the imperative. What Lakoff overlooks is that there exists a class of verbs which take the progressive but not the imperative, a class that would include inchoative predicates derived from States as in Lakoff (1970:98). This middle verb type, which is neither State nor Action, was later called Process by Chafe (1970:99) and Anderson (1971:43).

John Sowa (1984) speaks of a "SITUATION type with subtypes STATE, EVENT, or ACT" (1984:113). "*States* have duration, as opposed to Events, which are in flux" (1984:413); "*Events* include *Acts* by animate Agents as well as *happenings* like explosions, when an Agent may not be present" (1984:410); "an *Act* is an Event with an animate Agent" (1984:408). A similar three-way division is found in James Allen's *Natural Language Understanding* (1987). "Stative verbs, which describe **States**, cannot be freely used in the progressive aspect...Nonstative verbs, which describe **Events**, do take the progressive aspect readily...An important subclass of events are those describing **Actions** by Agents" (Allen 1987:196).

(31) Verb type hierarchy

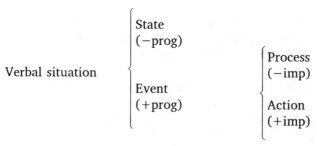

State verbs semantically describe a stative situation in which nothing is moving. This verbal situation can be captured with a still photograph. State verbs syntactically do not occur with the progressive or imperative. State verbs include most adjectives and verbs such as *know, want, like.*

Process verbs semantically describe a non-agentive dynamic event. Something is happening, but there is no Agent doing something. This verbal situation can only be captured by a camcorder. Process verbs syntactically may take the progressive but not the imperative. Process verbs include involuntary human actions like *sneeze, cough,* as well as most intransitives.

Action verbs semantically describe an agentive event in which an Agent can be said to be performing an action. Action events also require a camcorder. Action verbs syntactically take the progressive and imperative, and include most two-place transitive verbs. Action verbs also include action adjectives like *be (=act) rude, be (=act) polite.*

Semantic domains. In a dictionary verbs are listed alphabetically, and the many meanings of a verb are listed in any order within that entry. But in a thesaurus, verbs are listed according to semantic domain. There are four domains distinguished in the Case Grammar Matrix Model.

The Basic domain consists of those verbs which can be described in terms of Object alone, or Agent and Object. This domain will include State verbs (Os), Process verbs (O), and Action verbs (A,O).

The Experiential domain deals with sensation, emotion, cognition. It also includes verbs of communication. This domain includes State verbs (E,Os), Process verbs (E,O), and Action verbs (A,E,O).

The Benefactive domain includes those verbs which deal with possession or transfer of property. This domain will include State verbs (B,Os), Process verbs (O,B) and Action verbs (A,B,O).

The Locative domain deals with location in a place, or movement from one place to another. Locative verbs include State verbs (Os,L), Process verbs (O,L), and Action verbs (A,O,L).

Using the notion of domain, the State, Process, and Action verbs are further distinguished according to their meaning. In this classification, it has only been necessary to speak of five case roles. The primary cases are Agent and Object, the secondary cases are the Experiencer, Benefactive, and Locative which mark specific domains. The full list of cases is A-E-B-O-L. Within each case frame, cases are normally listed left-to-right according to a subject choice hierarchy.

Once the verb adicity, verb type, and verb domain are determined, the naming of the arguments can be simplified by a set of principles. Using these principles the case-labelling of most arguments is automatic; only the residue needs to be filled. These principles are as follows:

1. Every verb contains an argument labelled O for Object. This obligatory-O hypothesis is not in Fillmore or Chafe, but is strong in Anderson (1971) and the Gruber-Jackendoff system of Thematic relations.
2. If the verb is a State verb, then the obligatory Object is marked with a subscript as Os to indicate stativity. This marking is necessary in order to distinguish State verbs from Process verbs.
3. If the verb is an Action, then the first argument in the structure is always marked with A for Agent. Agent is not determined by any distinctive features, it is determined solely by the fact that the verb is an Action.

(32)   Case frame matrix

Verb types	Basic	Exp	Ben	Loc
State	Os be true	E,Os know	B,Os have	Os,L be in
Process	O die	E,O enjoy	B,O find	O,L move
Action	A,O read	A,E,O say	A,B,O give	A,O,L put

With verbs defined according to verb type in one dimension, and verbs defined according to semantic domain in another dimension, it is

possible to construct a preliminary Case Grammar matrix which will de-
fine all verb types in terms of type and domain. The question then arises:
Is this matrix necessary and sufficient for the description of all verbs in
all their individual senses? This question can only be addressed after the
variations in the model are fully explained. Only then can the model be
subject to extensive text analysis.

1.11. Case tactics

Once the case list is chosen, the case grammarian must determine in
what combinations cases may occur. The Case Grammar Matrix Model
uses the following set of tactics for the formation of case frames, adopted
from the work of nonlocalistic case grammarians.

1. A predication consists of a verb and one to three cases.
2. The Object (Theme) role is obligatory in every predication.
3. Sentences are embedded only under the Object (Theme) case.
4. No case except the Object may occur twice in the same frame.
5. Experiencer, Benefactive, Locative are mutually exclusive.
6. Cases are listed left-to-right in subject choice hierarchy order.

Rule one excludes zero-place predicates by insisting that in every case
frame "at least one case category must be chosen" (Fillmore 1968:24).
This rule permits one to three cases, with the maximum case frame made
up of Agent, Object (Theme), and a domain-marking case like E, B, L.

Rule two states the obligatory-O hypothesis as used in localist Case
Grammars proposed by Gruber (1976), Jackendoff (1972), and Anderson
(1971). Nonlocal systems, such as Fillmore (1968,1971), Chafe (1970),
do not propose an obligatory Object (Theme), but this tactic is recommended in Cook (1989). The use of the obligatory Theme forces a
greater use of deletable, coreferential, and lexicalized roles, since the
analyst must determine where the obligatory Object (Theme) is located.

Rule three is suggested by Fillmore when he uses "a symbol S as indicating an O (Object case) to which an S (sentence) has been embedded"
(1968:28). This is contradicted in Fillmore's later writings in which sentences are embedded under other cases. This rule makes it easy to
discover the Theme in sentences with clause complements, since the subject or object clause complement always fills the Object role.

Rule four states that Fillmore's well-known one-instance-per-clause principle applies to all cases except the Object case. The relaxation of Fillmore's principle for the Object case is based on John Anderson's analysis of
predicate nominals (1971:76) in which both nouns are assigned the Object

case. Later Anderson states that it may be necessary to relax the one-instance-per-clause principle "to allow up to two instances per proposition of just O, specifically to allow for equative sentences" (1977:54).

Rule five was originally derived from Chafe's discussion of secondary cases in chapter 12 (1970:144–66), in which he successively tests the Experiencer, Benefactive, and Locative cases to see if within these domains there are instances of State, Process, and Action verbs. Verb types within the Experiential, Benefactive, and Locative domains are established as distinct from the Basic verb types already developed in chapter 9 (1970:95–104).

Rule six establishes a subject choice hierarchy as A-E-B-O-L. Within the case frame, the cases required by the verb are listed in this order. The first case in the frame is then chosen as subject of the verb. If there is an A it is subject; if there is no A, then E or B is chosen as subject; if there is no A, E, or B, then O is chosen as subject. This subject choice hierarchy is merely a generalization which covers the unmarked choice. Marked choices which violate the subject choice hierarchy must be indicated in the lexicon by changing the order of cases in the case frame.

1.12. The revised Case Grammar matrix

With these tactics in mind, the Case Grammar model develops a matrix with verb type, State, Process, and Action, in one dimension, and semantic domain, Basic, Experiential, Benefactive, and Locative, in the other. This matrix contains twelve verb types. But there is variation within the various cells of the matrix, due to the existence of double-O frames, rank shifts in the order of cases, coreferential case roles, lexicalized case roles, and Time predicates.

Double-O frames. One extension of the matrix is the introduction of double-O frames in the Basic domain. Predicate nominals in *be* + N structure are Os,Os; predicate nominals in *become* + N structure are O,O. There are also action verbs with two complements, such as *elect,* listed as A,O,O. These additional frames are included in the revised matrix in (36).

Rank shifts. Rank shifts occur in the subject hierarchy. When a verb requires a subject different from that determined by the subject choice hierarchy, the cases are shifted to indicate the case that must be chosen as subject. These are the marked choices. Rank shifts for subject choice never involve the Agent, but rank shift does occur with State two-place predicates, in Os-E, Os-B, and L-Os frames, and with Process predicates, in O-E, O-B, and L-O frames. Rank shifts for object choice occur with all three-place predicates, permitting A-O-E, A-O-B, and A-L-O predicates. These additional frames are included in the revised Case Grammar matrix in (36).

Coreferential roles. Case frames within the matrix are modified to include frames with coreferential roles. Most coreference involves the Agent case coreferential with Object, Experiencer, Benefactive, or Locative cases. Many cases of coreference are Agentive reinterpretations of preexisting nonagentive structures. The only nonagentive coreferential roles that were discovered are found in the frame E,*Os /E=O, in such sentences as *John is (=feels) cold* (Anderson 1971:96).

Lexicalized roles. Case frames within the matrix are modified to include frames with lexicalized roles, in which a noun manifesting a case is incorporated into the verb. These include the lexicalization of the Object case with A-O, A-E-O, A-B-O, and A-O-L frames. The Locative case may also be lexicalized with O-L and A-O-L verbs.

Time predicates. The Time case, which is normally a modal case that can occur with virtually any predicate, is occasionally a propositional case. These include State Time such as *be* + Time, Process Time such as *last*, and Action Time such as *spend* (time). The matrix should be extended to include a Time dimension, with State, Process, and Action realizations.

(33) The meeting /is /on Wednesday.   Os,T
      Os   V T

(34) The play /lasted /an hour.   O,T
      O   V   T

(35) The surfers /spent /an hour /on the beach.   A=O,T
      A=O   V   T   Lm

The Case Grammar matrix is revised to include double-O structures and rank shifts in the subject choice hierarchy. Covert roles, such as deletable, coreferential, and lexicalized roles are not indicated in the matrix since they do not affect a change in case frame, only in its surface expression. The case frame matrix is extended to a time dimension in (37).

(36)   Revised case frame matrix

Verb type	Basic	Exp	Ben	Loc
State	Os be true Os,Os be + N	E,Os like Os,E be boring	B,Os have Os,B belong to	Os,L be in L,Os contain
Process	O die O,O become	E,O enjoy O,E amuse	B,O inherit O,B benefit	O,L come L,O leak
Action	A,O eat A,O,O elect	A,E,O say A,O,E amuse	A,B,O give A,O,B blame	A,O,L put A,L,O fill

(37)   Matrix extended to a Time domain

Verb type	— — — — —	Time
State	— — — — —	Os,T be + time
Process	— — — — —	O,T last
Action	— — — — —	A,O,T spend time

1.13–1.15 Derivation

Once predicates are classified according to case frames, and distributed in a matrix indicating verb type and domain, it becomes obvious that there are predicates derived from the same morphological root, such as the State verb *be open,* the Process verb *open,iv* and the Action verb *open,tv* and the question is raised: How are these verbs related? Although each item deserves an independent place in the lexicon (Jackendoff's full entry theory), it is necessary to show the relationships between these predicates. The first step is to identify the existence of related predicates, the next step is to specify the relationship between them. Some of these relationships can be made evident by lexical decomposition.

Derivation is simplified under the obligatory-O hypothesis in which the only verb types are State, Process, and Action. The bidirectional derivational system used by Chafe (1970) is reduced to four types of derivation. This derivational system is based on morphological and syntactic criteria of English and is therefore language specific.

1.13. Existence of related predicates

Within the vertical dimension of the case frame matrix there are often found related forms based on the same lexical root. The State forms, or BE forms, describe a stative situation, the Process forms, or BECOME forms, describe entering into that State, and the Action forms, or CAUSE BECOME forms, describe an Agent controlling the change of State. The chart in (38) indicates some of these related forms.

Lexical gaps, indicated by paraphrases with *become* and *cause,* are concepts for which there exists no single word lexical entry. Since a paraphrase exists, these gaps represent possible lexical items. A word may be coined in the future to fill such gaps. Along the color scale, verbs such as *whiten, redden, blacken* exist, but no verbs such as *bluen, greenen* exist.

Semantic gaps, indicated by blanks, are positions for which there is no corresponding concept. These semantic gaps have no expression, even by paraphrase. Verbs such as *slam, sneeze* have no underlying State from which they can be derived. There is no paraphrase such as *become slammed,* or *become sneezed,* and it is difficult to imagine a stative concept that would represent these verbs as a State.

(38)   Related predicates

State	Process	Action
BE	BECOME	CAUSE BECOME
be blue	(become blue)	(cause become blue)
be broken	break,iv	break,tv
be cool	cool,iv	cool,tv
be dead	die	(kill,tv)
be deaf	—	deafen,tv
be dry	dry,iv	dry,tv
be frozen	freeze,iv	freeze,tv
be hot	heat,iv	heat,tv
be open	open,iv	open,tv
—	slam,iv	slam,tv
—	sneeze,iv	(make sneeze)
be tight	tighten,iv	tighten,tv
be wide	widen,iv	widen,tv

1.14. Bidirectional derivation

Chafe (1970:132) devised a bidirectional system for relating different verb types. State verbs become Process by the inchoative derivation; Process verbs become States by the resultative derivation. Process verbs become Actions by the causative derivation; Action verbs become Process by the decausative derivation.

(39)   Chafe's derivations

	Inchoative>	Causative>
State	Process	Action
	<Resultative	<Decausative

		Inchoative>	Causative>
a.	State	+ inchoative	= Process
	wide,adj	+ inchoative	= widen,tv
b.	Process	+ resultative	= State
	break,iv	+ resultative	= broken,adj
c.	Process	+ causative	= Action
	widen,iv	+ causative	= widen,tv
d.	Action	+ decausative	= Process
	cut,tv	+ decausative	= cut,iv

Choosing a base form. Given a bidirectional derivational system, the analyst must then determine whether related State, Process, and Action forms exist, and if they exist, which of these forms is the basic form?

In choosing between State and non-State forms, the main rule is the simplicity of form criterion. In the pair *wide/widen,* the State form *wide* is basic and the Process form derived. In *break/broken,* the Process form *break* is basic and the State form derived. In the case of vowel change as in *hot/heat,* since the parallel forms *hot* and *heated* occur, *hot* is basic and the process *heat* is derived. If *heated* is formed by the resultative derivation, then *hot/heat* must be related by the inchoative derivation.

In choosing between process and action forms, the basic form is the Process form if that form occurs in normal intransitive use, as in the pair *break,iv/break,tv.* The basic form is the Action verb, if the Process form is pseudo-intransitive and requires manner adverbials, as in the pair *cut,iv/cut,tv.* Lyons states, "all pseudo-intransitive sentences are to be transformationally derived from transitive sentences. On the other hand...true intransitives may be taken as the source for the generation of transitive sentences" (1968:367).

Derivational features may be used to simplify the lexicon. One could list the basic form and its various derivations under a single entry. The method followed here is the full entry theory (Jackendoff 1976), which lists each item separately and supplements the lexicon with redundancy rules that relate these lexical entries to each other.

1.15. Lexical decomposition

Lexical decomposition is the process of analyzing predicates as consisting of more basic atomic predicates. Some of the atomic predicates suggested have been the causatives CAUSE and LET, inchoative COME ABOUT, and the durative REMAIN. If lexical predicates can be factored into simpler abstract predicates, the relationship between lexical items is made more evident. In lexical decomposition it is safer to work with predicates from the same root, based on morphology, and to use only with caution such suppletive sets such as the relation between *kill* and *die*.

Causative-inchoative paradigm. Lakoff (1970:32) suggests that some State verbs have corresponding Process forms, derived from the State by an inchoative derivation, and Action forms, derived from the Process by a causative derivation. The inchoative is represented as COME ABOUT. The causative is represented as CAUSE. Together these predicates form the causative-inchoative paradigm.

(40) The door is open.   be open Os
      BE OPEN (door)

(41) The door opened.   open,iv O
      COME ABOUT (BE OPEN (door))

(42) John opened the door.   open,tv A,O
      CAUSE (John, COME ABOUT (BE OPEN (door)))

The morphological root *open* occurs as a State verb *be open*. From this root the Process verb *open,iv* is derived by adding COME ABOUT. From this Process verb, the Action verb *open,tv* is derived by adding CAUSE. If the Process is COME ABOUT + State, and the Action is CAUSE + COME ABOUT + State, the relationship between these lexical items is made evident.

(43) Inchoative structure

The door opened.
= COME ABOUT (BE OPEN (door))

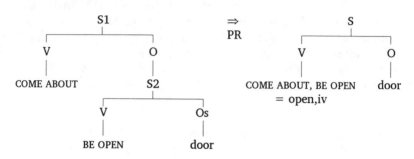

The original structure in (43) shows COME ABOUT as a one-place inchoative predicate with a sentence embedded as subject. The embedded sentence has a stative adjective predicate with the frame Os. To form the Process predicate the lower predicate BE OPEN is raised and joined to the COME ABOUT predicate to form the lexical item *open,iv*. By tree-pruning the empty S2 and its V are deleted and the lower subject becomes the subject of the new predicate which has the case frame O.

(44) Causative-inchoative structure

John opened the door.
= CAUSE (John, COME ABOUT (BE OPEN (door)))

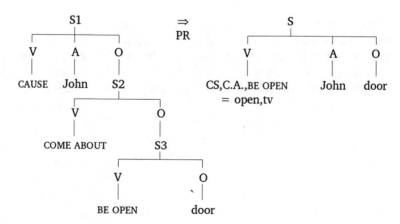

The original structure in (44) shows CAUSE as a two-place cause predicate with Agent and Object, COME ABOUT as a one-place inchoative predicate with Object only, and BE OPEN as a one-place stative predicate with Object only. To form the Action predicate according to McCawley's predicate raising rule, both lower predicates COME ABOUT and BE OPEN are raised and joined to the CAUSE predicate to form the lexical item *open,tv*. Tree-pruning is as follows: Both lower Vs are pruned away because they have no realization, S2 and S3 are deleted because no S can exist without a V, and the two lower Os are deleted because they are redundant. The resulting structure has A and O, which is the case frame for the verb *open,tv*.

Inchoative. According to Lakoff (1970:32) the inchoative lexical form, which is a Process, indicates the coming about of a State. This inchoative is represented by the abstract predicate COME ABOUT, a one-place predicate which takes a sentence as its subject complement (1965:34). This inchoative may or may not be incorporated into a single lexical item. When there is no lexical item that combines the inchoative + State, the inchoative predicate is lexicalized by a verb form such as *become, get, come to be,* as in sentence (45). These lexical forms are subject-raising predicates, which raise the subject of the complement to be the subject of the inchoative verb. When there is a lexical item available that can represent the combination inchoative + State, the inchoative predicate and the complement predicate are combined by McCawley's (1973:158) rule of predicate-raising and a single lexical item is substituted for the combined inchoative + State predicate, as in sentence (46).

(45) The sky became /got /came to be /dark.
      = COME ABOUT (BE DARK (sky))

(46) The sky /darkened.
      = COME ABOUT (BE DARK (sky))

Some inchoative predicates have no surface marking to distinguish them from the stative adjective, such as *cool/cool,iv* or *open/open,iv*. Other inchoatives are marked by the derivational affix *-en,* such as *hard/harden, thick/thicken, sick/sicken, red/redden, black/blacken.* Still others are marked with the suffix *-fy,* as *liquid/liquefy,* and *solid/solidify.*

David Dowty (1972:40) defines the predicate COME ABOUT in terms of the change-of-state calculus of Georg Henrik von Wright (1963). COME ABOUT is defined as $-p$ T p where p = a proposition, $-p$ is the negative of that proposition, and T is a dyadic operator meaning "and next." The inchoative predication *the door opened* is interpreted as *the door was not open* AND NEXT *the door was open*. In this interpretation, the former *not-open* state is presupposed and the later *open* state is asserted. This change of State takes place at some moment in time, with the result that the inchoative takes point adverbials but not durative adverbials.

Wallace Chafe (1970:119) distinguishes between absolute inchoatives, such as *open, red, deaf,* and relative inchoatives, such as *wide, loud, old.* In comparing the predicates *open,iv* and *widen,iv,* Chafe states that with *open* the change is from *not-open* to *open,* whereas with *widen* "the change is one in which the patient moves some distance along the continuum of wideness, from having a lesser degree of that quality to having a greater degree" (1970:121). "In *the road widened,* the road becomes not *wide,* but *wider.* After the change it may or may not be true that *the road is wide*" (1970:121). Dowty calls these inchoatives degree inchoatives (1972:57) and notes that unlike absolute inchoatives, they may occur with durative adverbs, as in *the soup cooled for hours.* It should also be noted that despite the definition of COME ABOUT as −p T p, degree inchoatives do not presuppose the negative of the proposition. *The road widened* does not presuppose *the road was not wide* (by some standard), it merely asserts the road is wider than it was before.

Chafe defines the inchoative as a derivational unit used "to turn a verb root which is intrinsically a State into one that is derivationally a Process" (1970:123). This definition applies to both absolute and relative inchoatives. It is consistent with Dowty's definition of inchoative as −p T p provided that the formula can be interpreted properly for degree relatives, not as a change from *not-wide* to *wide,* but from *not-as-wide* to *more-wide.*

Causative. Lakoff (1970:41) suggests that surface verbs like *cause* and *bring about* express an underlying CAUSE predicate, which occurs with the inchoative within its scope in the causative-inchoative paradigm. James McCawley suggests that State verbs are never directly in the scope of CAUSE. "The notion of causing which is relevant here is a relation between two Events, rather than between an Event and a State" (1973:344). And elsewhere "CAUSE corresponds to a relationship between a person and an event... However, CAUSE can also be used to express a relationship between an action or event, and an event" (1973:164, footnote 4). The verb *kill* is not analyzed as CAUSE, BE DEAD but as CAUSE, COME ABOUT, BE DEAD.

Gruber distinguishes between causative Agent and permissive Agent. For permissive Agents "the subject is still identified as a willful entity, but rather than being a cause, he permits the act" (1976:164). This distinction is codified in Jackendoff's Thematic Relations as the abstract predicates LET and CAUSE. "To represent the semantic notion of causation, we will use two semantic functions CAUSE (x,e) and LET (x,e). In the former x is a C-Agent and e is an event; in the latter x is a P-Agent and e is an event" (1976:105). This distinction is useful in differentiating causative predicates like *make, force, cause* from permissive predicates *let, allow, permit.* Jackendoff's definitions indicate the objects of causatives are Events not States. These definitions coincide with McCawley's statement that States are never the object of the predicate CAUSE.

Causative-durative paradigm. Parallel to the causative-inchoative paradigm is the causative-durative paradigm, in which the durative is represented not by derivational affixes but by separate durative verbs, such as *stay, keep, remain,* or by durational adverbials, such as *still, yet,* or by durational phrases, such as *for an hour, until tomorrow, since yesterday.* The underlying durative is represented as an abstract predicate REMAIN. The causative in a durative context is still represented as an abstract predicate CAUSE. Together these predicates form the causative-durative paradigm, shown in sentences (47)–(49).

(47) The door is open.   be open
      BE OPEN (door)

(48) The door stayed open.   stay,iv
      REMAIN (BE OPEN (door))

(49) John kept the door open.   keep,tv
      CAUSE (John, REMAIN (BE OPEN (door)))

The morphological root *open* occurs in adjective form as a State verb *be open.* From this root the durative-state form is derived by the addition of the abstract predicate REMAIN, represented in surface structure by the verb *stay,iv.* The verb *stay,iv* is a one-place predicate with a clause as its subject and the case frame O. By subject-raising rules the subject of the lower sentence is raised to be the subject of the durative verb. The raised subject is marked as NP since it has no case relationship to the raising verb.

(50)   Durative-state structure

The door stayed open.   O
= REMAIN (BE OPEN (door))

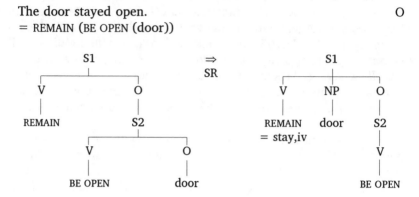

The morphological root *open* occurs in adjective form as a State verb *be open*. From this root the causative-durative-state form is derived by the addition of the abstract predicates REMAIN + CAUSE, represented in the surface structure by the verb *keep,tv*. The verb *keep,tv* is a two-place predicate with an Agent as its subject and an embedded sentence as its object. The case frame is A,O. By predicate raising (McCawley 1973:158) the abstract predicate REMAIN is raised and joined to the abstract predicate CAUSE. This combination is represented in surface structure by the durative verb *keep,tv*. The empty S2 with V and O labels are pruned to leave a two-verb structure.

(51) Causative-durative structure

John kept the door open.   A,O
= CAUSE (John, REMAIN (BE OPEN (door)))

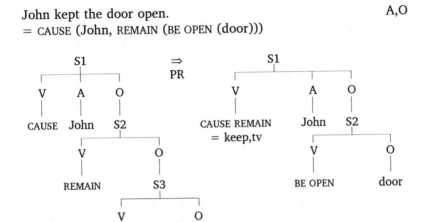

David Dowty (1972:43) defines the predicate REMAIN as parallel to the predicate COME ABOUT. Whereas COME ABOUT is defined as $-p$ T p, meaning it was not that way AND NEXT it is that way, REMAIN is defined as p T p, meaning it was that way AND NEXT it (still) is that way. REMAIN asserts a state of affairs and presupposes the same state of affairs at an earlier stage. *The door stayed open* means the door was open AND NEXT the door is still open. Durative predications are expressed in English using durative predicates, such as *stay, keep, remain.* Other duratives are recognized only by context, with or without durative adverbial phrases.

1.16–1.19 Covert case roles

Overt case roles are case roles required by the predicate that always occur whenever the verb is used. Covert case roles are case roles required by the meaning of the predicate that are sometimes or always missing from the surface structure. Partially covert roles are those roles which sometimes appear in surface structure and sometimes do not appear. These are called deletable roles. Totally covert roles are roles that never appear in the surface structure despite the fact that they are required by the meaning of the verb. They include coreferential roles and lexicalized roles.

(52)   Covert roles (Cook 1989:201)

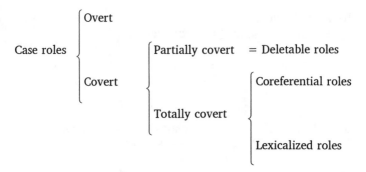

Covert roles assume greater importance in any theory that maintains the obligatory-O hypothesis. If the Object role can be sometimes deleted, or can be coreferential with another role, or can be lexicalized into the verb, then the analyst must look deeper to find the obligatory Object.

1.16. Deletable roles

Deletable roles are roles that sometimes occur in the surface structure and sometimes do not occur. The theory of deletable roles began with Fillmore's deletable object verbs (1968:29). The same case frame is given to the verb whether the Object is present as in sentence (53), or not present as in sentence (54). In both sentences, the case frame consists of the full complement of case roles required by the verb.

(53)   Mother /is cooking /potatoes.   A,O
         A   V   O

(54)   Mother /is cooking /(something).   A,O /O-del
         A   V   O-del

Anderson also speaks of deletable objects (1971:67), and in describing Locative verbs he suggests that this set of verbs "strongly select loc, i.e. **allowing for deletion,** loc is necessarily part of the frame into which such verbs are inserted" (1971:83).

In computational linguistics, it is important that multiple subcategorization patterns be handled by a single underlying predicate. Certain roles may be deleted in the surface structure. These deleted roles are referred to as implicit or open arguments. "Open thematic roles, we suppose, appear in the discourse model as indefinites, addresses in need of further identification or elaboration" (Carlson and Tanenhaus 1988:269).

(55) I /gave/(somebody)/(something)/at the office.   A,B,O /B-del,O-del
    A   V   B-del   O-del   L-modal

(56) The United Way /needed /the money.   B,Os
    B   V   Os

If the verb *give* requires a giver (Agent), a receiver (Benefactive), and a gift (Object), and the Benefactive and Object do not occur in the context of (55), then these two roles are left as open addresses. Sentence (56), which contains a Benefactive and an Object, can be related to sentence (55) with the result that the implicit Benefactive and Object arguments are made explicit.

Besides the advantage in resolving anaphora in discourse context, there is an obvious simplification if a single underlying predicate-argument structure is applied to many different surface subcategorization patterns. If the verb *tell* always requires a speaker (Agent), a hearer (Experiencer), and an what is said (Object), then one lexical entry with the full complement of case roles is sufficient, no matter what is deleted on the surface. The same case frame would apply to all four sentences (57)–(60).

(57) John /told /(somebody) /(something).   A,E,O /E-del,O-del
    A   V   E-del   O-del

(58) John /told /(somebody) /the story.   A,E,O /E-del
    A   V   E-del   O

(59) John /told /Mary /(something).   A,E,O /O-del
    A   V   E   O-del

(60) John /told /Mary /the story.   A,E,O
    A   V   E   O

Roles are marked as deletable when they are deleted from the active kernel sentence. Subjects are never marked as deleted, even in the passive. The Agent role, always in subject position, is never marked as a deletable role. The principal deletions are the Object case in direct object position, Experiencer and Benefactive roles in indirect object position, and Locatives with motion verbs.

1.17. Coreferential roles

Coreferential roles are defined as two roles that are applied to the same NP in the surface structure. The lower ranking of the two coreferential roles is never manifested in the surface structure. Fillmore had no coreference in his 1968 model. For this reason, Jackendoff chose Gruber's thematic relations over Fillmore's Case Grammar. "In Gruber's system of thematic relations, noun phrases can function in more than one thematic role within the same sentence" (1972:34). In sentence (61) an Object (Theme) is in motion; in sentence (62) there are two readings. The subject may be moving involuntarily and the thematic relations are the same as in sentence (61), or he may be moving intentionally as in sentence (63) and the subject is "both Theme and Agent" (1972:34).

(61) The rock /rolled /down the hill.   O,L
      O   V   L

(62) Max /rolled /down the hill (unintentionally).   O,L
      O   V   L

(63) Max /rolled /down the hill (intentionally).   A=O,L
      A=O V   L

Fillmore adopts coreferential roles in his later work. Anderson introduces coreferential roles as two case roles marked on the same NP. Within his localist system, Agent may be coreferential with any of the other four cases, Object, Location, Source, and Goal. Anderson (1971:121) cites three different case frames for the verb *move,* as in sentences (64)–(66).

(64) The rock /moved /(somewhere).   NonAgentive
      O   V   (L)

(65) John /moved /(somewhere).   Agentive reflexive
      A=O   V   (L)

(66) John /moved /the rock /(somewhere).   Agentive nonreflexive
      A   V   O   (L)

Anderson also cites coreference of Agent and Locative (1971:99) in sentences such as (67) and coreference of Experiencer and Object

(1971:96), which he calls reflexive (abstract) locative in one reading of sentence (68).

(67) His regiment /contained /the attack.   A,O,*L /A=L
      A=L   V   O

(68) a. John /is cold /(to the touch).   Os
         Os   V

      b. John /is (=feels) cold.   E=Os
         E=Os V

Coreference is not to be confused with reflexivization. Coreference is a deep structure configuration in which two case roles are applied to one NP. Reflexivization is a surface phenomena in which two NPs, each with its own case role, have the same referent. In fact, surface reflexivization is prima facie evidence that no coreferential roles are involved, since the reflexive rule involves two surface NPs and coreferential roles involve one NP with two case roles. Sentence (69) illustrates reflexivization. Note that the surface structure has two noun phrases, each with its own case role.

(69) Harry /washed /himself.   A,O
      A   V   O

1.18. Lexicalized roles

Lexicalized roles are totally covert roles that normally do not appear in the surface structure because they are incorporated into the verb. It was Gruber (1976:5) who first postulated a prelexical categorial base which through a process of incorporation become a single lexical item, as in *pierce* (= go through), *cross* (= go across). Most of Gruber's examples dealt with prepositions which mark thematic roles. But prelexical structure shows much more variation, as in the following example.

(70) V + Prep   go into   incorporated as enter,tv
      V + NP   eat dinner   incorporated as dine,iv
      V + NP + Prep   put water on   incorporated as water,tv
      V + Prep + NP   put in boxes   incorporated as box,tv

Anderson cites examples of V + NP + Prep in verbs like *help* = give help to and *thank* = give thanks to "in which the underlying nominative phrase is deleted, and its lexical content carried by the verb" (1971:142). Sentences (71a)–(71b) from Anderson illustrate lexical incorporation.

(71) a. Mary /gave /help /to anyone who asked.   A,B,O
          A   V   O   B

      b. Mary /helped   /anyone who asked.   A,B,*O /O-lex
          A   V (O-lex) B

The case grammarian, working within the context of prelexical structures, is principally interested in the lexicalization of nouns which
manifest propositional roles, not modal roles. Predicates occur which include lexicalized Object or Locative roles. The analyst is also interested
in the lexicalization of prepositions which are markers of essential cases,
particularly the Locative.

Lexicalized Object occurs in all four semantic domains: in the Basic
domain with A-O verbs, as in *work* = do work; in the Experiential domain with A-E-O verbs, as in *question* = ask questions of; in the
Benefactive domain with A-B-O verbs, as in *bribe* = give bribe to; in the
Locative domain with A-O-L verbs, as in *powder* = put powder on. With
A-O-L verbs the principal lexicalizations are in verbs of the put-on category, as in *powder, water, wax, polish* and the take-off category, as in *skin,
peel, scale, gut.*

One indication of lexicalized roles is the presence in the lexicon of
verbs and nouns with the same spelling. If the lexicon contains the verb
work and the noun *work,* it is highly probable that the verb *work* incorpo-
rates the noun. Another indication is the fact that the lexicalized role can
be forced to the surface. If the noun is not modified, its appearance in
the surface structure is redundant; but if modified it may appear as a
role copy, as in sentence (72b).

(72) a. Lucy /powdered /her nose /(*with powder).   A,*O,L /O-lex
          A   V (O-lex) L

      b. Lucy /powdered /her nose /with white powder.
          A   V (O-lex) L   O-copy

Lexicalized Locative occurs in the Locative domain with A-O-L verbs.
These lexicalized locatives occur with container nouns lexicalized. The
Object contained may be animate, as in *jail* (= put person in jail) or inanimate, as in *box* (= put object in boxes). As with lexicalized Object,
one expects the Locative noun to occur as both noun and verb, and

expects the Locative to be forced to the surface when the lexicalized noun is modified, as in 73b and 74b.

(73) a. Jake /bottled /the beer /(*in bottles)   A,O,*L /L-lex
     A   V (L-lex) O

   b. Jake /bottled /the beer /in green bottles.
     A   V (L-lex) O   L-copy

(74) a. The sheriff /jailed   /Robin Hood /(*in a jail). A,O,*L /L-lex
     A   V (L-lex) O

   b. The sheriff /jailed   /Robin Hood /in a dirty jail.
     A   V (L-lex) O   L-copy

Lexicalized prepositions occur with O-L and A-O-L verbs in the Locative domain. These hidden prepositions are indicators of the Locative case role, and often change the verb to transitive with the Locative noun as direct object, With these verbs the Locative case is not marked as lexicalized, since the Locative noun appears in the surface structure, as in sentence (75).

(75) John /entered /the room.   A,O,L /A=O
     A=O   V   L

Some verbs have lexicalized prepositions which act as full Locative case roles. No locative noun occurs in the structure, but the lexicalized preposition acts as an adverb of Location and is considered to be a lexicalized case. The case frame is O,*L /L-lex, as in sentence (76), where *set* = go down.

(76) The sun /set.   O,*L /L-lex
     O   V (L-lex)

1.19. Where is the Theme?

Sentences with no Object noun in the structure present a problem for any model which uses the obligatory-O hypothesis. The Theme (Object) case is often missing from the surface structure. A clearly defined theory of covert case roles is needed to find the missing Theme, so that the verb, even with a hidden case role, is defined in terms of its full complement of case roles. The analyst must make a decision as to where the

Theme (Object) is. How can the analyst distinguish between deletable roles, coreferential roles, and lexicalized roles?

Deletable object. When the Object noun is missing from the surface structure, one solution is to list these verbs as transitive with deletable object. Chafe (1970) calls these verbs completable. "The verb describes a certain action which, by its very nature, implies the existence of a certain nominal concept. Singing implies a song, playing implies a game" (1970:156). Fillmore (1968:29) lists verbs such as *cook* as "deletable object" verbs. The test used here for deletable object verbs is that deletable object verbs occur sometimes with an Object, and sometimes without an Object. Instead of positing two case frames for these two occurrences, the case frame A,O is given for both occurrences, which, when the object is missing, is listed as A,O /O-del. Verbs such as *cook, dance, play, sing* are deletable object verbs.

Coreferential roles. Another solution is to list verbs with no surface Object as having Agent and Object coreferential. With Action adjectives, coreferential roles are restricted to structures built upon already existing structures by adding an Agentive reinterpretation. With Action verbs in the basic domain, coreferential Agent and Object occur when involuntary human activities, classed as O, are voluntary in a given context. Some possible candidates are *breathe, cough, die, laugh, sleep, yawn.* It may be that all coreference is built on preexisting structures.

In the Experiential domain, verbs of sensation and cognition which are basically State E-Os verbs, such as *smell, taste, know, remember,* may receive an Agentive interpretation and be classed as A=E,O verbs when they are used in the active sense. Likewise, Psych movement verbs which are basic O-E Process verbs, such as *amaze, annoy, bore, interest,* may receive an agentive interpretation when the stimulus subject is acting deliberately.

In the Benefactive domain, verbs of acquisition which are basic B-O Process verbs, such as *acquire, receive,* may receive an Agentive interpretation when the subject instigates the activity, and are classed as A=B,O verbs.

In the Locative domain, this coreference occurs frequently when process motion verbs with inanimate subjects, classed as O,L, receive an Agentive interpretation with animate subjects and are classed as A=O,L. With motion verbs the Object (Theme) is always what is in motion. In A=O,L verbs the subject is both Agent instigating the activity and moving object.

Coreference also occurs when position verbs are reinterpreted agentively. Position verbs like *lie, sit, stand* are basically State verbs indicating the position of an Object, but when used with the meaning 'cause self to adopt a position' or 'cause self to remain in a position', they become action verbs with the Agent determining the position and are classed as A=O,L verbs.

Lexicalized Object. A third solution is to list these verbs as having a lexicalized Object case. Anderson, with the verb *work*, calls these reflexive ergative clauses and proposes coreferential Agent and Object because "the Agent operates in some sense upon itself" (1971:50). But given the fact that *work* is both a noun and a verb, the verb may be interpreted as an Action *do* verb with the particular nominal expressing the action incorporated into the verb. The verb *work* then would be interpreted as *do work,* much like John Ross' interpretation of *frogs croak* as *frogs do croaking* (1972:70). Some verbs with lexicalized Object include *act, cry, fish, gamble, work,* and these verbs are classed as A,O /O-lex.

Lexicalized objects occur in the Experiential domain, with verbs like *question, answer,* and are classed as A,E,O /O-lex, They also occur in the Benefactive domain, with verbs like *bribe, help,* classed as A,B,O /O-lex. In the Locative domain, the Object is lexicalized in put-on verbs like *water, powder* and take-off verbs like *skin, peel,* and are classed as A,O,L /O-lex.

1.20–1.22 Methodology

Once a Case Grammar model has been chosen, the model may be used to analyze the semantic context of texts. In the present work the model used is the Case Grammar Matrix Model (Cook 1989). This model presents a clear predicate-argument structure, builds a lexicon which distinguishes various verb senses, and not only describes arguments occurring in the text, but through covert roles, describes implicit arguments. This model is supplemented by the use of conceptual graphs, following the model described by John Sowa (1984).

1.20. Text analysis procedures

In order to analyze running text, the text must be broken down into single clauses. The clause, defined as a syntactic sequence containing one and only one predicate element, is the basic unit of information. The procedures for text analysis are as follows:

1. Separate the text into clauses.
2. Segment each clause into functioning phrase units.
3. Assign a case label to every unit except the verb.
4. Group the propositional cases as a tentative case frame.
5. Examine the case frame for possible covert roles.

These case frames are listed in a Case Grammar lexicon. Occurrences of the same verb are tested to see if the meaning is the same or different. This Case Grammar lexicon is then used for further text analysis.

Context. The case grammarian is involved in the same vicious circle as the dictionary maker. Which comes first, the meaning or the context? How do lexicographers write dictionaries? They list the meanings of the verbs in each context in which the verb is found. But once the dictionary is complete, it comes into general use. How do we use a dictionary? We look up the verb and see what meaning fits the context. The first process is inductive, discovering the meaning from context; the second is deductive, interpreting text according to the lexicon.

Likewise, in Case Grammar, the analyst assigns case frames to verbs as they are found in context, describing them according to a well-defined case model. These verbs and their case frames are then listed alphabetically in the lexicon. A second lexicon sorts the list according to case frames for the description of sets of verbs belonging to the same type. In text analysis, the analyst then uses the case lexicon to assign the case frame that is best suited to describe the meaning of each verb in the text. Ideally, the case frames are listed in the lexicon in order of frequency of occurrence.

1.21. Conceptual graphs

John F. Sowa, in his 1984 book, presents his theory of conceptual graphs as a synthesis of Case Grammar, semantic networks, and the graph logic of Charles S. Peirce. In these conceptual graphs, concept nodes are placed in boxes and represent entities; relation nodes are placed in circles and show how concepts are interrelated. In predicate-argument structure, concept nodes are the verb and related nouns, relation nodes are the case roles relating the arguments to the central predicate.

(77)   Conceptual graphs

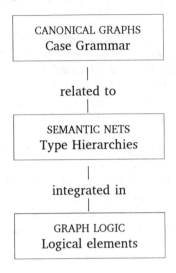

Conceptual graphs have a wider scope than Case Grammar. Examination of the thirty-seven conceptual relations in Sowa's appendix B3 (1984:415–19) shows not only essential cases like Agent, Experiencer, Object, but also modal cases, such as Manner, Material, Measure. There are relations for tense (PAST), modals (PSBL, NECS), aspect (PROG), negation (NEG), and modification relations for attributes (ATTR) and characteristics (CHRC). Case Grammar is restricted to the essential predicate-argument structure. Each of these five case roles of the matrix model subsume several of Sowa's conceptual relations.

(78)   Case Grammar   Conceptual relations

      Agent   Agent, Initiator, Instrument
      Experiencer   Experiencer
      Benefactive   Possession, Recipient
      Object   Object, Result, (Patient)
      Locative   Location, Source, Path, Destination

The present plan is to describe predicate-argument structure in terms of conceptual graphs, using only the five cases of the matrix model. The conceptual graph is more explicit in its distinction of concepts and relations, but adds no new information to the Case Grammar analysis. However, putting these structures in graph notation provides a basis, within conceptual graph theory, for representing the predicate-argument structure of propositions, which can then be expanded to include non-propositional elements.

In the lexicon, verbs in each of their senses are listed with their case frames. A case frame in Sowa is defined as "a canonical graph that shows the expected configuration of concepts and relations" (1984:224). What is expected of a verb is its full complement of case roles, even when all of these roles do not appear in a particular surface structure.

In parsing natural language there is a general tendency to name everything explicit in the current sentence, without identifying the implicit arguments demanded by the meaning of the verb. A parsing mechanism demands (1) a fixed list of cases, applied in depth to extended text analysis, (2) a clear distinction between propositional elements that are part of the predicate-argument structure and modal elements which may occur with virtually any predicate, and (3) a clear notion of verb type with its inheritance features, and verbal domain which groups together verbs of similar meaning.

Basic procedures. Case Grammar is written in conceptual graph format by placing the concepts (predicates, arguments) in boxes and relations (case roles) in circles. In linear notation boxes are represented by square brackets and circles by parentheses. The arrows in the notation point away from the predicate which is the source of the case relations. Within the noun concept box, the noun type is separated from the referent by a colon. The symbol # indicates a definite reference. The prepositional phrase is listed as a noun phrase concept, *the mat,* dominated by a preposition, *on.* It is the whole prepositional phrase, a phrase that can be replaced by the proform *there,* which bears the locative relation to the verb *sit.* Illustration (79a), adapted from Sowa 1984,[1] shows a conceptual graph along with the perception behind the utterance and the translation into two different languages. The linear notation is given in (79b).

---

[1] J. Sowa, *Conceptual Structures* (figure 2.3 from page 39). ©1984 Addison Wesley Longman. Reprinted by permission of Addison Wesley Longman.

(79) Perceptions, concepts, and language (Sowa 1984:39, adapted)

a.

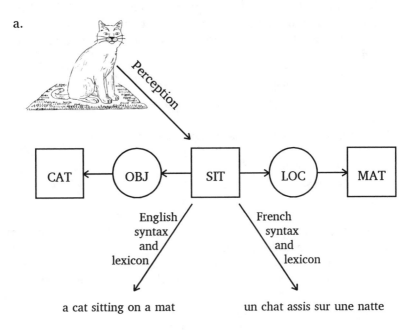

a cat sitting on a mat   un chat assis sur une natte

b. The cat /is sitting /on the mat.   Os,L

$$[\text{CAT}:\#]\leftarrow(\text{Os})\leftarrow[\text{SIT}]\rightarrow(\text{L})\rightarrow[\text{on } [\text{MAT}:\#]].$$

Although one-place and two-place predicates are easily written in linear notation, three-place predicates present a problem. In the notation
used in this work, all relational arrows are to be interpreted as relations
springing from the central verb. Proper nouns, such as *John,* will be written as concepts, but they are to be interpreted, in type: referent notation,
as [PERSON: John].

(80) John /told /Mary /the story.   A,E,O
      $[\text{JOHN}]\leftarrow(\text{A})\leftarrow[\text{TELL}]\rightarrow(\text{E})\rightarrow[\text{MARY}]\rightarrow(\text{O})\rightarrow[\text{STORY}:\#].$

Complex structures, with embedded predicates, may be written only
for the main verb if the embedded sentence is simply described as a
proposition. However, to represent both sentences in a single graph, the
main verb is listed on the first line, followed by a dash to indicate continuation, followed on succeeding lines by the case roles and arguments.

For the argument that is an embedded sentence, the proposition is listed in square brackets, the embedded verb is then listed, followed by a dash to indicate continuation, then the arguments of the verb are entered on successive lines. The proposition is closed with a square bracket and a period.

(81) John /told /Mary /that he was sick.   A,E,O
      [JOHN]←(A)←[TELL]→(E)→[MARY]→(O)→[PROPOSITION].

(82) John /told /Mary /that he was sick.   A,E,O
      [TELL] –
          (A)→[JOHN]
          (E)→[MARY]
          (O)→[[BE SICK]→(Os)→[JOHN]].

Covert roles. Covert case roles are not found in conceptual graphs although they are an important part of the predicate-argument structure. Deletable roles are easily incorporated using indefinite pronouns. Since these deletable roles occur elsewhere with their full complement of case roles, it is important to identify deletable roles, even if they remain empty addresses. In this way the verb is always entered with its full complement of case roles. In sentence (83) the deletable Object role, missing from the surface structure, is represented by a [NULL] symbol, indicating an open address.

(83) Adam /ate /(something).   A,O /O-del
      [ADAM]←(A)←[EAT]→(O)→[NULL].

Coreferential roles are not mentioned in Sowa's conceptual graphs, but are important in determining the verb type and verbal domain, and in identifying the presence of the obligatory theme. These coreferential roles never appear in the surface structure, but are entered in the case lexicon. Most coreferential roles involve an Agent and another role, and help to discriminate between agentive and nonagentive uses of the same verb.

(84) a. Harry /went /to the hospital.   O,L
      = Harry was unconscious and went in an ambulance.
      [HARRY]←(O)←[GO]→(L)→[to [HOSPITAL:#]].

    b. Harry /went /to the hospital.   A,*O,L /A=O
      = Harry went to visit his wife.
      [HARRY]←(A=O)←[GO]→(L)→[to [HOSPITAL:#]].

Lexicalized roles are not mentioned in Sowa's conceptual graphs, but are important in determining the presence of an obligatory Theme, when Object is lexicalized, and the verbal domain, when Locative is lexicalized. These lexicalized roles are never found in the surface structure unless the lexicalized noun is modified. Since Sowa's Conceptual graphs do not include lexicalized roles, a graph notation is suggested in sentences (85)–(86).

(85) Lucy /powdered /her nose.   A,*O,L /O-lex
      = put powder on
      [LUCY]←(A)←[POWDER /O-lex]→(L)→[NOSE:her].

(86) Bob /bottled /the beer.   A,O,*L /L-lex
      = put in bottles
      [BOB]←(A)←[BOTTLE /L-lex]→(O)→[BEER:#].

Nominalization will not be treated explicitly in this study, following Sowa's principle that "nominalized verbs inherit the case frames of the verbs they were derived from" (1988:7). It is to be hoped that in the future a full study of nominalizations will follow the analysis of the underlying verbs.

1.22. Case Grammar and conceptual graphs

Some of the differences between a case analysis based on the matrix model and conceptual graphs lie in the restricted environment of Case Grammar. Case Grammar is a more organized model than that represented in graphs, as in the following examples.

(87) A cat /is sitting /on the mat. (Sowa 1984:79)   Os,L

      Graph: [CAT]→(STAT)→[SIT]→(LOC)→[MAT].
      Case: [CAT]←(Os)←[SIT]→(L)→[on [MAT:#]].

In the graph, the STAT relation seems to link a physical object to a position (Sowa 1984:71, figure 3.2). The arrows indicate that the relation flows from the Object to the predicate expressing position. In the case description there is no STAT relation. Position verbs belong to a State locative class and require two cases flowing from the verb, an Object and its Location. Verb centrality is maintained (all case relations flow from the verb), and the verb is classified according to verb type, State, and verbal domain, Locative.

Principle: All conceptual relations flow from the central verb.

(88)   The cat /chased /the mouse. (Sowa 1984:202)   A,O,L

Graph: [CAT:#]←(AGT)←[CHASE]→(OBJ)→[MOUSE:#].
Case: [CAT:#]←(A)←[CHASE]→(O)→[MOUSE:#]→(L)→[NULL].

In the graph, the verb appears as a two-place predicate with Agent and Object, but *chase* is a motion verb. The cat chased the mouse somewhere. All motion verbs refer to an Object, which is in motion, and a Location, which is the path of the motion. An Agent may or may not be included in the structure. Therefore, in the case description of the verb *chase* the deletable Locative role should be inserted. Only by inserting the deletable Locative role is the verb placed in the proper semantic domain. The verb in sentence (88) is the same as the verb in *the cat chased the mouse around the house.*

Principle: Include deletable roles in case descriptions.

1.23. Conclusion

Case Grammar Theory (Cook 1989) describes the Case Grammar models of Fillmore, Chafe, Anderson, Gruber, Jackendoff, and some tagmemicists as contrasting models within Case Grammar theory. Each model is examined with regard to (1) its logical structure, (2) the list of cases used, (3) tactics for case frame formation, (4) rules for derivation within verb types, and (5) the use of covert roles. The final chapter explains the Case Grammar Matrix Model, which is formed by choosing from these contrasting models what is arguably the best structure, case list, case tactics, derivation, and covert roles.

Chapter 1 of the present work, intended as a companion volume to *Case Grammar Theory,* presents the matrix model in summary form and introduces conceptual graph representation. The reasons behind the methodology presented can be found in the *Case Grammar Theory* text. This methodology is then tested in extended textual analysis.

The next four chapters treat verbs in the Basic, Experiential, Benefactive, and Locative domains. Each verb type will have a generalized conceptual graph to indicate the predicate-argument structure. Each example in the text will contain the canonical graph of that sentence using the verb and nouns as concepts and the case labels as the verb-to-noun relations.

Case grammarians choose their own lists of cases. Still, the examples in the next four chapters should indicate that the five case labels used in the Case Grammar Matrix Model are necessary and sufficient for the description of all the verbs of the language. Localistic case grammarians, and analysts with other lists of case, should be able to translate the examples in the text into their own particular semantic model.

2
The Basic Domain

The basic domain consists of those predicates which require only the Object concept, or the Agent and Object concepts, to complete their meaning. The absence of Experiencer, Benefactive, and Locative roles indicates that the predicate belongs in the Basic domain. In a survey of 5,000 clauses in Hemingway's *The Old Man and the Sea*, 1,833 clauses (37%) were in the Basic domain. Of these clauses 750 (15%) were Basic States, 241 (5%) were Basic Process, and 842 (17%) were Basic Actions. The figure (89) shows the types of verbal situation which occur in the Basic domain, including Basic State, Basic Process, and Basic Action.

(89)   The Basic domain

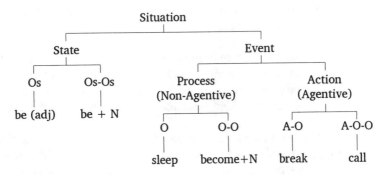

Basic State (750 clauses). Basic State verbs express a stative situation which can be fully captured with a still photograph. Nothing in the scene is moving or changing. Basic State predications require either a single Object marked for stativity as Os, or two Objects marked as Os, Os.

The Os frame. Predicate adjective structures have the Os case frame. Simple intransitive predicate adjectives have to be distinguished from adjectives which express actions (Lakoff 1966) and adjectives which express an experience. Simple predicate adverbs fall into the same category. There are, in addition, a few intransitive verbs with an Os frame, including verbs of existence and certain one-place raising predicates.

The Os-Os frame. Predicate noun structures have the Os-Os case frame. Within the lexicon these predicate nominals are simply listed as be + Noun. In addition, there are certain transitive adjectives, such as the comparatives which are two-place predicates. A few verbs are two-place stative predicates, including *cost, weigh,* and *mean.*

Basic Process (241 clauses). Basic Process verbs express a dynamic situation which does not involve an Agent. Since the situation is changing, these situations cannot be captured by a still photograph, but only by a video recording. Basic Process predications require either a single Object role, marked as O, or two Object roles, marked as O,O.

The O frame. Predicate adjective structures with the linking verb *become* are analyzed as complex structures. The verb *become* represents an underlying inchoative with the O case frame. The adjective is listed separately as a State predicate with the Os frame. Verbs with the O frame also include intransitive verbs of occurrence, intransitives with inanimate subjects, intransitives with involuntary animate subjects, and intransitive forms of the aspectual verbs.

The O-O frame. Predicate nominal structures with the linking verb *become* are listed as structures with the O-O case frame. Other verbs with the O-O frame include causatives in which one event causes another event. Both events may be embedded sentences, embedded under the O-case.

Basic Action (842 clauses). Basic Action verbs express a dynamic situation which involves an Agent. Since the situation is changing, these situations cannot be captured by a still photograph, but only by a video recording. Basic Action predications require an Agent role and an Object role.

The A,*O /A=O frame. Intransitive adjectives interpreted as Actions have the A-O case frame with A=O coreference. The be + adjective structure in context is reinterpreted as act + adverb. Sentences such as *John is polite* are reinterpreted in context as *John is acting politely.* Action adjectives are found in the work of George Lakoff (1966) and John Anderson (1971:55). Action verbs also occur when animate activities which are normally involuntary are reinterpreted as voluntary, as in *John coughed politely.*

The A,*O /O-lex frame. The Object case is often lexicalized into the verb. This lexicalization is evident when the word indicating the activity occurs as both a noun and a verb in the lexicon. In this context, the verb is considered a *do* verb with the noun lexicalized, such as *work = do work.*

The A,O frame. Some action adjectives are transitive, with both the Agent and Object roles overt. Transitive Action verbs also occur with both roles overt. Among these verbs are the transitive forms of the aspectual verbs *begin,tv, keep,tv, stop,tv.*

The A,O,O frame. Double objects occur with a very small set of Action verbs, including *call, name, elect.* These verbs are three-place predicates with the A-O-O case frame.

The A + A,O structure. Certain Action verbs are complex double Agent structures. The Agent of the main verb controls the Agent of the embedded verb, in such verbs as *walk,tv* in *he walked the dog.*

2.1–2.2 Basic State verbs

State verbs describe a static situation in which there is no change. State verbs in the basic domain are State verbs which do not include an Experiencer, Benefactive, or Locative. Basic State verbs occur with a single Object (Os) or double Object (Os,Os).

2.1. State with single Os

Basic State predicates with single Object are one-place predicates. The structure of the predication is shown in the graph in (90), which links an ENTITY called the Object with its predicate.

(90)   ┌───┐
       │ [ENTITY]   ←   (Os)   ←   [STATE-VERB]   │
       └───┘

Basic States with single Os include: predicate adjectives, apparent passives, intransitive verbs, and predicate adverbs. Most Basic State verbs are adjectives or participles, very few are verbs.

Predicate adjectives. Adjectives in English can be used in a predicate adjective structure with the copula *be*. These adjectives are listed in the lexicon with *be* preceding the adjective to indicate predicative use. The basic adjective predicate is classed as Os, as in sentence (91). Some one-place predicates may take an embedded sentence as subject, as in sentence (92). Special classes of adjectives include weather adjectives, epistemic adjectives, and contrasting adjectives.

(91)   Adam /is tall.   Os
       [ADAM]←(Os)←[BE TALL].

(92)   To err /is human.   Os
       [BE HUMAN]–
          (Os)→[[PERSON]←(O)←[ERR]].

Weather adjectives. A special type of basic State predicate is the adjective referring to the weather. These predicates require pronominal *it* as subject referring to the weather environment. Fillmore (1968:42) suggests that meteorological predicates with weather *it* have the case frame L indicating the place where the weather condition holds. Chafe (1970:101) claims that there is no noun in these "ambient" structures and that the case frame is empty. Anderson (1971:50, footnote 3) suggests that weather *it* represents "an underlying though perhaps empty" Theme. The case frame for weather State is Os. These adjectives are specified in the lexicon as weather related, such as *be cold (w)*. (See also §2.3 Inanimate process, for weather process verbs.)

(93)   It /is cold.   Os
       = The weather is cold.
       [WEATHER: IT]←(Os)←[BE COLD].

Weather adjectives require only the Object case referring to the weather or temperature. Time and Place expressions that occur with weather *it* are interpreted as circumstantial and are not part of the essential proposition.

(94) It /is hot /in the studio.   Os
      = (It is in the studio that) it is hot.
      [TEMPERATURE: IT]←(Os)←[BE HOT].

Epistemic adjectives. Some adjectives take an embedded sentence as subject and assert the truth value of the subject proposition. These subject complements may be in the form of a that-clause, for/to clause, or poss/ing clause. By a rule of extraposition this embedded sentence is moved to the end of the sentence and replaced by the dummy pronoun *it.* The extraposition rule applies to embedded that-clauses and for/to infinitives, but not to the poss/ing structure. These predicates include *be false, be possible, be true.*

(95) That Ben broke the dish /is true.   Os
      = It is true that Ben broke the dish.
      [BE TRUE] -
          (Os)→[[BEN]←(A)←[BREAK]→(O)→[DISH:#]].

A limited number of these epistemic predicates allow subject raising. The subject of the lower verb is raised to become the subject of the higher verb and the lower verb becomes an infinitive. They include *be likely, be certain.*

    This epistemic use of the adjective *be certain* (Os) is to be distinguished from the use of *be certain* (E,Os) as a cognitive adjective meaning 'be sure of'. (See §3.1 Cognitive states with E-subject.)

(96) Edward /is certain /to break the vase.   Os
      = It is certain that Edward will break the vase.
      [BE CERTAIN] -
          (Os)→[[Edward]← (A)←[BREAK]→(O)→[VASE:#]].

Contrasting adjectives. Although most predicate adjectives are Basic State verbs with the case frame Os, some adjectives, such as *be kind, be polite,* are used as action adjectives. Action adjectives include an Agent and are listed in the lexicon as *be kind (A)* and have the case frame A=O. Other adjectives, such as *be happy, be sad,* are inherently Experiential. They are listed in the lexicon as *be happy (E)* and have the case frame E=Os. Other adjectives express State relative to an Experiencer. They have the case frame Os,E.

    Action adjectives are those adjective predications in which the copula *be* is interpreted as *act* and the adjective is interpreted as a manner adverb. These adjectives occur with the imperative and progressive. The subject is both Agent and Object. Action adjectives describe activities rather than qualities. These actions include adjectives like *be kind, be polite, be rude.*

(97)   Adam /is polite.   Os
       = Adam is a polite person.
       [ADAM]←(Os)←[BE POLITE].

(98)   Adam /is being polite.   A=O
       = Adam is acting politely.
       [ADAM]←(A=O)←[BE (= act) POLITE].

Agentive reinterpretation. Juhani Rudanko (1989:60) uses the term AGENTIVE REINTERPRETATION to describe the Agentive interpretation of the Process verb *sleep* in sentences such as *John tried to sleep,* in which the verb *sleep,* which is normally a Process verb, is interpreted as an Action when controlled by the action verb *try.* One of the basic conditions for agentive reinterpretation is that there exists a nonagentive reading before reinterpretation. Extending this notion to sentences (97) and (98), sentence (97) is a Basic State with the case frame Os. This Basic State is reinterpreted in sentence (98) as a Basic Action with the case frame A=O. This reinterpretation is obligatory when the predicate adjective occurs in the progressive, *John is being polite,* or in the imperative *be polite, John.* In the reinterpretation the verb *be* is interpreted as *act,* and the predicate adjective is interpreted as the manner adverb, *politely.* The principle of agentive reinterpretation can also be applied to involuntary human activities, normally Process verbs with the case frame O, reinterpreted in certain contexts as deliberate actions, as in *John coughed politely.*

Experiential adjective (E=Os). State experiential adjectives with an Experiencer as subject are adjective predications in which the copula *be* is interpreted as *feel.* The subject has coreferential Experiencer and Object roles. Experiential adjectives are States and do not take the progressive. These include emotional adjectives *happy, sad, angry* and are listed in the lexicon as *be happy (E).* State experiential adjectives are inherently experiential, they have no other interpretation. (See §3.1 State Experiential with E-Subject.)

(99)   Adam /is happy.   E=Os
       = Adam feels happy.
       [ADAM]←(E=Os)←[BE (=feel) HAPPY].

State Experiential adjective (Os,E). State adjective predicates (Os) are distinguished from State experiential predicates (Os,E) with stimulus (Os) subject and implied Experiencer (E) as indirect object. These adjectives are two-place predicates, but sometimes have the Experiencer case role deleted. These adjectives often take embedded sentences as their subject. They include *be good for, be bad for, be hard for, be difficult for, be easy for.* Some of these predicates take object raising, so-called tough movement. (See §3.2 State Experiential with Os-subject.)

(100) The pollen /is bad for /the old man.   Os,E
     [POLLEN:#]←(Os)←[BE BAD FOR]→(E)→[MAN:#]

(101) It /is hard /for Dan /to like Lucy.   Os,E
     [BE HARD FOR] -
       (Os)→[[DAN]←(E)←[LIKE]→(Os)→[LUCY]]
       (E)→[DAN]

Apparent passives. In a formal approach to English grammar all constructions that include the auxiliary *be* and the past participle of a transitive verb are called passives. Quirk et al. (1985:171) place these passives on a gradient from central passive to semi-passive to pseudo-passive to statal passive. In a semantic approach a choice must be made between a passive interpretation, which implies an Agent, and a stative interpretation, which does not imply an Agent. A true passive predication describes an activity, but a stative predication describes the state of the object as a result of that activity. The gradient involved is the degree to which this ambiguity can be resolved by structural clues in context. Passive sentences from which the *by*-phrase has been deleted are called "short passives" (Anderson 1971:47). These sentences are ambiguous between a passive and a stative interpretation. Quirk et al. (1985:170) calls the latter "statal passives." These are really not passives at all, but resemble passives in form.

(102) The lock was broken during the night.   A,O /(P)
     = The lock was broken by someone.
     Passive
     [PERSON]←(A)←[BREAK]→(O)→[LOCK:#].

(103) The lock was broken.   Os
     = The lock was in a broken state.
     Resultative State
     [LOCK:#]←(Os)←[BE BROKEN].

The ambiguity is structural. In (102) the sentence is interpreted as a subject-predicate structure with the predicate position filled by a verb in the passive form, *was broken*. The *-en* is an inflectional affix indicating passive. In (103) the sentence is interpreted as a subject-be-adjective structure in which the adjective position is filled by a derived adjective, *broken*. The *-en* is a derivational affix indicating resultative state, that is, a state as the result of an action or process. The ambiguity is occasioned by the loss of the inflectional system. In an inflected language (102) would appear as a verb inflected for passive, whereas (103) would show agreement between the predicate adjective and its subject. But with no system for marking agreement the ambiguity can only be resolved by context (Cook 1990:25, Ambiguity of the short passive).

Adjectives derived from intransitive verbs. A resultative adjective may be derived from a Process verb. Some States are derived from intransitive Process forms and cannot be confused with the passive, since intransitive verbs have no passive. These include *dead/die, gone/go, alive/live, asleep/sleep*.

(104) Shakespeare /is dead.   Resultative Os
      = Shakespeare is in a dead state.
      [SHAKESPEARE]←(Os)←[BE DEAD].

Adjectives derived from transitive verbs. The most common derived adjectives come from those verbs that have transitive use as an Action verb and intransitive use as a Process verb. These include *broken/break, closed/close, frozen/freeze, melted/melt*. The resultative adjectives derived from Action verbs are often ambiguous with the passive past participle. The passive implies a deleted Agent phrase and may take the progressive. The resultative State resembles a simple adjective and has the meaning of state-as-a-result-of-a-process. The resultative adjectives are listed with other simple adjectives, generally Os; the passive forms are listed as action verbs in the passive, such as A,O /(P).

(105) The sail /is patched.   Resultative Os
      = The sail is in a patched state.
      [SAIL:#]←(Os)←[BE PATCHED].

Whether or not the ambiguity is resolved, there is a clear-cut choice between two well-defined structures. Interpretation and translation of the sentence demand that the analyst make this choice and resolve the ambiguity one way or the other. The meaning of the stative construction is totally different from the meaning of the passive construction. Passives imply an Agent, statives do not imply an Agent. Structural clues include immediate and remote context. Present tense forms tend to be states; past tense forms remain ambiguous. States do not take the progressive; passives may take the progressive. State adjectives permit intensifiers like *very;* passives do not. If all these fail the analyst resorts to remote context to determine if the sentence is describing an activity by some person or simply describing the state of the object. The key question to ask is whether the passive form invokes the question: by whom?

By-phrases occurring with the past participle do not necessarily denote an Agent, but only denote a down-graded subject. In *the truth is known by many people* the downgraded subject is an Experiencer. All by-phrases do not denote downgraded subjects. The preposition may be locative, as in (106).

(106) The house /is situated /by the sea.   Os,L
      = *The sea situates the house.
      [HOUSE:#]←(Os)←[BE SITUATED]→(L)→[by [SEA:#]].

Intransitive verbs. Although the majority of State verbs are adjective forms, there are a few verbs which are basic States. These include existence predicates and a few raising predicates. These intransitive State verbs are contrasted with similar forms with which they might be confused.

Existence verbs. Existence is predicated of a subject with the verb *exist,* or the verb *be* (= *exist*). The subject noun in the sentence is the Theme (Os) and the predicate is *exist.* The verb *exist* occurs optionally with existential *there,* but the verb *be* (= *exist*) is ungrammatical without the use of existential *there.*

(107) Green giants /exist.   Os
      = There exist green giants.
      [GIANTS]←(Os)←[EXIST].

(108) There /are /green giants.   Os
      = *Green giants are.
      [GIANTS]←(Os)←[BE (= **exist**)].

Contrast with occurrence. Existential *be* contrasts with *be* = *occur* which predicates the existence of an ongoing event. The verb *be* in this context is a Process verb, and requires the insertion of existential *there* since the verb *be* cannot occur in final position.

(109) There /was /much betting.   O
    = *Much betting was (=occurred).
    [BETTING]←(O)←[BE (= occur)].

Contrast with durative. Existential *be* also contrasts with *be* = *remain* which predicates the duration of an ongoing event. The verb *be* in this context is a Process verb, and requires the insertion of existential *there*. In the conceptual graph, @2 means the set has two members.

(110) There are two hours until sunset.   O
    = *Two hours /are (=remain) /until sunset.
    [HOURS:@2]←(O)←[BE (= remain)].

Contrast with locative. Existential *there* occurs optionally in State locative predications, in which existential *there* is inserted as part of a focussing rule and is not part of the logical structure.

(111) There /is /a book /on the table.   Os,L
    = A book is (located) on the table.
    [BOOK]←(Os)←[BE-LOC]→(L)→[on [TABLE:#]].

Raising verbs. There are a few basic State verbs which are raising predicates which always have an embedded sentence as their subject. These include the verbs *happen, tend.* The subject of the embedded sentence is raised to become the subject of the raising verb. The raising verb *happen* in sentence (112) contrasts with the verb *happen* = *occur* in sentence (113) which is a Process verb which takes an event noun as its subject. (See §2.3 Process verb with single O.)

(112) Edward /happened /to break the vase.   Os
    = It is the case that Edward broke the vase.
    [HAPPEN] -
      (Os)→[[EDWARD]←(A)←[BREAK]→(O)→[VASE:#]].

(113) An accident /happened.   O
    [ACCIDENT]←(O)←[HAPPEN = occur].

Predicate adverbs. Predicate adverbs are often linked to their subjects by the copula *be.* Manner adverbials function like the predicate adjectives. The lexical entry for manner adverbials when used as predicate adverbs is *be* + adverb.

(114) David /is in bad shape.   Os
      = be in bad shape (David).
      [DAVID]←(Os)←[BE IN BAD SHAPE].

Contrast with Time. When Time adverbials are predicated of a subject, the structure is interpreted as Os,T. The meaning of the *be* predicate is 'be located in time', and the time adverb is an essential argument. Expressions of Time are also essential arguments with a few Process and Action verbs. (See §1.12 Revised Case Grammar matrix, time predicates.)

(115) The meeting /is /on Wednesday.   Os,T
      = The meeting is (located in time) on Wednesday.
      [MEETING:#]←(Os)←[BE-TEMP]→(T)→[on [WEDNESDAY]].

Contrast with Place. When Place adverbials are predicated of a subject, the structure is interpreted as Os,L. The meaning of the *be* predicate is 'be located in space', and the place adverbial is an essential argument. (See §5.1 State Locative with Os-subject.)

(116) The play /is /at the Kennedy Center.   Os,L
      = The play is (located) at the Kennedy Center.
      [PLAY:#]←(Os)←[BE-LOC]→(L)→[at [KENNEDY CENTER:#]].

Text analysis of State verbs with single Os (599). In the Hemingway novel Basic State predicates with single Os included adjectives and verbs. Most adjectives were one place intransitive predicates, and were distinguished from Action adjectives and Experiential adjectives.

Adjectives (410). In the Basic domain there were 410 occurrences of one place intransitive adjectives. Among these adjectives the most frequent were be strong (16), be good (13), be long (12), and be clear (12).

(117) But are you strong enough now for a truly big fish?   14:22
      [PERSON:you]←(Os)←[BE STRONG].

(118) And your eyes are good.   14:20
      [EYES:your]←(Os)←[BE GOOD].

Verbs (53). In the Basic domain there were 53 occurrences of one-place intransitive verbs.The most frequent was the verb *be (= exist)* (52). There was one occurrence of the verb *shine (= appear) silver.*

(119) And there are many tricks.   14:24
      [TRICKS:many]←(Os)←[BE (=exist)].

(120) The tuna shone silver in the sun.   38:3
      [SHINE (=appear)] -
        Os→[[TUNA:#]←(Os)←[BE SILVER]].

2.2. State with double Os

Some State verbs are two-place predicates. These verbs are analyzed as two Object roles related by the predicate *be*. The structure of the predication is shown in the following graph, which links one ENTITY called the Object with another ENTITY called Object.

(121)

Basic states with double Os include predicate nouns, transitive adjective predicates, and transitive stative verbs. These verbs are characterized as Os,Os.

Predicate nouns. Predicate nouns are linked to their subjects by the copula *be*. This forms a two argument structure in which the Object role is used for both the subject NP and the predicate noun. These structures are listed as *be* + Noun and are characterized as Os,Os. Fillmore was committed to the principle that "no case category appears more than once" in a case frame (1968:24), consequently he struggled to find a label for the predicate noun. Chafe (1970:141, 201) claims that the predicate noun becomes a verb by a predicativizer derivation. Anderson (1971:76) suggests that predicate nominal structures include two occurrences of the Object case. Later, Anderson (1976:38, 54) states that it may be necessary to relax Fillmore's one-instance-per-clause condition "to allow up to two instances of just Object," specifically to allow for equative sentences. According to Anderson, the O-case may be repeated in any case frame, but all other cases follow the well-known Fillmore one-instance-per-clause principle.

(122) Carl /is /a teacher. Os,Os
[CARL]←(Os)←[BE-IDENT]→(Os)→[TEACHER]

Some predicate nominal constructions show an identity between two nouns that are generally used to express Time. These nouns do not place an event in time, but indicate identity between two nouns.

(123) Today /is /Wednesday. Os,Os
[TODAY]←(Os)←[BE-IDENT]→(Os)→[WEDNESDAY]

In predicate nominal structures with *be,* the predicate nominal position, or the subject position, or both, may be filled by a sentence embedded under the Object case. These structures are listed as *be +* *clause.*

(124) This /is /what I saw. Os,Os
[BE-IDENT] -
(Os)→[THIS]
(Os)→[[PERSON:#I]←(E)←[SEE]→(Os)→[WHAT]].

Transitive adjective predicates. Some two-place adjectives constitute a comparison between two noun phrases. These include *be better/ worse than, be equal/inferior/superior to, be like/unlike, be made of.* This structure is characterized as Os,Os.

(125) Summer /is better than /winter. Os,Os
[SUMMER]←(Os)←[BE BETTER THAN]→(Os)→[WINTER].

Most transitive adjectives can take embedded sentences in subject or object position or both. In the conceptual graph notation for embedded sentences, the main verb is placed on the first line with a dash to indicate continuation, and the two Objects being related are placed on following lines. The following graph shows embedded sentences in both subject and object position.

(126) Doing research /is better than /working. Os,Os
[BE BETTER THAN] -
(Os)→[[PERSON]←(A)←[DO]→(O)→[RESEARCH]]
(Os)→[[PERSON]←(A)←[DO]→(O)→[WORK]].

Transitive stative verbs. A small set of verbs take a double Object role. With the relaxation of the one-instance-per-clause principle for the

Object case, these structures may be characterized as Os,Os and include *cost, weigh, measure, make (=form), mean.* Chafe uses *cost* and *weigh* as examples of verbs that take his Complement case, and the verbs are called completable. "*Weigh* must be accompanied by a complement expressing weight, *cost* by a complement expressing a price" (1970:157). However, since Complement is not an available subject choice, it is considered in the present model to be a variant of the Object (Theme) case.

(127) The box /weighs /two pounds.   Os,Os
      [BOX:#]←(Os)←[WEIGH]→(Os)→[POUNDS:@2]

(128) The trees /make /a circle around the house.   Os,Os
      = The trees form a circle.
      [TREES:#]←(Os)←[MAKE = **form**]→(Os)→[CIRCLE].

Certain transitive verbs take subject or object complements filling the Theme role (Os) in either or both positions. These include *indicate, mean, signify.*

(129) This data /means /that the economy is falling.   Os,Os
      = This data means the proposition (the economy is falling).
      [MEAN] -
      (Os)→[DATA:#]
      (Os)→[[ECONOMY]←(O)←[FALL = **decrease**]].

Text analysis of State verbs with double Os (293). Basic State predicates with double Os include adjectives and verbs. Adjectives with double Os (37) are two place transitive predicates that make a comparison between two entities. The most common were *be better than* (3) and *be like* (10). The most dominant verbs with double Os (256) were the BE + NOUN (212) and the BE + CLAUSE (16) structures. Others were *cost* (2) and *be = cost* (1), *weigh* (3) and equivalents *be = weigh* (2) and *dress out = weigh* (2), and *mean* (11).

(130) He was feeling much better.   65:15
      = He felt himself to be better than before.
      [FEEL] -
      (E)→[PERS:#he]
      (O)→[[PERS:#he]←(Os)←[BE BETTER THAN]→(Os)→[NULL]].

2.3–2.4 Basic Process verbs

Process verbs in the basic domain describe an on-going situation in which there is change. Basic Process verbs include both one-place (O) and two-place (O,O) predicates. Process verbs may occur with the progressive inflection, but may not take the imperative.

2.3. Process with single O

Basic Process predicates with single Object are one-place predicates. The structure of the predication is shown in the following graph, which links an ENTITY called the Object with its predicate.

(131) | ENTITY | ← Ⓞ ← | PROCESS-VERB |

Basic Process verbs with single Os include: (1) occurrence verbs, (2) animate process verbs, (3) inanimate process verbs, (4) intransitive aspectual verbs, (5) derived process verbs, and (6) become + adjective. There are no Process adjectives.

Occurrence verbs. Occurrence verbs refer to an ongoing event. These include the process verb *be = occur* which does not occur in progressive form. This meaning of the verb *be* often occurs with existential *there* in subject position. This verb set also includes the verbs *happen* and *occur*, which do occur in progressive form. These verbs are generally accompanied by an event noun. Any expressions of place and time that occur are modal.

(132) There /is /a hurricane /in the Atlantic.   O
      = A hurricane is occurring in the Atlantic.
      [EVENT:hurricane]←(O)←[BE = **occur**].

The Process verb *happen (=occur)* contrasts with the stative verb *happen*, a raising predicate in which the stative verb has the meaning *It is the case that...* (See §2.1 Intransitive verbs, Raising verbs.)

(133) What /is happening /on campus /this weekend?   O
      = What event is happening?
      [WHAT]←(O)←[HAPPEN = **occur**].

Animate process. Intransitive Process verbs occur which describe an animate person undergoing an involuntary process. They occur freely with the progressive, but are not Agentive, since the activity is not within the person's control. These include *breathe, cough, die, laugh, sleep, sneeze, yawn.*

(134) The man /is dying.   O
    = DIE (man)
    [MAN:#]←(O)←[DIE].

Although these verbs are Process verbs, they may become Actions by a causative derivation, which will then allow them to be used in the imperative. In this use the person is in control of the activity, and either permits or causes the otherwise involuntary action. (See §2.5 Action with A=O coreference.)

(135) Sleep well, old man.   A=O
    = Let yourself sleep.
    [PERSON:#you]←(A=O)←[SLEEP].

Inanimate process. Intransitive Process verbs describing an inanimate object undergoing a process are frequent and are paired with a transitive form which is causatively derived from them. These include *break,iv, close,iv, cook,iv, freeze,iv, grow,iv, melt,iv, shine,iv.*

(136) The sun /is shining.   O
    [SUN:#]←(O)←[SHINE].

A special subset of these intransitive events are the "haunted house" verbs, which are unique in that they have no underlying state. These include *bang,iv, creak,iv, howl,iv, pop,iv, rustle,iv, shriek,iv, slam,iv.*

(137) The door /slammed.   O
    ≠ *The door is in a slammed state.
    [DOOR:#]←(O)←[SLAM].

Another subset of inanimate process verbs are weather process verbs, such as *It is raining.* Although the concept of *raining* and its semantic representation in a case frame is the same for all languages, the syntactic realization of this concept varies from language to language. Some languages use an NP subject, some a pronominal subject, and some no subject at all. Where there is a subject, a case relation is demanded;

where there is no subject, the semantics overrides the syntax and postulates an understood subject. In a case theory in which there are no empty case frames and in which Object is obligatory, there can be no zero-place predicates. (See also §2.1 Weather adjectives for the position taken on this subject by Fillmore and Chafe.) Anderson's explanation is perhaps the clearest. Weather *it* represents "an underlying though perhaps empty theme."

(138) It is raining
    [Weather:IT]←(O)←[RAIN].

Aspectual verbs. An important subset of Process verbs are intransitive aspectual verbs. Events have a beginning, a middle, and an end. These aspects of events are marked by inceptive, durative, and terminative predicates with an event noun or an embedded complement in their scope. State verbs do not take inceptive or terminative aspects.

(139) Aspectual verbs

Verb type	Inceptive	Durative	Terminative
State	—	stay, iv	—
Process	begin, iv	keep, iv	stop, iv
Action	begin, tv	keep, tv	stop, tv

Inceptives. The inceptive predicates mark the beginning of an event. They are aspectual verbs which must have an event noun or event sentence in their scope. These include *begin, commence, start*. Perlmutter (1970) demonstrates that aspectual predicates like *begin* are used both intransitively and transitively even when no complementation is involved. *Begin,iv* is a process verb with an event noun as its subject. *Begin,tv* is an action verb with an Agent as subject and an event noun as the direct object. Newmeyer (1975) suggests that the transitive form is derived from the intransitive by a causative derivation.

(140) The play /began.   O
    [PLAY:#]←(O)←[BEGIN,**iv**].

(141) They /began /the play.   A,O
    [PERSON:#they]←(A)←[BEGIN,**tv**] → (O) → [PLAY:#].

Intransitive inceptive predicates are raising predicates and take reduced complements, infinitives, or participles, as their subject. The
intransitive form is recognized by the fact that the embedded proposition
is a Process, never a State or an Action. *Begin,iv* is a one-place predicate.
The subject of the lower Process verb is raised and becomes the subject
of *begin*.

(142) It /began /to rain.   O
    = BEGIN (RAIN (It))
    [BEGIN,iv] -
        (O)→[[WEATHER:IT]←(O)←[RAIN]].

The inceptive *commence,iv* accepts the participle form, but is doubtful
with the infinitive. The inceptives *begin,tv* and *start,iv* take both the infinitive and the participle complement.

(143) The leaves began /?commenced /started to fall.   O
      The leaves began /commenced /started falling.   O
      [BEGIN,tv] -
          (O)→[[LEAVES:#]←(O)←[FALL]→(L)→[NULL]].

Inceptive predicates sometimes seem to have a State within their scope.
The embedded proposition is not State, but a Process. States do not have
a beginning, only a Process has a beginning and an end.

(144) It /started /to be light.   O
      [START,iv] -
          (O)→[[WEATHER: IT]←(O)←[BE (=become) LIGHT]].

The intransitive inceptive predicates, which are Process verbs with a
Process verb within their scope, must be distinguished from the transitive inceptive predicates, which are Action verbs with an Action within
their scope. The Agent is both the Agent of starting and the Agent of the
activity. The transitive form is recognized by the fact that the embedded
proposition is an Action. *Begin,tv* is a two-place predicate. The subject of
begin,tv is interpreted as the PRO-subject of the embedded Action.

(145) David /began /to read /the book.   A,O
    = BEGIN (David, READ (David, book))
    [BEGIN,tv] -
        (A)→[DAVID]
        (O)→[[DAVID]←(A)←[READ]→(O)→[BOOK: #]].

(146) John /started /to clean the house.   A,O
 = START (John, CLEAN (John, house))
 [START,tv] -
  (A)→[JOHN]
  (O)→[[JOHN]←(A)←[CLEAN]→(O)→[HOUSE:#]].

Duratives. The durative predicates mark the continuance of an event. They are aspectual verbs which may have a State, Process, or Action verb within their scope, since States, Processes, and Actions may all continue. These verbs include *continue, keep, remain, stay.*

(147) The opera /continued.   O
 [OPERA:#]←(O)←[CONTINUE,iv].

(148) They /continued /the opera.   AO
 [PERSON:#they]←(A)←[CONTINUE,tv]→(O)→[OPERA:#].

Intransitive durative predicates take reduced infinitive or participle complements as their subject when the embedded proposition is a State. The durative predicate may occur with durative adverbial phrases like *for, since, until.* The predicate *stay,iv* is a one-place raising predicate with a State verb within its scope. With adjective State predicates, the infinitive marker *to* and the verb *be* are deleted. The durative predicate *remain,iv* is also used in this context, but the durative predicate *keep,iv* is ungrammatical.

(149) The water stayed /*kept /remained calm.   O
 = REMAIN (BE CALM (water))
 [STAY,iv] -
  (O)→[[WATER:#]←(Os)←[BE CALM]].

The predicate *remain,iv* is also a one-place raising predicate and may have a State or a Process verb within its scope. It is the only durative predicate that is used with predications including predicate nouns.

(150) Henry *stayed /*kept /remained a doctor.   O
 = REMAIN (BE (Henry, doctor)
 [REMAIN] -
  (O)→[[HENRY]←(Os)←[BE]→(Os)→[DOCTOR]].

The predicate *keep,iv* is a one-place predicate and has a Process verb within its scope. It is also a subject-raising predicate, and the embedded verb is a participle. The durative predicate *keep,iv* may be replaced by *continue,iv, go on,iv, keep on,iv.* Infinitive complements may only occur with the Process verb *continue,iv.*

(151) The water *stayed /kept /*remained /running.   O
     =The water *stayed /*kept /*remained to run.
     [KEEP,iv] -
         (O)→[[WATER:#]←(O)←[RUN]].

(152) The water /continued /running.   O
     = The water continued to run.
     [CONTINUE,iv] -
         (O)→[[WATER:#]←(O)←[RUN]].

Terminatives. The terminative predicates mark the end of an event. They are aspectual verbs which have a Process within their scope. They have either an event noun or an embedded Process sentence as subject. These verbs include *cease,iv, finish,iv, quit,iv,* and *stop,iv.*

(153) The music /stopped.   O
         [MUSIC:#]←(O)←[STOP,iv].

The intransitive terminative predicates take reduced complements, infinitives, or participles. The embedded proposition is always a Process. Verbs such as *cease,iv, finish,iv, quit,iv, stop,iv* are raising predicates. The verb *cease,iv* marginally takes an infinitive complement.

(154) It ceased /finished /stopped /quit /raining.   O
     It ceased /*finished /*stopped /*quit /to rain.   O
     = STOP (RAIN (IT))
     [STOP,iv] -
         (O)→[[WEATHER:IT]←(O)←[RAIN]].

Derived process. According to Wallace Chafe (1970:122), Process verbs may be derived from State verbs by the inchoative derivation, or they may be derived from Action verbs by a decausative derivation. George Lakoff (1970:32), in comparing Process verbs with State verbs for such pairs as *thick/thicken,iv,* suggests the difference is contained in an abstract inchoative predicate, later designated as COME ABOUT, and defined by David Dowty (1972:40).

Process derived from State. A Process verb may be derived from a State verb by the inchoative derivation. These Process verbs may be one word Process verbs marked by the derivational ending *-en.* One-word Process verbs are derived from stative adjectives and appear in the lexicon as intransitive verbs. There are other two-word Process predicates consisting of the verbs *become, get,* or *turn* with predicate adjectives. For semantic purposes these may be considered to be a single lexical entry.

(155) The road /widened.   O
    = The road became wide.
    [ROAD:#]←(O)←[WIDEN,iv].

Some derived forms in *-en* are never used as intransitive verbs, but they are used as transitive Action verbs. These include *cheapen,tv, deaden,tv, deafen,tv, fatten,tv, roughen,tv, sicken,tv.*

(156) The noise /deafened /George.   A,O
    = The noise caused George to become deaf.
    [NOISE:#]←(A)←[DEAFEN,tv]→(O)→[GEORGE].

Some derived forms are marked by vowel change, like *hot/heat.* The intransitive verb *heat,iv* is derived from *hot* by the inchoative derivation, but *heated* is derived from the verb *heat* by the resultative derivation.

(157) The water /heated.   O
    = The water became hot.
    [WATER:#]←(O)←[HEAT,iv].

Some derived forms are zero marked. The adjective State form is spelled the same as the derived intransitive verb form. This class includes *clean,iv, dry,iv, open,iv, thin,iv.* The transitive forms of these same verbs are formed by the causative derivation.

(158) The door /opened.   O
    = The door became open.
    [DOOR:#]←(O)←[OPEN,iv].

Process derived from Action. Process verbs are derived from Action verbs by the decausative derivation which removes the Agent from the structure. Verbs of this class include *cut, handle, kick, polish, wash.*

(159) The dishes /wash /easily.   O
    [DISHES:#]←(O)←[WASH,iv].

Become + adjective. Some Process verbs are complex and consist of two words, an inchoative verb and an adjective. Inchoative verbs occurring in English include *become, get,* and *turn.* These inchoative predicates combine with adjectives and constitute a problem for the lexicon.

The *become* + adjective structure may constitute a single entry in the lexicon, parallel to the *-en* inchoative derivation. In this case the two-word structure becomes a single lexical entry with the case frame O. The meaning of the two structures is the same, only the form is different. David Dowty's (1972:40) definition of the inchoative predicate COME ABOUT has already been cited under §1.15 Lexical decomposition. The inchoative *thicken,iv* is interpreted as "The soup was not thick, and next, the soup was thick." The inchoative presupposes it was not that way, and then asserts it became that way. The same interpretation can be given to the combination *become thick.*

(160) The soup /thickened.   thicken,iv = O
    = COME ABOUT (BE THICK (soup))
    [SOUP:#]←(O)←[THICKEN,iv].

(161) The soup /became thick.   become thick = O
    = COME ABOUT (BE THICK (soup))
    [BECOME] -
    (O)→[[SOUP:#]←(Os)←[BE THICK]]].

Although the two-word structure is sound semantically, it creates problems for the lexicon. The *become* + adjective structure is an open-ended structure which can be applied to virtually any adjective, causing excessive duplication in the lexicon. An alternative solution is to separate *become* from its adjective and list the two elements as two separate predicates. The verb *become,* followed by an adjective, is a one-place predicate expressing the inchoative. The stative adjective predication is within the scope of the inchoative predicate. The verb *become* would be listed with the case frame O, with the meaning COME ABOUT, and the adjective would be listed with the case frame proper to other adjectives of its class. The conceptual graph shows the stative proposition embedded as subject to the inchoative *become.* The same interpretation would be given to *get* + adjective and *turn* + adjective, as in *He's getting confused,* or *It's turning cold.*

(162) The sky /became /blue.
    a. BECOME (sky (BE BLUE))   O
    b. BE BLUE (sky)   Os
    [BECOME] -
        (O)→[STATE: [SKY:#]←(Os)←[BE BLUE]].

2.4. Process with double O

Some Process verbs are two-place predicates. The structure of the predication is shown in the following graph, which links one ENTITY called Object with another ENTITY called Object.

(163)
| ENTITY | ← | (O) | ← | PROCESS-VERB | → | (O) | → | ENTITY |

Basic Process verbs with double O include: become + predicate noun and causative predicates where one event causes another event. If an Agent causes the event, the verb is classified as A,O.

Become + noun. The *become* + noun structure does not involve the same problem as the *become* + adjective structure. The predicate *become* is a two-place predicate relating the two nouns in the structure. In the lexicon this predicate is listed as *become* + *noun* with the case frame O,O. A small number of Process verbs occur with predicate nouns to form a double Object structure. These verbs include *become, change into, turn into.*

(164) The boy /became /a doctor.   O,O
    = BECOME (boy, doctor)
    [BOY:#]←(O)←[BECOME]→(O)→[DOCTOR].

(165) The coach /turned into /a pumpkin.   O,O
    = BECOME (coach, pumpkin)
    [COACH:#]←(O)←[TURN INTO]→(O)→[PUMPKIN].

Causative predicates. Causative predicates with embedded sentences as subjects are always two-place Process verbs, since the sentences are embedded under the Object case. The subject is an inanimate object or an embedded sentence. Verbs in this structure include *make, cause.*

(166) Susan's screaming /made /Harry drop the tray.   O,O
    = CAUSE (SCREAM (Susan), DROP (Harry, tray))
    [EVENT:#1]←(O)←[CAUSE]→(O)→[EVENT:#2].
    [MAKE = cause] -
        (O)→[[SUSAN]←(A)←[SCREAM /O-lex]]
        (O)→[[HARRY]←(A)←[DROP]→(O)→[TRAY]←(L)←[NULL]].

Text analysis of Process verbs with single O (219). Basic Process predicates with single O are one-place intransitive predicates. Some high frequency verbs in this category include *be = occur* (8), *be = remain* (6), *come = occur* (21), *die* (7), *happen* (7), *rise = occur* (8), *sleep* (26). Many have a corresponding transitive form which functions as an Action verb, such as *begin,iv* (7), *break,iv* (8), *dry,iv* (6), *open,iv* (6), *start,iv* (5), and *wake,iv* (9).

There is a set of Basic Process predicates which are equivalent to the inchoative predicate *become*. These verbs are generally followed by an adjective and are treated as one place raising predicates, in which the subject of the adjective predicate is raised to be subject of the inchoative. These include *be = become* as in *become light* (5), *become* (4), *come to = become*, (1) *get = become* (4), *go into = become* (1), *reach = become* (1), and *turn = become* (1).

(167) I will eat the tuna after it gets light.   50:24
    [GET = become] -
        (O)→[[SKY:#]←(Os)←[BE LIGHT]].

2.5–2.9 Basic Action verbs

Action verbs in the basic domain describe an active situation in which there is Agent-directed activity. Basic Action verbs require both the Agent and Object, but the Object may be (1) coreferential with the Agent, (2) lexicalized into the verb, or (3) freely deletable. Action verbs with an Agent subject and no other noun visible in the structure present a problem for the obligatory-O hypothesis. With verbs like *play, sleep, work*, used intransitively, the analyst is faced with the problem of determining where is the obligatory Object case.

2.5. Action with A=O coreference

Some Action predicates are two-place predicates with A=O coreference. The structure of the predication is shown in the following graph, which links a PERSON that is both Agent and Object with an Action predicate.

(168)

| PERSON | ← | (A=O) | ← | ACTION-VERB |

Basic Action verbs with A=O coreference include: action adjectives, which are an agentive reinterpretation of basic adjectives, and action verbs, in which the subject is both Agent and Object.

Action adjectives. Traditional grammarians described adjectives as indicating States and verbs as indicating Actions. In his 1966 article, Lakoff points out that, although this is generally true, there are adjectives which describe Actions and verbs which describe States. States do not take the progressive or the imperative; Actions take both progressive and imperative. Some adjectives occur with progressive and imperative, and therefore describe Actions.

Lakoff (1966) lists twenty-eight action adjectives, but analysts can determine their own list by testing the adjective with the progressive or imperative. Adjectives are either States or Actions, there are no Process adjectives. Consequently, every occurrence with the progressive indicates an Action adjective. Some adjectives, such as *be tall, be old* are never used as Actions, since they are unacceptable in contexts such as *John is being tall.* But other adjectives such as *be careful, be polite* may be interpreted as Actions, since they are acceptable in contexts such as *John is being careful.*

Lakoff points out that these same adjectives, without the progressive or the imperative, are ambiguous between a stative and an active interpretation. They may describe a quality, or they may describe an activity. Consequently, there are no adjectives which are inherently Action, but many adjectives which can be interpreted as Action in context. Action adjectives then constitute an agentive reinterpretation (Rudanko 1989) of a Basic State structure. Action adjectives are marked for agency in the lexicon as *be kind (A).*

(169) David is kind.   Os
    = David is kind by nature.
    [DAVID]←(Os)←[BE KIND].

(170) David is being kind.   A=O
    = David is acting in a kind manner.
    [DAVID]←(A=O)←[BE (= act) KIND].

John Anderson also treats adjectives that take the progressive and the imperative as Action adjectives, and assigns to them a case frame with A=O coreferential (1971:56).

(171) Egbert /was being cautious.   A=O
    = Egbert was acting in a cautious manner.
    [EGBERT]←(A=O)←[BE CAUTIOUS].

Anderson makes a distinction between intransitive Action adjectives like be cautious and transitive Action adjectives like be careful with. To the transitive adjectives he assigns the case frame A,O with no coreference.

(172) Egbert /was being careful with /the vase.   A,O
    [EGBERT]←(A)←[BE CAREFUL WITH]→(O)→[VASE:#].

Adjectives used with the progressive are always interpreted as actions. Adjectives without the progressive are to be analyzed as actions whenever the BE + ADJECTIVE structure is interpreted as act + adverb, for example, when be polite = act politely. The subject is both Agent and Object. Since the Agent is added to an already well-formed structure, the structure is A=O.

Action verbs with A=O coreference. Verbs with no surface object may have Agent and Object roles coreferential. With action adjectives, coreferential roles are restricted to structures built upon already existing structures by adding an agentive reinterpretation. With Action verbs in the basic domain, coreferential Agent and Object occur when involuntary human activities, normally classed as Process (see §2.3 Animate Process), are interpreted as voluntary in a given context. Some possible candidates are breathe, cough, die, laugh, sleep, yawn.

(173) John /coughed.   O
    = John coughed involuntarily.
    [JOHN]←(O)←[COUGH].

(174) John /coughed politely.   A,*O/ A=O
    = John coughed deliberately to attract attention.
    [JOHN]←(A=O)←[COUGH].

Text analysis of Basic Action with A=O coreference (29). Coreference of Agent and Object case occurred both with adjectives (28) and with verbs (1). Action adjectives are an agentive reinterpretation of simple adjectives and in this use may take both the imperative and progressive. The only verbs with coreference were agentive reinterpretations of natural processes, such as *sleep*. Action adjectives included *be calm* (5), *be careful* (2), and *be steady* (2).

2.6. Action with O-lexicalized

Some Action verbs are two-place predicates with O-lexicalized into the verb. The structure of the predication is shown in the following graph, which links a PERSON who is an Agent with an Action predicate that includes a lexicalized Object.

(175) | PERSON | ← (A) ← | ACTION /O-LEX |

Lexicalized Object. Some verbs may have a lexicalized Object case. Anderson, with the verb *work*, calls these reflexive ergative clauses and proposes coreferential Agent and Object because "the Agent operates in some sense upon itself" (1971:50). But when a word is listed in the lexicon as both a noun and a verb, it is likely that the noun is incorporated into the verb. Since *work* is listed as both a noun and a verb, the verb may be interpreted as an Action *do* verb with the nominal expressing the Action incorporated into the verb. The verb *work* then would be interpreted as *do work*, much like John Ross' interpretation of *frogs croak* as *frogs do croaking* (1972:70). Some verbs with lexicalized Object include *act, cry, fish, gamble, work.*

(176) Father /is working.   A,*O /O-Lex
        [FATHER]←(A)←[WORK /O-lex].

(177) Father /is doing /work.   A,O
        [FATHER]←(A)←[DO]→(O)→[WORK].

Contrast with motion verbs. Fillmore (1971b:41) suggested that motion verbs, like *drive, ride, run, swim, walk,* should receive two different case analyses, depending upon whether they describe types of activities or types of movement. Motion verbs as types of activity do not require a Locative role and are characterized as A,*O /O-lex.

(178) Max was driving for an hour.   A,*O /O-lex
= Max was doing driving.
[MAX]←(A=O)←[DRIVE /O-lex].

Motion verbs as types of movement are not interpreted as *do driving,*
that is, as the performance of an activity. They are interpreted as *go-by-
driving* and require a Locative role, as variants of the verb *go.* These verbs
are then characterized as A,*O,L /A=O.

(179) Max drove to the mountains.   A,*O,L /A=O
= Max went-by-driving to the mountains.
[MAX]←(A=O)←[DRIVE]→(L)→[to [MOUNTAINS:#]].

Text analysis of Basic Action with O-lexicalized (92). When the
Object role does not appear in the surface structure, it is often lexicalized
into the verb, and the verb remains intransitive. High frequency verbs in
this category included *fish* (16), *swim* (10), *work* (12), and *rest* (15).

2.7. Action with both roles overt

Most Action verbs occur with both roles overt. The structure of the
predication is shown in the following graph, which links a PERSON who is
an Agent with an ENTITY called the Object.

(180) | PERSON | ← Ⓐ ← | ACTION-VERB | → Ⓞ → | ENTITY |

Action verbs with both roles overt are two-place transitive predicates
and include: transitive action adjectives, deletable object verbs, transitive verbs, aspectual verbs, and transitive verbs with complements.

Transitive action adjectives. Action adjectives may be transitive.
The Agent and direct object both appear in the surface structure. One example of these Action adjectives is *be careful with* (Anderson 1971:62).

(181) Len /is careful with /the vase.   A,O
[LEN]←(A)←[BE CAREFUL WITH]→(O)→[VASE].

Deletable object verbs. Deletable object verbs occur sometimes
with and sometimes without an object. These verbs are listed as transitive with deletable object. Chafe (1970) calls these verbs completable.
"The verb describes a certain action which, by its very nature, implies

the existence of a certain nominal concept. Singing implies a song, play-ing implies a game" (1970:156). But elsewhere he lists *sing* as intransitive Action (1970:98). Fillmore (1968:29) lists verbs such as *cook* as "deletable object" verbs. The test used here for deletable object verbs is that deletable object verbs occur sometimes with an Object and some-times without an Object. Instead of positing two case frames for these two occurrences, the case frame A,O is given for both occurrences, which, when the object is missing, is given the frame A,O /O-del. Verbs like *cook, dance, play, sing* have deletable objects.

(182) Maria /is dancing.   A,O /O-del
    = DANCE (Maria, dance)
    [MARIA]←(A)←[DANCE]→(O)→[NULL].

(183) Maria /is dancing /the tango.   A,O
    = DANCE (Maria, tango)
    [MARIA]←(A)←[DANCE]→(O)→[TANGO:#].

Transitive verbs. Most transitive verbs have an Object role which appears in the surface structure. The object noun may be neutral, as in *read,* or created by the action, as in *write,* or affected by the action, as in *kill.* Whatever meaning the Object (Theme) role may have, the case analysis does not distinguish these structures, but classes them all as A,O. The Object nouns are in complementary distribution, and vary with the meaning of the verb.

(184) Nathan /read /the book.   A,O /neutral O
    = READ (Nathan, book)
    [NATHAN]←(A)←[READ]→(O)→[BOOK].

(185) Helen /wrote /a poem.   A,O /created O
    = WRITE (Helen, poem)
    [HELEN]←(A)←[WRITE]→(O)→[POEM].

(186) Omar /killed /the lion.   A,O /affected O
    = KILL (Omar, lion)
    [OMAR]←(A)←[KILL]→(O)→[LION].

Transitive aspectual verbs. Action aspectual verbs are the causative version of Process aspectual verbs. They require an Agent as subject, and an embedded proposition with the Agent as subject of the lower verb.

Inceptive Actions. The transitive inceptive predicates mark the beginning of an activity. These include *begin,tv, commence,tv, start,tv.*

(187) Peter /began /working.   A,O
    = Peter began (Peter work).
    [BEGIN,tv] -
      (A)→[PETER]
      (O)→[[PETER]←(A)←[WORK /O-lex]].

Durative Actions. The transitive durative predicates mark the continuing of an activity. These include *continue,tv, keep,tv, remain,tv.* The verb *keep,tv* is used with both like and unlike subjects. The verb *stay,tv* is limited to static situations with like subjects.

(188) Stay (keep) /off the grass.   A,O
    = Keep yourself (like subject) off the grass.
    [STAY,tv] -
      (A)→[PERS:#you]
      (O)→[[PERS:#you]←(Os)←[BE-LOC]→(L)→[off [GRASS:#]].

(189) Keep (*stay)/ the children /off the grass.   A,O
    = Keep some one else (unlike subject) off the grass.
    [KEEP,tv] -
      (A)→[PERSON:#you]
      (O)→[[CHILDREN]←(Os)←[BE-LOC]→(L)→[off [GRASS]].

Terminative Actions. The transitive terminative predicates mark the end of an activity. These include *cease,tv, finish,tv,* and *stop,tv* followed by an action participle.

(190) Peter /stopped /being cautious.   A,O
    = Peter stopped (Peter be cautious).
    [STOP,tv] -
      (A)→[PETER]
      (O)→[[PETER]←(A=O)←[BE CAUTIOUS]].

Action verb with complement. Some transitive Action verbs take reduced object complements. The subject of the higher verb may be same as or different from the subject of the embedded verb.

Like-subject predicates. Some transitive Action verbs take reduced complements with the same subject as the main verb, such as *attempt,,try.*

Since the subject of the main verb is an Agent, the subject of the lower verb is interpreted as an Agent and the lower verb is an Action.

(191) Paul /tried /to open the door.   A,O
    = Paul tried (Paul open door).
    [TRY] -
      (A)→[PAUL]
      (O)→[[PAUL]←(A)←[OPEN]→(O)→[DOOR]].

Ambiguous causality. Agents permit or cause Events. Permissive action verbs include *allow, let, permit.* When the permitted Event is a process, the permissive verb is a two-place predicate, classed as A,O, with the meaning *let happen.* But when the caused Event is an Action, the verb is a three-place predicate, classed as A,B,O, with the meaning *let some one do something.* (See §4.5 Action Benefactive verbs.) The interpretation of the action predicate as a two-place or three-place predicate depends upon the nature of the verb within its scope.

(192) Helen /let /the water run into the tub.   A,O
    = Helen let happen (water run into the tub).
    [LET **happen**] -
      (A)→[HELEN]
      (O)→[[WATER:#]←(O)←[RUN]→(L)→[into [TUB:#]].

(193) Helen /let /James /do his homework.   A,B,O
    = Helen let James do (James do homework).
    [LET **do**] -
      (A)→[HELEN]
      (B)→[JAMES]
      (O)→[[JAMES]←(A)←[DO]→(O)→[HOMEWORK]].

Causative action verbs include *cause, force, make.* When the caused Event is a process, the causative verb is a two-place predicate, classed as A,O, with the meaning *make happen.* But when the caused Event is an Action, the verb is a three-place predicate, classed as A,B,O, with the meaning *make some one do something.* The interpretation of the Action predicate as a two-place or three-place predicate depends upon the nature of the verb within its scope.

(194) Harold /made /the water run into the tub.   A,O
    = Harold make happen (water run into the tub).
    [MAKE happen] -
      (A)→[HAROLD]
      (O)→[[WATER:#]←(O)←[RUN]→(L)→[into [TUB:#]].

(195) Harold /made /James /do his homework.   A,B,O
    = Harold make James do (James do homework).
    [MAKE do] -
      (A)→[HAROLD]
      (B)→[JAMES]
      (O)→[[JAMES]←(A)←[DO]→(O)→[HOMEWORK]].

Hammer-flat structure. There is an Action verb structure which has an adjective as its final element. The adjective cannot be an attributive adjective for it follows the noun it modifies. It must be a predicate adjective. This embedded adjective predication is the object of the main verb. The main verb means *cause* and has a lexicalized modality. These constructions include *hammer x flat,* meaning *cause-by-hammering x to be flat* and *sweep x clean* meaning *cause-by-sweeping x to be clean.* James McCawley describes these structures as causative with "means-incorporation" (1971:31). Georgia Green translates these structures as "subject CAUSE direct object to COME TO BE State by verb-ing direct object" (1974:218). Whatever the main verb may be, the meaning is *cause,* and the verb chosen expresses the means used.

(196) Susan /swept /the house clean.   A,O
    = Susan caused-by-sweeping the house to be clean.
    [CAUSE by sweeping] -
      (A)→[SUSAN]
      (O)→[[HOUSE:#]←(Os)←[BE CLEAN]].

(197) Harry /hammered /the metal flat.   A,O
    = Harry caused-by-hammering the metal to be flat.
    [CAUSE by hammering] -
      (A)→[HARRY]
      (O)→[[METAL:#]←(Os)←[BE FLAT]].

Derived action predicates. Action verbs may be derived from State verbs, usually by derivational suffixes, or from Process verbs, generally with a zero-marked causative derivation (Chafe 1970:128; Lakoff 1970:41).

Action derived from State. Actions are derived from stative adjectives by the inchoative and causative derivations. Derived Action predicates include *enable,tv, encode,tv, enlarge,tv; cheapen,tv, deafen,tv, thicken,tv, clarify,tv, falsify,tv, purify,tv, simplify,tv, equalize,tv, formalize,tv.*

(198) The computer /formalized /the new data.   A,O
    = The computer caused the new data to be formal.
    [COMPUTER:#]←(A)←[FORMALIZE]→(O)→[DATA:#].

Action derived from Process. Action verbs are also derived from Process verbs by a causative derivation. As intransitives they are Process, as transitives they are Actions. These verbs include *break, cook, open, shut.*

(199) Henry /broke /the window.   A,O
    = Henry caused the window to break.
    [HENRY]←(A)←[BREAK,tv]→(O)→[WINDOW:#].

In contrast, some Process verbs are derived from Action verbs, reversing the order of derivation. Lyons calls these derived Process forms pseudo-intransitive (1968:366). Pseudo-intransitives are recognized by the fact that these predications acquire a generic sense and require manner adverbials. According to Chafe (1970:131) the Agent is removed from the structure by a decausative derivation. Anderson (1971:68) calls the clauses "something of a mystery." They include Basic verbs *cut, wash,* and Benefactive verbs like *sell.*

(200) This sweater /washes /easily.   O
    = This sweater washes (generic) easily.
    [SWEATER:#this]←(O)←[WASH,iv].

Text analysis Basic Action with both roles overt (690). This category contained a few transitive adjectives such as *be worthy of,* and many verbs. This A,O category is the most prominent in the novel. High frequency verbs were *eat,tv* (69), *do,tv* (55), *kill,tv* (40), *make,tv* (32), *keep,tv* (29), *hit,tv* (26): True passives of A-O verbs (30) which implied an Agent occurred. These are distinguished from Stative adjectives which are derived from Process verbs.

2.8. Action with double O

Some Actions are three-place predicates with an Agent and two Objects. The structure of the predication is shown in the following graph, which links a PERSON who is an Agent with two ENTITIES called Objects.

(201)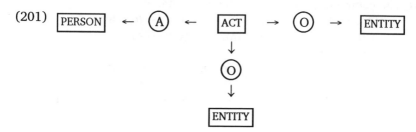

Action verbs with double Objects are three-place ditransitive verbs with the case frame A,O,O. The passive of these verbs, with the elimination of the Agent, becomes an Os,Os structure. They include *call, name, elect, make.* Sentence (202) illustrates the active, sentence (203) the passive.

(202) The people /elected /Clinton /President.   A,O,O
       [ELECT] -
          (A)→[PEOPLE:#]
          (O)→[CLINTON]
          (O)→[PRESIDENT]

(203) Cicero /is called /Tully.   Os,Os
       [PERSON: Cicero]←(Os)←[BE CALLED]→(Os)→[NAME:Tully]

Text analysis of Basic Action with double O (8). A few verbs occurred with double Object roles. These included *call* (5), *identify* (1), and *make into* (1). There was one passive form with double Object, *be called* (1).

(204) They called this part of the ocean the great well.   28:19
       [PERSON:#they]←(A)←[CALL]→(O)→[OCEAN]→(O)→[WELL].

(205) The royal palm is called guano.   15:21
       [PALM:#]←(Os)←[BE CALLED]→(Os)→[GUANO].

2.9. Action with double Agent

A small subclass of transitive verbs requires two occurrences of the Agent role. These verbs are normally intransitive. When they are used transitively, a second Agent is added to the structure. These include verbs like *march,tv, walk,tv, work,tv*. John Lyons (1968:365) describes these structures as action verbs with Agentive objects, and compares "double-Agentive" sentences like *John walked the horse* with similar double-Agentive sentences like *John made the horse walk*. The difference is that sentence (206) is a single clause with a double Agent, whereas sentence (207) can easily be broken into two Agentive clauses with the verb *make* as A,O and the verb *walk,iv* as A,*O.

(206) John /walked /the horse.   A + A,*O /O-lex
      = CAUSE (John, WALK (horse))
      [CAUSE] -
         (A)→[JOHN]
         (O)→[[HORSE:#]←(A)←[WALK /O-lex]].

(207) John /made /the horse walk.   A + A,*O /O-lex
      = CAUSE (John, WALK (horse))
      [MAKE = **cause**] -
         (A)→[JOHN]
         (O)→[[HORSE:#]←(A)←[WALK /O-lex]].

John Anderson claims that similar sentences like *He marched the prisoners around the yard* are "derived via a double causation" (1971:183), but labels the subjects of these causatives as Source rather than Agent. The transitive verb *march,tv* is factored into *cause + march,iv*. The domain here is Locative.

(208) He /marched /the men /around the yard.   A + A=O,L
      = CAUSE (Guard, MARCH (men, around the yard))
      [CAUSE] -
         (A)→[PERSON: he]
         (O)→[[MEN:#]←(A=O)←[MARCH]→(L)→[around [YARD:#]].

3
The Experiential Domain

The Experiential domain consists of those predicates which require the Experiential role, combined with the Object role, or with the Agent and Object roles. The presence of the Experiencer role indicates that the predicate belongs in the Experiential domain. In a survey of 5,000 clauses in Hemingway's *The Old Man and the Sea,* 1,380 clauses or 28% were in the Experiential domain. Of these clauses 727 or 15% were States, 148 or 3% were Process, and 505 or 10% were Actions.

(209) The Experiential domain

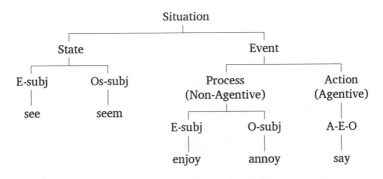

State Experiential (727 clauses). State Experiential verbs express a stative situation, in which a person experiences sensation, emotion, or cognition. Basic Experiential verbs require an Object and an Experiencer. The Object case is marked with the subscript (s) to show stativity.

State Experiential verbs with the E,Os frame regularly require the Experiencer as subject and include verbs and adjectives dealing with sensation, emotion, and cognition. These are all classified as states since they do not take the progressive and express a static situation. A subclass of E,Os verbs have E=Os and sometimes are an experiential reinterpretation of Os verbs. In experiential *be* + adjective structures, *be* is interpreted as *feel.*

State Experiential verbs with the Os,E frame show a rank shift in the subject choice hierarchy. The Object role, which represents the stimulus of the experience is promoted to subject over the Experiencer role. Since the Object is an entity or an event, and the Experiencer is a person, there is no problem in determining when this rank shift occurs. Predicates with the Os,E frame include sensation states such as *look, sound,* emotive states such as *be good for, be bad for,* and cognitive states such as *seem.*

Process Experiential (148 clauses). Process Experiential verbs express ongoing experience without an Agent. Process experiential verbs require an Object and an Experiencer. The Object in direct object position indicates the content of the experience, but the Object case when rank-shifted into subject position is interpreted as the stimulus for the experience.

Process Experiential verbs with the E,O frame regularly take the Experiencer as subject. These include emotive verbs such as *enjoy, feel,* and cognitive verbs such as *learn.* No sensation verbs were found that could be classified as a Process. These Process verbs are distinguished from States in their ability to freely take the progressive.

Process experiential verbs with the O,E frame show a rank shift in the subject choice hierarchy. The Object role, which represents the stimulus of the experience, is promoted to subject over the Experiencer role, the person undergoing the experience. Rank shift is detected when the Experiencer role occurs in a nonsubject position. The principal set of verbs with the O,E frame are the psych movement verbs (see list in (307)).

Action Experiential (505 clauses). Action Experiential verbs express change directed by an Agent. Action experiential predications require an Agent, an Experiencer, and an Object. Communication verbs are listed as experiential since they require a speaker, a hearer, and what is said. The speaker is the Agent, the hearer is the Experiencer, and the Object is what is being communicated. Action Experiential verbs include

A,E,O verbs with A = E coreference, A,E,O verbs with A=O coreference, A,E,*O verb with O-lexicalized, and A,E,O verbs with all roles overt.

Action Experiential verbs with A=E include State verbs of sensation which are reinterpreted as voluntary Action. Sensation may occur involuntarily, as with *see, hear* and are classed as E,Os. But the same sensations in the form of *watch, listen to* imply voluntary acceptance of the sensation, and are classed as A,*E,O /A=E. The subject is both an Agent, acting voluntarily, and an Experiencer, undergoing a sensation.

Action Experiential verbs with A=O include Process psych movement verbs which are reinterpreted as voluntary Action. If the psych movement verb has a nonagentive entity as stimulus subject the verb is classed as O,E, but if that entity is a person acting intentionally as a stimulus then the verb is classed as an Action with the frame A,E,*O /A=O.

Action Experiential verbs with O-lex include verbs of communication in which the Object role is incorporated into the verb such as *question* = ask questions of, *answer* = give answer to.

Action Experiential verbs with all roles overt are principally verbs of communication such as *say, tell.* There are a few verbs in this class that may be treated as causatives such as *show, teach.*

3.1–3.3 State Experiential verbs

State Experiential verbs describe a static experiential situation. They require the Experiencer role for the person in the experiential state and an Object role expressing the content of the experience. State Experiential verbs occur with E-subject or with O-subject.

3.1. Experiential state with E-subject

Experiential states with Experiencer subjects are two-place predicates relating an Experiencer to an Object. The structure of the predication is shown in the following graph, which links a PERSON called the Experiencer with an ENTITY called the Object. The Object is the content of the experience.

(210)   PERSON   ←   (E)   ←   EXP-VERB   →   (Os)   →   ENTITY

Experiential states with the Experiencer as subject include sensation states which deal with the five senses, emotive states which deal with human emotions, and cognitive states which deal with mental activity.

Sensation states (E,Os). Experiential states with Experiencer as subject express the sensation experience that the person undergoes. The Object case describes the content of the sensation experience. These predicates may be adjectival or verbal.

Sensation adjectives with E-subject. Experiential adjectives with Experiencer as subject include adjectives of sensation that express general feelings of cold, warmth, hunger, or thirst. Some adjectives such as *be hungry, be thirsty* are inherently experiential. Other adjectives, such as *be cold, be warm* are ambiguous between basic and experiential meaning. In their basic meaning they describe qualities of the subject and have the case frame Os. (See §2.1 Basic State with Os-Subject.)

In their experiential meaning these adjectives describe what the subject feels. In this second meaning, the *be* form is interpreted as *be = feel,* the Experiencer is coreferential with the Object, and the case frame is E=Os. This interpretation is based on John Anderson (1971:96). Experiential adjectives are listed in the lexicon with an E to indicate Experiential. The descriptive adjective *be cold* is distinguished from the Experiential adjective *be cold (E).* The case frame of the former is Os; the case frame of the latter is E=Os.

(211) John /is cold.   Os
      = John is cold (to the touch).
      [JOHN]←(Os)←[BE COLD].

(212) John /is cold.   E=Os
      = John feels cold.
      [JOHN]←(E=Os)←[BE COLD (E)].

Sensation verbs. Sensation verbs deal with the five sensations: sight, hearing, smell, taste, and touch. Sensation is expressed as a State verb with an E-subject, as a State verb with an O-subject, and as an Action verb with an A-subject when the sensation is actively invoked. In English, for the sensations of sight and hearing, the verb form is different for each use. For the sensations of smell, taste, and touch, however, the verb form is the same whether the subject of the verb is an E-subject, O-subject, or A-subject, and the meaning must be determined by context.

(213) Verbs of sensation

Sense verb	O-subject	E-subject	A-subject
sight	look	see	look at
hearing	sound	hear	listen to
smell	smell	smell	smell
taste	taste	taste	taste
touch	feel	feel	feel

Sense verbs with E-subject constitute the basic sense predication with Experiencer as subject and the content of the experience as Object. They are characterized as E,Os.

(214) Michael /saw /the falling star.   E,Os
    [MICHAEL]←(E)←[SEE]→(Os)→[STAR:#].

Sense verbs with O-subject will normally be found in a VERB + ADJEC- TIVE structure with the Experiencer as a deletable indirect object. The structure is characterized as Os,E with the Object role filled by the adjective predication. The subject of the adjective is raised to become the subject of the sense verb and the infinitive *to be* is deleted. The meaning of the sentence *The falling star looked beautiful to Michael* is: The star is beautiful, at least it looks that way to Michael. Sense verbs with an O- subject have the same palliative effect as the verb *seem*. The inclusion of *sounds* (to me), *looks* (to me) softens the force of the predication in the same way as *seems* (to me).

(215) The falling star /looked /beautiful /to Michael.   Os,E
    = It looked to Michael that the falling star was beautiful.
    [LOOK] -
      (Os)→[[STAR:#]←(Os)←[BE BEAUTIFUL]]
      (E)→[to MICHAEL].

Sense verbs with A-subject indicate active participation in the sense experience in which the Experiencer subject receives an agentive reinter- pretation. The Agent role is coreferential with the Experiencer role. This structure is characterized as A=E,O. The verb *see* is stative, but the verbs *watch, look at* are active. The verb *hear* is stative but the verb *listen to* is active. (See §3.6 Experiential actions with A=E coreference.)

(216) Michael /watched /the falling star.   A=E,O
      = Michael (deliberately) saw the falling star.
      [MICHAEL]←(A=E)←[WATCH]→(Os)→[STAR:#].

Unmarked infinitives. Sense verbs take an unmarked infinitive structure. This structure has a noun in the objective case as subject of the
embedded clause and an infinitive without the *to* marker as predicate.
Sense verbs in their most literal meaning take no other type of complement. These verbs are characterized as E,Os, except *feel*, which is E,O.

(217) He /heard /the lion roar.   E,Os
      = He heard (him (to) roar).
      [HEAR] -
          (E)→[PERSON:#he]
          (Os)→[[LION]←(A=O)←[ROAR]].

(218) He /saw /flying fish spurt out of the water.   E,Os
      = He saw (them to spurt out of the water).
      [SEE] -
          (E)→[PERSON:#he]
          (Os)→[[FISH]←(O)←[SPURT]→(L)→[out of [WATER:#]]].

(219) He /felt /the boat shiver.   E,O
      = He felt (boat to shiver).
      [FEEL] -
          (E)→[PERSON:#he]
          (O)→[[BOAT:#]←(O)←[SHIVER]].

The infinitive occurs without *to* with the sense verbs, *hear, see, feel,*
and with the causatives *make, let.* The marker *to* is required with *allow,
permit,* and *cause.* These are regular rules which are observable in normal
use of the English language. The omission of the infinitive marker *to*
with some verbs is not a sufficient reason to create a small clause of the
type suggested by Radford (1988:324). A further argument against small
clauses is the existence of verbs like *help* which occur with and without
to with no change in meaning. There is no reason to postulate two different structures when the only difference is the presence or absence of the
infinitive marker.

(220) Bill /helped /Jane /do her homework.   A,B,O
    = Bill helped Jane (to) do her homework.
    [HELP] -
        (A)→[BILL]
        (B)→[JANE]
        (O)→[[JANE]←(A)←[DO]→(O)→[HOMEWORK:#her]].

Unmarked infinitives are sometimes followed by an -*ing* participle. This seems to be the progressive form of the infinitive, and not the possessive and gerund construction. The simple infinitive refers to the act of crossing in general, the progressive form indicates seeing the man in the act of crossing.

(221) I /saw /the man cross the street.   E,Os
    = I saw him (to) cross the street.
    [SEE] -
        (E)→[PERSON:#I]
        (Os)→[[MAN:#]←(A=O)←[CROSS]→(L)→[STREET:#]].

(222) I /saw /the man crossing the street.   E,Os
    = I saw him (to be) crossing the street.
    [SEE] -
        (E)→[PERSON:I]
        (Os)→[[MAN:#]←(A=O)←[CROSS]→(L)→[STREET:#]].

That-complements. Sensation verbs with that-complements are often interpreted as cognitive states, rather than sense verbs. The verb *feel (that)* is interpreted as *believe,* the verb *see (that)* is interpreted as *notice,* and the verb *hear (that)* is interpreted as *learn.* When a that-clause occurs with a sense verb, the meaning changes. These cognitive State verbs are described as E,Os. These verbs should be classed with cognitive state verbs such as *know* and *think.* (See §3.1 Cognitive states.)

(223) He /felt /that he was already dead.   E,Os
    = He believed that he was already dead.
    [FEEL = **believe**] -
        (E)→[PERSON:#he]
        (Os)→[[PERSON:#he]←(Os)←[BE DEAD]].

(224) He /saw /that no land was visible.   E,Os
  = He noticed that no land was visible (to him).
  [SEE = notice] -
    (E)→[PERSON:#he]
    (Os)→[[LAND:no]←(Os)←[BE VISIBLE]→(E)→[NULL]].

(225) He /heard /that a storm was coming.   E,Os
  = He learned that a storm was coming.
  [HEAR = learn] -
    (E)→[PERSON:#he]
    (Os)→[[STORM]←(O)←[COME = occur]].

Emotive states (E,Os). Experiential states with Experiencer as subject express the emotion that the Experiencer undergoes. The Object case describes the content of the experience. Predicates may be adjectival or verbal.

Emotive adjectives with E-subject. Experiential adjectives expressing emotion are generally transitive. These adjectives are two-place predicates with the Experiencer role as subject and the Object role, expressing the content of the experience, as direct object. These adjectives include *be fond of,* which is ungrammatical without its obligatory Object and *be afraid (of)* which may occur either with or without its optional Object.

(226) John /is fond of /Mary.   E,Os
      *John is fond.
      [JOHN]←(E)←[BE FOND OF]→(Os)→[MARY].

(227) The child /is afraid of /the dark.   E,Os
  = The child is afraid.
      [CHILD:#]←(E)←[BE AFRAID OF]→(Os)→[DARK:#].

Experiential adjectives expressing emotion may be derived from state verbs with E-subject. Adjectives derived from Experiential state verbs are often paraphrases of the verb construction. Many adjectives ending in -ful, -ive, or -ous belong to this class. These adjectives include *be appreciative of* from the verb *appreciate, be desirous of* from the verb *desire,* and *be fearful about,* from the verb *fear.*

(228) Pat /is fearful about /the results.   E,Os
  = Pat fears the results.
      [PAT]←(E)←[BE FEARFUL ABOUT]→(Os)→[RESULTS:#].

(229) The company /is appreciative of /your cooperation.   E,Os
      = The company appreciates your cooperation.
      [COMPANY:#]←(E)←[BE APPRECIATIVE OF]→(Os)→[COOPERATION].

(230) The staff /is desirous of /a vacation.   E,Os
      [STAFF:#]←(E)←[BE DESIROUS OF]→(Os)→[VACATION].

Transitive adjectives may take a noun or an embedded sentence as
their object. The embedded sentence takes the form of a that-clause or
preposition + participle. The prepositions are lexically specified for each
adjective. These prepositions occur with noun phrases or participle but
are deleted before a that-clause.

(231) Mark /is afraid of /seeing ghosts.   E,Os
      = Mark is afraid that he will see ghosts.
      [BE AFRAID OF] -
        (E)→[Mark]
        (Os)→[[MARK]←(E)←[SEE]→(Os)→[GHOSTS]].

(232) Michael /is happy /that he won the race.   E,Os
      = Michael is happy about winning the race.
      [BE HAPPY ABOUT] -
        (E)→[Michael]
        (Os)→[[MICHAEL]←(A=B)←[WIN]→(O)→[RACE:#]].

Emotive verbs with E-subject. Emotive verbs deal with human emotions. Emotion is expressed with an E-subject denoting the person
experiencing the emotion and with an O-object denoting the content of
the emotion. Emotive verbs are generally stative, do not take the progressive, and are characterized as E,Os. The most frequent emotive verbs
are *like, love, wish, want.* One of the most unusual experiential states is
have = experience, which is distinguished from *have = possession* by the
nature of the direct object. Expressions such as *have faith* do not deal
with physical possession but with inner experience. To *have faith* is to *experience faith.*

(233) Lionel /loves /Agatha.   E,Os
      [LIONEL]←(E)←[LOVE]→(Os)→[AGATHA].

(234) The child /has /faith.   E,Os
      [CHILD:#]←(E)←[HAVE = **experience**]→(Os)→[FAITH].

The more frequent emotive verbs take infinitive complements, such as *like to, love to, wish to, want to.* Some of these verbs occur with a like-subject condition in which the subject of the main verb is the same as the subject of the lower verb. The syntactic structure is described as NP-VERB-INFINITIVE. Some verbs, such as *want to,* allow both like and unlike subjects in the embedded sentence and occur in the language with the structure NP-VERB-NP-INFINITIVE.

(235) Harry /wants /to leave /this place.   E,Os
    = Harry wants (Harry to leave)
    [WANT] -
       (E)→[HARRY]
       (Os)→[[HARRY]←(A=O)←[LEAVE]→(L)→[PLACE:#]].

(236) Harry /wants /Jim to leave /this place.   E,Os
    = Harry wants (Jim leave)
    [WANT] -
       (E)→[HARRY]
       (Os)→[[JIM]←(A=O)←[LEAVE]→(L)→[PLACE:#]].

The verb *have* with complement is ambiguous between experiential and active interpretations. The verb *have* meaning *to experience unwillingly* is a State E,Os verb; the verb *have* meaning *to cause something to happen* is an Action A,O verb. (See §2.7 Basic Action with both roles overt.)

(237) Harry /had /his watch stolen.   E,Os
    = Harry experienced (someone stole his watch)
    [HAVE = **experience**] -
       (E)→[HARRY]
       (Os)→[[PERSON]←(A)←[STEAL]→(O)→[WATCH]→(B)→[NULL]].

(238) Harry /had /his hair cut.   A,O
    = Harry caused (some one cut his hair).
    [HAVE = **cause**] -
       (A)→[HARRY]
       (O)→[[PERSON]←(A)←[CUT] → (O) → [HAIR:his]].

Cognitive states (E,Os). Experiential states with Experiencer as subject may express the present state of mind of the Experiencer. The Object case describes the content of the cognitive experience.

Cognitive adjectives with E-subject. Some adjectives with E-subject express mental states such as *be sure (of), be aware (of).* They take simple noun phrases or complements as their direct object. With that-complements, the preposition is deleted. The structure is described as E,Os.

(239) Harry /is aware of /the danger.   E,Os
     [HARRY]←(E)←[BE AWARE OF]→(Os)→[DANGER:#].

(240) Edward /is sure /that he will win.   E,Os
     [BE SURE] -
       (E)→[EDWARD]
       (Os)→[[EDWARD]←(A=B)←[WIN]→(O)→[NULL]].

One set of adjectives derived from psych movement verbs "involves endings in *-ed* and postadjectival prepositional phrases in *with, at, of, about,* or *by*" (Postal 1971a:41). The choice of preposition is lexically determined. These derived adjectives have the case frame E,Os. They include both cognitive and emotive predicates. Although similar to passives in form, these adjectives have different prepositions introducing the Object case, and allow the intensifier *very.* For passives, the former subject is introduced by the preposition *by,* and intensifiers are not allowed. For a complete listing, see (307) Psych movement verbs.

(241) Sam / is interested/ by theory.   O,E /(P)
     Passive of the verb *interest.*
     [THEORY]←(O)←[INTEREST]→(E)→[SAM].

(242) Sam /is very interested /in theory.   E,Os
     Adjective derived from the verb *interest.*
     [SAM]←(E)←[BE INTERESTED IN]→(Os)→[THEORY].

(243) Helen /is bored /by this class.   O,E /(P)
     Passive of the verb *bore.*
     [CLASS:#]←(O)←[BORE]→(E)→[HELEN].

(244) Helen /is very bored with /this class.   E,Os
     Adjective derived from the verb *bore.*
     [HELEN]←(E)←[BE BORED WITH]→(Os)→[CLASS:#].

Cognitive verbs with E-subject. Cognition may be expressed with an E-subject and an Os-object denoting the content of the thought. Frequent

cognitive verbs are *believe, know, remember, think.* Although these verbs
are basically States, they are subject to agentive reinterpretation to indicate active mental activity. In their active meaning these verbs take both
the progressive and the imperative. (See §3.6 Experiential action with
A=E.)

(245) John /knows /the answer.   E,Os
      ≠*John is knowing the answer.
      [JOHN]←(E)←[KNOW]→(Os)→[ANSWER:#].

(246) Know the answer by tomorrow.   A=E,O
      = Cause yourself to know the answer by tomorrow.
      [CAUSE] -
        (A)→[PERSON:#you]
        (O)→[[PERSON:#you]←(E)←[KNOW]→(Os)→[ANSWER:#]].

Most cognitive verbs with complements take either that-clause complements or infinitive complements. The verb *think* followed by a
that-clause is invariably stative E,Os. The verb *think,* followed by prepositions *of* and *about,* generally refers to the active use of the cognitive
faculty and is an Action.

(247) Fred /thought /that he would soon leave the country.   E,Os
      ≠*Fred was thinking that...
      [THINK] -
        (E)→[FRED]
        (Os)→[[FRED]←(A=O)←[LEAVE]→(L)→[COUNTRY:#]].

(248) Fred /was thinking about /the good old days.   A=E,O
      = Fred was (deliberately) thinking about...
      [FRED]←(A=E)←[THINK ABOUT]→(O)→[DAYS:#].

Indirect discourse. Direct and indirect discourse occur with verbs of
saying and thinking. In direct discourse with verbs of saying the proposition is enclosed in double quotes; with verbs of thinking, the proposition
is separated from the main verb by commas. In indirect discourse the
embedded proposition is normally a that-clause. These verbs, whether
the discourse is direct or indirect, have the same semantic structure and
are represented by the same conceptual graph. The verb *think* is characterized as E,Os; the verb *say* as A,E,O. The verbs *say* and *think* are high
frequency verbs. (See §3.9 Action Experiential verbs with all roles overt.)

(249) The old man, he thought, is sick.   E,Os
     = direct discourse

(250) He thought that the old man was sick.   E,Os
     = indirect discourse
     [THINK] -
         (E)→[PERSON:#he]
         (Os)→[[MAN:#]←(Os)←[BE SICK]].

(251) "The old man is sick," he said.   A,E,O
     = direct discourse

(252) He said that the old man was sick.   A,E,O
     = indirect discourse
     [SAY] -
         (A)→[PERSON:#he]
         (E)→[NULL]
         (O)→[[MAN:#]←(Os)←[BE SICK]].

Impression verbs. There is a small set of impression verbs which relate an Experiencer to a proposition. Verbs like *regard* and *consider* have the Experiencer as subject; verbs like *strike* and *impress* have the Experiencer as direct object. The proposition consists of two noun phrases, or noun phrase and adjective, linked by *as (= to be)* or with the link *to be* not expressed. Chomsky (1965:162) considers the relation between *strike* and *regard* in the sentences *I regard John as pompous* and *John strikes me as pompous,* and he makes the suggestion "In some sense the relation of John to *strike* is the same as that of John to *regard* and the relation of *strike* to *me* is the same as that of *regard* to *I*" (1965:163).

For the verbs *regard* and *consider,* the Experiencer is subject and the proposition is direct object. The case frame is E,Os. For the verbs *strike* and *impress,* the Experiencer is direct object, and the subject of the proposition is raised to become the subject of the main verb. The case frame is Os,E.

(253) I /regard /John as pompous.   E,Os
     = I regard John (to be) pompous.
     [REGARD] -
         (E)→[PERSON:#I]
         (Os)→[[JOHN]←(Os)←[BE POMPOUS]].

(254) I /consider /John pompous.   E,Os
   = I consider John (to be) pompous.
   [CONSIDER] -
      (E)→[PERSON:#I]
      (Os)→[[JOHN]←(Os)←[BE POMPOUS]].

(255) John /strikes /me /as pompous.   Os,E
   = It strikes me that John is pompous.
   [STRIKE] -
      (Os)→[[JOHN]←(Os)←[BE POMPOUS]]
      (E)→[PERSON:#me].

(256) John /impresses /me /as pompous.   Os,E
   = It is my impression that John is pompous.
   [IMPRESS] -
      (Os)→[[JOHN]←(Os)←[BE POMPOUS]]
      (E)→[PERSON:#me].

In Case Grammar terms, "the relation of *strike* to *me* is the same as that of *regard* to *I*" in that both are animate Experiencers receiving an impression. The difference is *regard* has an E-subject and *strike* has an E-object. "The relation of *John* to *strike* is the same as that of *John* to *regard*" in that in both cases *John* is the subject of the embedded adjective in logical structure.

Text analysis of Experiential State with E-subject. In the text of the Hemingway novel many of the Experiential States were found with E-subject. Intransitive adjectives had the frame E=Os, transitive adjectives and verbs had the frame E,Os. With adjectives the copula *be* was interpreted as *feel.*

Adjectives found with the frame E=Os included sensation adjectives *be cold, be warm, be comfortable, be hungry, be sore, be stiff, be thirsty,* and emotion adjectives *be angry, be confident, be desperate, be excited, be fearless, be happy, be panicked, be pleased, be sad, be worried.* The following are typical.

(257) There was a Norther and he was (=felt) cold.   81:14
   [PERSON:#he]←(E=Os)←[BE COLD (E)].

(258) The older fishermen looked at him and were (=felt) sad.   11:9
   [FISHERMEN:#]←(E=Os)←[BE SAD (E)].

Adjectives found with the frame E,Os included the emotion adjectives *be afraid of, be fond of, be glad that, be proud of, be sorry for* and also the cognitive adjective *be sure that.* The following sentences are typical.

(259) The old man was afraid that the fish would cut the line.   49:15
      [MAN:#]←(E)←[BE AFRAID]→(Os)→[PROPOSITION]

(260) He was sure that no local people would steal from him.   15:12
      [PERSON:#he]←(E)←[BE SURE]→(Os)→[PROPOSITION]

Verbs with the frame E,Os included sensation verbs *hear, see* (130 times), *smell,* emotion verbs *care, fear, hate, have (=exp), know (fear), like, love, miss, pity, rather (=prefer), want, wish,* and cognitive verbs *believe, comprehend, consider, doubt, have wrong, know* (91 times), *mind be on, note, notice, realize, recognize, remember, suppose, tell (=notice), think* (170 times), *trust,* and *understand.*

(261) He saw the native boats come riding through the surf.   24:25
      [PERSON:#he]←(E)←[SEE]→(Os)→[PROPOSITION]

(262) He knows (=feels) no fear of anything.   106:2
      [PERSON:#he]←(E)←[KNOW]→(Os)→[FEAR:no]

(263) I want to be out before it is light.   14:6
      [PERSON:I]←(E)←[WANT]→(Os)→[PROPOSITION]

3.2. Experiential state with Os subject

Experiential states with Os as subject are two-place predicates relating an Experiencer and an Object. The structure of the predication is shown in the following graph, which links an ENTITY called the Object with a PERSON called the Experiencer. The Object is the stimulus for the experience.

(264)

Experiential states with Os as subject include sensation states, emotive states, and cognitive states. These experiential states with Os-subject may be adjectives or verbs.

Sensation states (Os,E). Sensation states will normally be found in a VERB + ADJECTIVE structure with the Experiencer as a deletable indirect object. The sense of sight is expressed by *look,* the sense of hearing is represented by *sound.* The other senses are represented by the same verb form that is used for State verbs with E-subject. The verb is characterized as Os,E with the Object role filled by the adjective predication. The subject of the adjective is raised to be the subject of the sense verb and the infinitive *to be* is obligatorily deleted, unlike *seem,* which optionally allows *to be.*

(265) The poet /looked /sad /to me.   Os,E
      = It looked to me that the poet was sad.
      [LOOK] -
         (Os)→[[POET:#]←(Os)←[BE SAD]]
         (E)→[TO [PERSON:#me]].

(266) The music /sounds /good /to me.   Os,E
      = It sounds to me that the music is good.
      [SOUND] -
         (Os)→[[MUSIC:#]←(Os)←[BE GOOD]]
         (E)→[TO [PERSON:#me]].

(267) The carpet /felt /soft /to Bruce.   Os,E
      = It felt to Bruce that the carpet was soft.
      [FEEL] -
         (Os)→[[CARPET:#]←(Os)←[BE SOFT]]
         (E)→[TO [BRUCE]].

Emotive states (Os,E). State Experiential predicates with Os stimulus as subject and Experiencer as indirect object are different from Basic State predicates (see §2.1 Basic State) in that these adjectives require an Experiencer. They include many adjectives which are derived from psych movement predicates, such as *be pleasant, be amusing.*

(268) It /was pleasant /on the terrace.   Os,E
      = It was pleasant (for people) on the terrace.
      [WEATHER:It]←(Os)←[BE PLEASANT]→(E)→[NULL].

(269) Watching clowns /is amusing /(to me).   Os,E
      [BE AMUSING] -
         (Os)→[[PERSON:#I]←(A=E)←[WATCH]→(O)→[CLOWNS]]
         (E)→[NULL].

Tough movement. A special subset of emotive states with Os subject are the tough movement adjectives. In *Current Issues in Linguistic Theory* (1964), Chomsky presented two sentences which seem to be identical in their surface structure, but have two different underlying structures.

(270) John is eager to please.   E,Os
   = BE eager (John, PLEASE (John, people))
   = John is subject of please.

(271) John is easy to please.   Os,E
   = BE EASY FOR (PLEASE (people, John)) people)
   = John is object of please.

In *Cross-over Phenomena* Postal describes a transformation which he calls "tough movement" (1971a:27) which moves a noun phrase out of the predicate complement and inserts it as subject of the sentence. This rule applies to a set of adjectives including *difficult, easy, hard, impossible, simple, tough.* Postal derives the sentence by applying extraposition, moving the subject complement to the end of the sentence, and then applying tough movement, raising the lower Object to subject position.

(272) To please John /is easy.   Os,E
   = It /is easy /to please John.   by extraposition
   = John /is easy /to please.   by tough movement

Postal (1971a:29) claims that there are two different surface structures with the following sentences, depending upon whether the *for*-phrase is associated with the adjective predicate or with the embedded sentence. According to Postal (1970:29) "the difference in meaning is real though subtle." The first sentence (273) "seems to associate the difficulty directly with Tony personally. The second (274) allows for a more generic attribution of difficulty."

(273) It was difficult for Tony /to rob the store.   Os,E
   = Tony is indirect object of difficult

(274) It was difficult /for Tony to rob the store.   Os,E
   = Tony is subject of the infinitive to rob.

Another explanation is that the *for*-phrase serves two functions: it is the indirect object of the main predicate and at the same time it is the subject of the infinitive complement. The lower subject is deleted by

Equi-NP deletion. The indirect object is later deleted because it is indefinite and adds no new information. Extraposition is then applied, followed by tough movement.

(275) For some one to please John /is easy /for some one.
      ⇒ To please John /is easy /for some one.   by Equi-NP deletion
      ⇒ To please John /is easy.   by Object deletion
      ⇒ It /is easy /to please John.   by extraposition
      ⇒ John /is easy /to please.   by tough movement

In a Case Grammar analysis, tough movement adjectives like *easy* are two-place predicates with the Object case as subject and the Experiencer case as indirect object. The case frame for *be easy for* is Os,E. This structure contrasts with two-place predicates like *eager* with the Experiencer case as subject and a complement as direct object. The case frame for *be eager* is E,Os. The contrast is shown in the following two conceptual graphs which show *John* as subject of *please* with *be eager*, but as object of *please* with *be easy for*.

(276) John /is eager /to please.   E,Os
    = John is eager to please (people).
    [BE EAGER] -
      (E)→[JOHN]
      (Os)→[[JOHN]←(A=O)←[PLEASE]→(E)→[NULL]].

(277) John /is easy /to please.   Os,E
    = It is easy (for people) to please John.
    [BE EASY FOR] -
      (Os)→[[PEOPLE]←(A=O)←[PLEASE]→(E)→[JOHN]]
      (E)→[NULL].

Cognitive states with Os-subject. Experiential sensation states with Os subject, such as *look, sound, feel,* have the Experiencer as indirect object. The subject is raised from the embedded complement to become the subject of the sensation predicate. (See §3.2 Experiential state with Os-subject: Sensation states.) The cognitive counterpart of these sense verbs is the verb *seem.* This verb is the principal cognitive state verb with Os subject. The verb *seem* is a two-place predicate with an embedded sentence as subject and an Experiencer object as indirect object. The case frame is Os,E. This verb has the same meaning in all its occurrences and occurs in only two possible structures. The verb *seem* is a discourse palliative. It is inserted into the discourse to soften the force of the predication by limiting the truth of the predication to the opinion of the speaker. Its force is determined by removing it from the predication and comparing the meaning of the underlying structure with the meaning of the *seem* structure.

The verb *seem* can then be codified into one of two structures. The first structure places the predication in a that-clause and applies obligatory *it* extraposition. The underlying structure graphs the components of the structure before extraposition. The case frame is Os,E.

(278) It /seems /to me /that the report is accurate.   Os,E
    = The report is accurate, it seems to me.
    [SEEM] -
      (Os)→[[REPORT:#]←(Os)←[BE ACCURATE]]
      (E)→[TO [PERSON:#me].

The second structure changes the predicate of the underlying clause to an infinitive, and raises the subject of the lower clause to become the subject of the higher clause. The graphic representation and case frame are unchanged. In this structure the elements *to be* may be freely omitted with adjectives.

(279) The report seems accurate.   Os,E
    = The report seems (to me) to be accurate.
    [SEEM] -
      (Os)→[[REPORT:#]←(Os)←[BE ACCURATE]]
      (E)→[NULL].

According to a survey of the verb *seem* from the Francis corpus, the that-clause occurs 10% of the time and the infinitive with subject raising occurs 90% of the time. The indirect object Experiencer is freely omitted and only occurred 5% of the time. But the phrase *to me* is clearly implied and can be added to any *seem* predication without change in meaning or grammaticality.

The logical structure of sentence (279) is shown in (280). The raised subject has no case label, and the *to me* phrase is deleted. The logical structure of sentence (278) is the same, but different rules are applied. By extraposition the proform *it* is placed in subject position, and the embedded clause becomes a that-clause and is moved to the end of the sentence.

(280) The verb SEEM.
The report seems accurate (to me).
= SEEM (BE ACCURATE (report), to me)

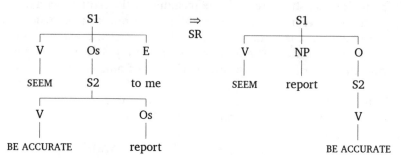

Psych movement adjectives. Another set of adjectives derived from psych movement verbs "involves adjectival endings in -*ing* (occasionally -*some* and -*ive*) and postadjectival phrases with *to*" (Postal 1970:41). These derived adjectives have the case frame Os,E. They include both cognitive and emotive predicates. Although similar to the progressive in form, these adjectives have the Experiencer as a freely deletable indirect object, and allow the use of intensifiers like *very*. The progressive form has Experiencer as direct object, and does not allow intensifiers like *very*. These adjectives may also take subject complements. For a complete listing see (307) Psych movement verbs.

(281) This theory /is interesting /Sam.   O,E
[THEORY:#]←(O)←[INTEREST]→(E)→[SAM].

(282) This theory /is very interesting /to Sam.   Os,E
[THEORY:#]←(Os)←[BE INTERESTING TO]→(E)→[SAM].

(283) This class /is boring /Helen.   O,E
[CLASS:#]←(O)←[BORE]→(E)→[HELEN].

(284) This class /is very boring /to Helen.   Os,E
[CLASS:#]←(Os)←[BE BORING TO]→(E)→[HELEN].

(285) Storms at sea /are frightening /to me.   Os,E
[STORMS]←(Os)←[BE FRIGHTENING]→(E)→[TO [PERSON:#me].

(286) It /is exhilarating /to ride the coaster.   Os,E
= It is exhilarating (for people) to ride the coaster.
[BE EXHILARATING] -
   (Os)→[[PEOPLE]←(A)←[RIDE]→(O)→[COASTER:#]]
   (E)→[NULL].

Text analysis of Experiential state with Os-subject. In the text of
the Hemingway novel some Experiential states were found with Os-
subject. The Experiencer role is downshifted out of subject position and
becomes a freely deletable indirect object. Intransitive adjectives have an
Os-subject and Experiencer as indirect object. This object is often deleted
but is understood in context. These include sensation adjectives *be bad-
smelling, be beautiful-looking, be comfortable, be coppery (tasting), be hard-
feeling, be hot, be imperceptible, be in sight, be nourishing, be out of sight, be
sweet (tasting), be sweet-smelling, be visible.* Emotion adjectives include *be
cheerful, be disgraceful, be humiliating, be painful, be pleasant, be intolerable,
be unavoidable, be wonderful.*

(287) He thought of it as almost comfortable.   47:13
   [POSITION:it]←(Os)←[BE COMFORTABLE]→(E)→[NULL].

(288) It was sunny and pleasant on the terrace.   12:2
   [WEATHER:it]←(Os)←[BE PLEASANT]→(E)→[NULL].

Transitive adjectives found in the text include mostly cognitive adjectives *be bad for, be better for, be difficult for, be easy for, be good for, be
hard for.* The Experiencer occurs as the object of the preposition *for.*

(289) A sardine's head was difficult to break from the hook.   42:5
= It was difficult to break a sardine's head from the hook.
= To break a sardine's head from the hook was difficult.
   [PROPOSITION]←(Os)←[BE DIFFICULT FOR]→(E)→[NULL].

Verbs with an Os-subject and Experiencer as indirect object included
the sensation verbs *look, show, taste* and the cognitive verbs *matter* and
seem. The indirect object is often omitted.

(290) The dolphin looks green (to me) of course.   72:4
= It looks to me that the dolphin is green.
= That the dolphin is green looks to me.
   [PROPOSITION]←(Os)←[LOOK]→(E)→[NULL].

(291) The creases did not show so much when he was asleep.   18:20
= The creases were not visible to anyone.
[CREASE:#]←(Os)←[SHOW]→(E)→[NULL].

(292) And pain does not matter to a man.   84:21
[PAIN]←(Os)←[MATTER]→(E)→[TO [MAN]].

3.3. Experiential state with double Os

Many apparent three-place Experiential verbs with Os as subject, such as the impression verb *strike*, can be reduced to two-place predicates by the rule of subject-raising. But some verbs with three nouns in the structure cannot be reduced.

The action verb *remind* is a three-place predicate with the meaning "cause someone to remember." The meaning includes an Agent as subject who does the reminding, an Experiencer as indirect object who is reminded, and an embedded proposition as direct object which is the content of the reminder. The complement object may be a that-clause or an infinitive. The case frame is A,E,O. (See §3.9 Experiential Action with all roles overt.)

(293) John /reminded /me /to lock the door.   A,E,O
= REMIND (John, me, (LOCK (I, door)))
[REMIND (+agt)] -
    (A)→[JOHN]
    (E)→[PERSON:#me]
    (O)→[[PERSON:#I]←(A)←[LOCK]→(O)→[DOOR:#]].

(294) Mary /reminded /me /that today was her birthday.   A,E,O
= REMIND (Mary, me, (BE (today, birthday)))
[REMIND (+agt)] -
    (A)→[MARY]
    (E)→[PERSON:#me]
    (O)→[[TODAY]←(Os)←[BE]→(Os)→[BIRTHDAY:her]].

The State verb *remind (of)* has the meaning "strikes one as similar to" (Postal 1971b:181). The State verb *strike* is a two-place predicate with an embedded sentence as subject and the Experiencer as object. The subject of the embedded clause is raised to become subject of the higher clause. The case frame is Os,E. (See §3.1 State Experiencer: Impression verbs.)

(295) Harry /strikes /me /as similar to my father.   Os,E
    = It strikes me that Harry is similar to my father.
    = STRIKE (BE SIMILAR (Harry,father), me)
    [STRIKE] -
        (Os)→[[HARRY]←(Os)←[BE SIMILAR TO]→(Os)→[FATHER:my]]
        (E)→[PERSON:#me].

Despite the similarity in meaning with the impression verb *strike*, the State verb *remind (of)* seems to be a three-place predicate. The three nouns in the structure are the subject, which is one of the entities being compared, the direct object which is the Experiencer, and the noun in the of-phrase, which is the other entity being compared. But this structure cannot be reduced to a two-place structure with subject raising. The only alternative is to interpret the case frame as E,Os,Os, but with Os-subject. The verb *resemble,* which is a two-place Os,Os predicate, is different from *remind* in that there is no reference, even indirectly, to an Experiencer who might be the person who detects the resemblance.

(296) Harry /reminds /me /of my father.   E,Os,Os
    = REMIND (Harry, me, father)
    [REMIND (−agt)] -
        (Os)→[HARRY]
        (E)→[PERSON:#me]
        (Os)→[FATHER:#my]

3.4–3.5 Process Experiential verbs

Process Experiential verbs describe a dynamic Experiential situation. They require the Experiencer role for the person undergoing the experience, and an Object role expressing the content of the experience. Process verbs may occur with E-subject or with O-subject.

3.4. Experiential process with E-subject

Experiential process verbs are two-place predicates relating an Experiencer to an Object. The structure of the predication is shown in the following graph, which links a PERSON called the Experiencer with an ENTITY called the Object.

(297) [PERSON] ← (E) ← [EXP-VERB] → (O) → [ENTITY]

Experiential process verbs with the Experiencer as subject include emotive verbs or cognitive verbs, but not sensation verbs. These predicates occur freely with the progressive.

Emotive process verbs. Some emotive verbs are process rather than state, as they occur freely with the progressive. Among these are the verbs *enjoy* and *feel.*

(298) Martha /is enjoying /the play.   E,O
      [MARTHA]←(E)←[ENJOY]→(O)→[PLAY:#].

(299) John /is feeling /fine.   E,O
      From: John feels (himself to be) fine.
      [FEEL] -
          (E)→[JOHN]
          (O)→[[JOHN]←(Os)←[BE FINE]].

Cognitive process verbs. Although cognitive process verbs are rare, there are occasions where the state cognitive verb is used to convey the meaning of coming into that state. In this use the verb is a process and takes the progressive.

(300) Harold /is understanding /more /every day.   E,O
      = Harold is coming to understand more.
      COME ABOUT (UNDERSTAND (Harold, more))
      [HAROLD]←(E)←[UNDERSTAND]→(O)→[MORE].

(301) Max /is learning /the meaning of life.   E,O
      = Max is coming to learn.
      COME ABOUT (LEARN (Max, meaning))
      [MAX]←(E)←[LEARN]→(O)→[MEANING].

The verb FEEL. The verb *feel* is a Process Experiential verb relating an Experiencer with the stimulus of that experience. Unlike most sensation verbs, the verb is considered to be a Process because in all of its occurrences the simple tenses can be replaced by the progressive tenses. *He feels sick* can always be replaced by *he is feeling sick.* Therefore, in all contexts except the combination *feel that,* assume that *feel* is a process verb.

feel + *noun.* This structure is an E-O structure with a personal subject and the emotion which is felt as its direct object. The subject has the Experiencer role and the emotion felt has the Object role.

(302) Thomas suddenly felt fear.   E,O
     [THOMAS]←(E)←[FEEL]→(O)→[FEAR].

feel + *adverb.* This structure is an E-O structure with a personal subject and the emotional state represented by an adverbial phrase. The subject has the Experiencer role and the adverb has the Object role.

(303) Albert feels badly.   E,O
     [ALBERT]←(E)←[FEEL]→(O)→[BADLY].

feel + *adjective.* Rather than enter combinations in the lexicon such as *feel confident, feel faint,* it seemed better to list *feel* as distinct from the adjectives, *be confident, be faint* to avoid unnecessary duplication. This structure is considered to be a complex structure consisting of two predicates, the verb *feel,* which has a person as subject and a sentence as object, and the adjective predication, which has the same subject as the main verb *feel.* The surface structure is derived by Equi-NP deletion.

(304) Martha felt faint.   E,O
     = Martha felt [herself to be faint].
     [FEEL] -
        (E)→[MARTHA]
        (O)→[[MARTHA]←(E=Os)←[BE FAINT]].

feel + *adjective /adverb, body part subject.* When the subject of the verb *feel* is a part of the body, the body part assumes the Object role, and the Experiencer role is a hidden indirect Object. The frame is O,E.

(305) His back feels bad (to him).   O,E
     = [His back is bad] feels to him.
     [FEEL] -
        (O)→[[BACK:#his]←(Os)←[BE BAD]]
        (E)→[NULL].

3.5. Experiential process with O-subject

Experiential process verbs are two-place predicates relating an Experiencer and an Object. The structure of the predication is shown in the following graph, which links an ENTITY called the Object with a PERSON called the Experiencer. The Object in subject position is interpreted as the stimulus for the experience.

(306)

Experiential process verbs with O-subject include predicates of emotion and cognition, but not sensation. Verbal predicates with O-subject are called "psych movement verbs." They are called "psych" because they deal with mental activity, and they are called "movement" because the Experiencer case is moved from subject to direct object position.

Paul Postal (1971a:41) lists seventeen psych movement predicates: *amaze, amuse, bore, confuse, disgust, excite, frighten, gratify, horrify, irritate, nauseate, puzzle, rile, surprise, terrify, threaten, worry*. Psych movement verbs have two State adjective derivatives, one with Os-subject and one with E-subject. The *-ing* form with Os-subject is a derived adjective, not a progressive. It takes intensifiers like *very*, and has the Experiencer as the indirect, not direct, object. (See §3.2 Cognitive states with O-subject.) The *-ed* form with E-subject is a derived adjective, not a passive. This form takes prepositions other than *by*. (See §3.1 Cognitive states with E-subject.) Forty psych movement verbs and their derivatives are listed in (307).

Jane Grimshaw (1990:175, chapter 2, note 3) lists fifteen psych movement predicates: *amaze, amuse, anger, annoy, appall, astonish, disgust, (dis)please, enrage, entertain, infuriate, intrigue, irritate, shock, terrify*, described as the *frighten* class, in which "the Experiencer appears as a postverbal object, and the Theme occupies the subject position" (1990:8). These verbs are opposed to the *fear* class, which in English includes the verbs: *abhor, admire, adore, appreciate, deplore, despise, detest, enjoy, hate, like, love, scorn, resent, respect* (1990:175, chapter 2, note 2), in which "the Experiencer is realized as subject, and the Theme as an object" (1990:8).

In discussing the psych movement verbs, Grimshaw attempts to provide reasons why the rank shift occurs which places the Object (Theme) as a subject. Her argument is that since the Object (Theme) role expresses the cause of the emotion, it must be moved to subject position. "Verbs in the *frighten* class are causative...the *frighten* class follows the rule: assign subject realization to a cause argument" (1990:24). In sentences such as *the storm frightened us*, *the storm* must be chosen as subject since it is the cause of the fright emotion. But there is a chicken-and-egg problem here. Is *storm* subject because it is cause, or is *storm* interpreted as cause because it is subject? The contrary opinion is that the Object (Theme) case focusses upon the content of the experience when in object position and focusses upon the stimulus (cause) of the experience when in subject position. But in sentences like *John enjoyed the show*, *the show* is still the cause of the enjoyment even though *the show* is not rank-shifted to subject position. It is my opinion that rank shifts can be described as facts of the language, but cannot be explained.

(307) Psych movement verbs

State: O-Subject Os,E	Process O,E	State: E-Subject E,Os
be amazing to	amaze	be amazed at
be amusing to	amuse	be amused at
be annoying to	annoy	be annoyed with
be appalling to	appall	be appalled at
be boring to	bore	be bored with
be bothersome to	bother	be bothered with
be captivating to	captivate	be captivated with
be charming to	charm	be charmed with
be cheering to	cheer	be cheered at
be comforting to	comfort	be comfortable with
be confusing to	confuse	be confused at
be debilitating to	debilitate	be debilitated at
be deceptive to	deceive	be deceived about
be delightful to	delight	be delighted with
be disgusting to	disgust	be disgusted with
be exciting to	excite	be excited at
be exhilarating to	exhilarate	be exhilarated at
be exhausting to	exhaust	be exhausted with
be frightening to	frighten	be frightened of
be grievous to	grieve	be grieved at
be horrifying to	horrify	be horrified at
be hurtful to	hurt	be hurt about
be interesting to	interest	be interested in
be irritating to	irritate	be irritated at
be mystifying to	mystify	be mystified at
be nauseating to	nauseate	be nauseated at
be offensive to	offend	be offended at
be painful to	pain	be pained at

be pleasing to	please	be pleased at
be puzzling to	puzzle	be puzzled at
be refreshing to	refresh	be refreshed at
be shocking to	shock	be shocked at
be surprising to	surprise	be surprised at
be terrifying to	terrify	be terrified at
be threatening to	threaten	be threatened with
be tiring to	tire	be tired of
be troubling to	trouble	be troubled with
be warming to	warm	be warmed at
be wearisome to	weary	be wearied at
be worrisome to	worry	be worried about

This large class of psych movement verbs violates the normal subject choice hierarchy of A-E-B-O-L by moving the Object (Theme) into subject position and downgrading the Experiencer to the direct object position. Most case grammarians consider this a fact of the language and consider all of these examples of rank shift as lexically determined.

Text analysis of Experiential Process. In the text of the Hemingway novel Experiential Process was found with E-subject and with O-subject. Since there are no Process adjectives, all of the entries were full verbs.

The E-O frame. Verbs with the E,O frame included emotion verbs such as *enjoy, expect, feel* (25), *hope, suffer, tire, worry* and cognitive verbs such as *bear, dream, endure, learn, picture, take* (=*endure*), *wonder.*

(308) Many of the older fishermen will worry (about you).   115:6
    [FISHERMEN:@many]←(E)←[WORRY ABOUT]→(O)→[NULL].

(309) He dreamed that he was in the village on his bed.   81:13
    [DREAM] -
        (E)→[PERSON:#he]
        (O)→[[PERSON:#he]←(Os)←[BE-LOC]→(L)→[in [VILLAGE:#]].

The O-E frame. The O-E verbs included sensation verbs *attract, burn, exhaust, hurt, nauseate,* emotion verbs *affect, annoy, bore, encourage, humiliate, please, worry,* and cognitive verbs *fascinate* and *start* (=*startle*).

(310) But I have no light to attract the fish.   66:3
= the light attracts the fish.
[LIGHT]←(O)←[ATTRACT]→(E)→[FISH:#].

(311) There was no one that his thoughts could annoy.   39:18
= His thoughts could annoy no one.
[THOUGHTS:#his]←(O)←[ANNOY]→(E)→[NO ONE].

(312) Watching the shark always fascinated the old man.   112:1
[FASCINATE] -
(O)→[[MAN:#]←(A=E)←[WATCH]→(O)→[SHARK:#]]
(E)→[MAN:#].

The *make* + adjective structure was treated as a complex structure
with *make* as a main verb and an event represented by the adjective
predication. These predications are the causative-inchoative variants of
the simple adjective. They include *make desperate, make happy, make
lonely, make sad.*

(313) It made the boy sad to see the old man.   9:9
[MAKE = cause] -
(O)→[[BOY:#]←(E)←[SEE]→(Os)→[MAN:#]]
(O)→[[BOY:#]←(E=Os)←[BE SAD]].

3.6–3.9 Action Experiential verbs

Action experiential verbs describe an active experiential situation.
They require the Agent role, the instigator of the activity, the Experiencer role, for the person undergoing the experience, and an Object role
expressing the content of the experience. The Agent may be coreferential
with the Experiencer case, or with the Object case.

3.6. With A=E coreference

Action Experiential predicates with A=E coreference are two-place
predicates. The structure of the predication is shown in the following
graph, which links a PERSON who is Agent and Experiencer with an ENTITY
called the Object, the content of the experience.

(314) | PERSON | ← (A=E) ← | EXP-VERB | → (O) → | ENTITY |

Action Experiential verbs with A=E coreference include active sense verbs and active cognitive verbs. The direct object may be a complement. The case frame is A=E,O. Many have a corresponding State form, E,Os.

Active sense verbs. Sense verbs have corresponding active forms to describe sensation actively perceived. The verb *see* becomes *look at* or *watch*, the verb *hear* becomes *listen to*. The verbs *smell, taste, feel* keep the same form but are interpreted as actions in context.

(315) Max /smelled /the odor from the fish factory.   E,Os
      = unintentional smell.
      [MAX]←(E)←[SMELL]→(Os)→[ODOR:#].

(316) Smell /the roses.   A,*E,O /A=E
      = deliberate smell.
      [PERSON:#you]←(A=E)←[SMELL (A)]→(O)→[ROSES:#].

(317) He /tasted /garlic in the soup.   E,Os
      = accidental taste.
      [PERSON:#he]←(E)←[TASTE]→(Os)→[GARLIC].

(318) Taste /your coffee.   A,*E,O /A=E
      = deliberate taste.
      [PERSON:#you]←(A=E)←[TASTE (A)]→(O)→[COFFEE].

(319) She /felt /the wind in her hair.   E,Os
      = accidental feeling.
      [PERSON:#she]←(E)←[FEEL]→(Os)→[WIND:#].

(320) Bruce /felt /the rug /with his toes.   A,*E,O /A=E
      = deliberate feeling.
      [BRUCE]←(A=E)←[FEEL (A)]→(O)→[RUG:#].

Active cognitive verbs. Many cognitive verbs that describe cognitive States receive an agentive reinterpretation in which they are cognitive Actions. Included in this set are the verbs *believe, forget, know, remember, think*. These verbs take both the progressive and the imperative.

(321) He /forgot /it was her birthday.   E,Os
      = accidentally forget.
      [PERSON:#he]←(E)←[FORGET]→(Os)→[BIRTHDAY:her].

(322) Forget /your troubles.   A,*E,O /A=E
      = deliberately forget.
      [PERSON:#you]←(A=E)←[FORGET (A)]→(O)→[TROUBLES].

(323) She /remembered /her appointment.   E,Os
      = accidentally remember.
      [PERSON:#she]←(E)←[REMEMBER]→(Os)→[PROPOSITION].

(324) Remember /the Alamo.   A,*E,O /A=E
      = deliberate recall
      [PERSON:#you]←(A=E)←[REMEMBER (A)]→(O)→[ALAMO:#].

3.7. With A=O coreference

Action Experiential predicates with A=O coreference are two-place
predicates. The structure of the predication is shown in the following
graph, which links a PERSON who is both Agent and Object with a PERSON
called the Experiencer in direct object position.

(325) | PERSON | ← (A=O) ← | EXP-VERB | → (E) → | PERSON |

Action experiential verbs with A=O coreference are generally psych
movement verbs in which the Object stimulus is a person acting intentionally. The stimulus has an active reinterpretation. Some sentences are
ambiguous between the nonagentive reading, as in sentence (326), and
the agentive reading, as in sentence (327).

(326) John /frightened /the baby.   O,E
      = accidentally frighten.
      [JOHN]←(O)←[FRIGHTEN]→(E)→[BABY:#].

(327) John /frightened /the baby.   A,E,*O /A=O
      = deliberately frighten.
      [JOHN]←(A=O)←[FRIGHTEN (+agt)]→(E)→[BABY:#].

3.8. With O-lexicalized

Action Experiential verbs with O-lexicalized are two-place predicates relating an Agent to an Experiencer. The structure of the predication is shown in the following graph which links a PERSON called the Agent with a PERSON called the Experiencer in direct object position.

(328) $\boxed{\text{PERSON}}$ ← Ⓐ ← $\boxed{\text{VERB/*O-lex}}$ → Ⓔ → $\boxed{\text{PERSON}}$

Action experiential verbs with O-lexicalized include those verbs which occur in the lexicon with a corresponding noun, such as *answer, blame, praise, question, thank*. In a simple two-place structure the subject is the Agent, the direct object is Experiencer, and the Object case is lexicalized into the verb.

(329) The police /questioned /the suspect.   A,E,*O /O-lex
= The police asked questions of the suspect.
[POLICE]←(A)←[QUESTION /O-lex]→(E)→[SUSPECT:#].

(330) Mary /thanked /John (for the flowers).   A,E,*O /O-lex
= Mary expressed thanks to John.
[MARY]←(A)←[THANK /O-lex]→(E)→[JOHN].

3.9. With all roles overt

Action Experiential predicates with all roles overt are three-place predicates involving an Agent, an Experiencer, and an Object. The structure of the predication is shown in the following graph, which links a PERSON who is Agent with a PERSON called the Experiencer and with an ENTITY called the Object in direct object position.

(331) $\boxed{\text{PERSON}}$ ← Ⓐ ← $\boxed{\text{VERB}}$ → Ⓔ → $\boxed{\text{PERSON}}$
↓
Ⓞ
↓
$\boxed{\text{ENTITY}}$

Action experiential verbs with all roles overt are principally verbs of communication, but there are a few A-E-O verbs that appear to be causatives, such as *show* = *cause to see,* and *teach* = *cause to learn.*

(332) Helen /showed /Jane /the picture.   A,E,O
    [HELEN]←(A)←[SHOW]→(E)→[JANE]→(O)→[PICTURE:#].

(333) Adam /taught /Eve /Greek.   A,E,O
    [ADAM]←(A)←[TEACH]→(E)→[EVE]→(O)→[GREEK].

Action experiential verbs with all roles overt which are verbs of communication have an Agent as speaker, an Experiencer as hearer, and an Object, what is said. These include the communication verbs *admit, agree, ask, call, explain, promise, say, speak, talk,* and *tell.* The Object, or what is said, is frequently an object complement.

(334) Martin /asked /Lisa /to leave the house.   A,E,O
    [ASK] -
        (A)→[MARTIN]
        (E)→[LISA]
        (O)→[[LISA]←(A=O)←[LEAVE]→(L)→[HOUSE:#]].

Although there are many verbs of communication in English, these verbs represent a different focus. This focus is indicated by the relative order of constituents, and by the deletability of constituents (see Cook 1985:30).

With the verb *tell,* the Object may be deleted, but not the Experiencer, as in *Joe told me.* The preferred order is Experiencer-Object, as in *Joe told me the story.* The focus of the verb is on the Experiencer, the hearer.

(335) Joe /told /me /that he was coming.   A,E,O
    [TELL] -
        (A)→[JOE]
        (E)→[PERSON:#me]
        (O)→[[JOE]←(A=O)←[COME]→(L)→[NULL]].

With the verb *say,* the Experiencer may be deleted, but not the Object, as in *Joe said he was coming.* The preferred order is Object-Experiencer, as in *Joe said this to me.* The focus is on the Object, what is said.

(336) Joe /said /to me /that he was coming.   A,E,O
     [SAY] -
        (A)→[JOE]
        (E)→[TO [PERSON:#me]]
        (O)→[[JOE]←(A=O)←[COME]→(L)→[NULL]].

With the verb *speak*, either the Experiencer or the Object, or both may
be deleted, as in *Joe spoke*. There is no preferred Experiencer-Object order, as they occur in either order. Since the focus is on neither the
Experiencer nor the Object, the focus is on the Agent, the speaker.

(337) Joe /spoke /to me /about this.   A,E,O
     = Joe spoke about this to me.
     [JOE]←(A)←[SPEAK]→(E)→[TO[#me]]→(O)→[ABOUT[#THIS]].

Text analysis of Experiential Action. Experiential Action verbs occur with A=E or A=O coreference, O-lexicalized, or all roles overt.
   Verbs with the A,*E,O /A=E frame include sensation verbs *feel* (10),
look at, smell, take a look, take (=endure), touch, and *watch,* emotion adjectives *be confident, be fearless,* and cognitive verbs *check, consider,
decide, forget, imagine, judge, know, learn, make (decision), make sure, mean
(=intend), pay attention, see (=find out), tell (=discern),* and *think of* (37).

(338) He carefully felt the pull of the fish.   52:13
     [PERSON:#he]←(A=E)←[FEEL (A)]→(O)→[PULL:#].

(339) You better be fearless and confident yourself, old man.   84:5
     [PERSON:#you]←(A=E=O)←[BE=ACT **fearless and confident**].

(340) Don't forget to tell Pedrico the head is his.   126:10
     [FORGET] -
        (A=E)→[PERSON:#you]
        (O)→[[TELL] -
           (A)→[PERSON:#you]
           (E)→[PEDRICO]
           (O)→[[HEAD]←[BELONG TO]→[PERSON:#him]].

Verbs with the A,E,*O /A=O frame consisted mainly of pysch movement verbs, with the frame O-E, reinterpreted as Agentive. These
included *bother, deceive, disturb,* and *hurt.*

(341) But I have hurt them both badly.   114:7
    [PERSON:#I]←(A=O)←[HURT (A)]→(E)→[SHARK:@both].

Verbs with the A,E,*O /O-lex frame found in the text were rare. These
verbs included *hail* (= *say hail to*), and *pray* (= *say prayers to*).

(342) Pray for us sinners.   65:11
    [PERSON:#you]←(A)←[PRAY /O-lex]→(E)→[PERSONS:#us].

Verbs with the A,E,O frame with all roles overt included communication verbs *add, admit, agree, ask* (16), *ask for, call, call on, convince,
explain, promise, say, shout, speak* (10), *talk* (11), *tell*, also *show* and *teach*.

(343) The old man had taught the boy to fish.   10:12
    [MAN:#]←(A)←[TEACH]→(E)→[BOY:#]→(O)→[TO FISH].

4
The Benefactive Domain

The Benefactive domain consists of those predicates which require the Benefactive concept, combined with the Object concept, or with the Agent and Object concepts. The presence of the Benefactive role indicates that the predicate belongs in the Benefactive domain. In a survey of 5,000 clauses in Hemingway's *The Old Man and the Sea*, 301 clauses or 6% were in the Benefactive domain. Of these clauses 93 or 2% were States, 20 or 0% were Process, and 188 or 4% were Actions.

(344) The Benefactive Domain

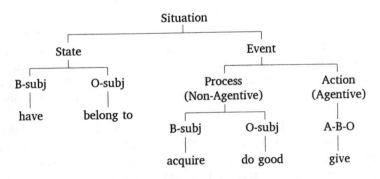

State Benefactive (93 clauses). State Benefactive verbs express a stative situation, in which a person is in possession of an Object. Basic Benefactive verbs require an Object and an Benefactive possessor. The Object case is marked with the subscript (*s*) to show stativity.

State Benefactive verbs with the B,Os frame regularly choose the Benefactive as subject. These include verbs dealing positively with possession such as *have, possess, own,* or verbs dealing negatively with absence of possession, such as *need, lack.* These verbs are all classified as States since they do not take the progressive and express a static situation.

State Benefactive verbs with the Os,B frame show a rank shift in the subject choice hierarchy. The Object role, which represents the possessed entity is promoted to subject over the Benefactive role indicating the person who possesses the Object. Since the Object is an entity and the Benefactive is a person, there is no problem in determining when this rank shift occurs. Predicates with the Os,B frame include *belong to,* and the structure represented as *be + possessive* such as *be mine.* These predicates also express a static situation and do not take the progressive.

Process Benefactive (20 clauses). Process Benefactive verbs express transfer of property without an Agent. Process Benefactive verbs require an Object and a Benefactive. The Object is the property changing possession, the Benefactive is the person to whom the transfer of property is directed. In Process predications there is no Agent in control of the transfer.

Process Benefactive verbs with the B,O frame regularly take the Benefactive as subject. Some Process verbs such as *acquire, inherit* seem to be inherently nonagentive. Other verbs are Process only when used in their nonagentive sense, such as *win, lose, receive, find.* These Process verbs are distinguished from States in their ability to freely take the progressive.

Process Benefactive verbs with the O,B frame show a rank shift in the subject choice hierarchy. The Object role, which represents the property transferred, is promoted to subject over the Benefactive role, the person who gains or loses in the transfer. Rank shift is detected when the Benefactive role occurs in a nonsubject position. Verbs with the O,B frame are quite rare. Possible candidates are *become + possessive,* such as *become mine.* Another possibility is the structure *do good to, benefit (someone).*

Action Benefactive (188 clauses). Action Benefactive verbs express a change of property directed by an Agent. Action Benefactive predications require an Agent, a Benefactive, and an Object. The Agent directs the transfer of property, the Benefactive is the "other party" in the transfer of property, and the Object is the property transferred. Action Benefactive verbs include A-B-O verbs with A=B coreference, A-B-O verbs with O lexicalized, and mainly A-B-O verbs with all roles overt.

There may occur a rank shift in the nonagentive roles with the case frame A,O,B.

Action Benefactive verbs with A=B include Process benefactive verbs which are reinterpreted as voluntary Action, such as *look for* and *find*, or voluntarily *receive*. When the Agent and Benefactive roles are coreferential the Agent is acquiring something for self.

Action Benefactive verbs with O-lex include verbs of transfer of property in which the Object role is incorporated into the verb such as *blame* = put the blame on and *bribe* = give a bribe to.

Action Experiential verbs with all roles overt are the most frequent, and include such common verbs as *give, buy,* and *sell.* The Agent may be the Source or Goal of the transaction, the Benefactive is the other party in the transfer, and the Object is the property transferred.

Although the Agent is never downshifted from subject position, rank shift may occur between the Benefactive and Object cases, placing the Object above Benefactive and creating the A,O,B case frame, as in *blame Fred for the mess,* with A,B,O order, rank-shifted to *blame the mess on Fred,* with A-O-B order.

4.1–4.2 State Benefactive verbs

State Benefactive verbs describe a static possession situation. They require the Benefactive role, for the person in possession, and an Object role expressing the object possessed. State benefactive verbs occur with B-subject or with Os-subject.

4.1. State with B-subject

Benefactive states are two-place predicates relating a Benefactive to an Object. The structure of the predication is shown in the following graph, which links a PERSON called the Benefactive with an ENTITY called the Object. The Object is the thing possessed.

(345) | PERSON | ← (B) ← | BEN-VERB | → (Os) → | ENTITY |

State Benefactive verbs with B-subject may be (1) positive, indicating the possession of an object, or (2) negative, indicating the lack or need for an object. The verbs *have, own, possess* are possession verbs, the verbs *need, lack, owe, require* are lack of possession verbs.

The verb HAVE. The verb *have*, indicating positive possession, according to the *Computational Analysis of Present Day American English* (Francis and Kucera 1967) is, after the verb *be*, the most frequent verb form in English. This count includes the use of *have* as perfect auxiliary, *have to* as a modal verb, and *have* as a main verb. The uses of *have* as an auxiliary or modal verb are not included in a Case Grammar analysis.

(346) Tom Clancy /has written/ a few books.   Perfect auxiliary
      = Present perfect of the verb *write*.

(347) Albert /has to go /to work.   Modal auxiliary
      = must go to work.

The verb HAVE + NP. The verb *have* as a main verb is transitive and may take a noun phrase or sentence as its object. When the verb *have* has as its direct object a noun phrase referring to a physical object, it is interpreted as a State Benefactive verb with the case frame B,Os. The verbs *own* and *possess* are also State Benefactive verbs, but refer more concretely to physical ownership. The verb *have* with an NP object is in some contexts interpreted as an Experiential verb or a Locative verb.

(348) John /has /eight children.   B,Os
      [JOHN]←(B)←[HAVE]→(Os)→[CHILDREN:@8].

(349) Ben /owns /a watch.   B,Os
      = owns a watch.
      [BEN]←(B)←[OWN]→(Os)→[WATCH].

Other uses of the verb HAVE. When the verb *have* has an object which can be experienced, it is interpreted as a State Experiential verb with the case frame E,Os. In this context, the verb *have* can be paraphrased as *experience*. (See §3.1 State Experiential with E-subject.)

(350) Carl /has /faith.   E,Os
      = experiences faith.
      [CARL]←(E)←[HAVE = **exp**]→(Os)→[FAITH].

(351) Ned /has /high hopes of winning.   E,Os
      = experiences hope.
      [NED]←(E)←[HAVE = **exp**]→(Os)→[HOPE].

The verb *have* is also used in the sense of *have (located)*. As noted by Fillmore (1968:48), the verb *have (located)* is used as the reverse of the stative *be* + locative structure. The direct object may be followed by a copy of the locative subject, expressed in a prepositional phrase. (See §5.2 State with L-subject.)

(352) The children /are /with Mary.   Os,L
    [CHILDREN:#]←(Os)←[BE-LOC]→(L)→[WITH [MARY]].

(353) Mary /has /the children /(with her).   L,Os
    [MARY]←(L)←[HAVE-LOC]→(Os)→[CHILDREN].

(354) There is /a lock /on the door.   Os,L
    [LOCK]←(Os)←[BE-LOC]→(L)→[ON [DOOR:#]].

(355) The door /has /a lock /(on it).   L,Os
    [DOOR:#]←(L)←[HAVE-LOC]→(Os)→[LOCK].

The verb HAVE + *complement.* When the verb *have* takes a sentence as object complement, it does not have Benefactive meaning. With a complement the verb *have* means "experience" when the embedded situation is a Process and the case frame is E,Os, but when the situation is an Action, the verb *have* means "cause" and the frame is A,O. (See §3.1 Emotive states with E-subject.)

The verb NEED. The verb *need* is used as a main verb, but is an auxiliary in the phrase *need to* = be obliged. As a main verb, *need* is a transitive verb which indicates lack of possession and has the frame B,Os. Similar verbs are *lack* and *require*.

(356) Frank /needs to /study more.   Modal
    = has an obligation.

(357) George /needs /a new hat.   B,Os
    = requires but has no possession of.
    [GEORGE]←(B)←[NEED]→(Os)→[HAT].

(358) Henry /lacks /understanding.   B,Os
    = does not possess.
    [HENRY]←(B)←[LACK]→(Os)→[UNDERSTANDING].

(359) This matter /requires /consideration.   B,Os
    = is in need of
    [MATTER:#]←(B)←[REQUIRE]→(Os)→[CONSIDERATION].

Text analysis of State Benefactive with B-subject. In the novel State
Benefactive verbs were found with B-subject, such as *have* = *possess* (60)
and the verbs *need* (9) and *lack* (= not possess). The verb *have* is indiffer-
ent to the distinctions of availability, alienable, and inalienable
possession. The verbs *own* and *possess* refer to possession. Adjectives include derivatives of the verb *to arm* = to provide arms for. The case
frame is B,Os /O-lex. The lexicalized Object case are the arms provided.
Other adjectives include *be against* (some obstacle), *be good for* (be a
benefit to), *be immune to* (have immunity to), and *be left* (be remaining
to).

(360) This fish was strong and well-armed.   101:5
    = has sufficient arms.
    [FISH:#]←(B)←[BE WELL-ARMED/ **O-lex**].

(361) The fish is against something he does not comprehend.   76:15
    = has as an obstacle.
    [FISH:#]←(B)←[BE AGAINST]←(Oσ)←[ΣOMETHINΓ].

The verb *have* is easily identified as *have* of possession when the Object is a physical entity, as in *have food, have radio.* Possession is
extended to characteristics, as in *have cutting edge,* or *have speed* and to
body parts as in *have brains, have heart.* More marginal cases are *have
courage, have plans,* or *have credit, have luck,* or *have* (people) as in *have
friends, have enemies.*

(362) I'll be back when I have the sardines.   17:7
    = have in my possession.
    [PERSON:I]←(B)←[HAVE]→(Os)→[SARDINES:#].

(363) I have such a heart too.   37:9
    = have as possession.
    [PERSON:#I]←(B)←[HAVE]→(Os)→[HEART].

(364) The flying fish have little chance.   34:19
    = possess chance.
    [FISH:#]←(B)←[HAVE]→(Os)→[CHANCE].

(365) They have other men of the team.   21:16
    = possess baseball players.
    [PERSON:#they]←(B)←[HAVE]→(Os)→[MEN:other].

The verb *have* is used with inanimate subjects to describe characteristics of that object. The verb *have* occurs in such contexts as *the sun has force, the meat has strength, the situation has its perils.*

(366) The teeth had razor sharp cutting edges on both sides.   101:3
    = have as characteristic.
    [TEETH:#]←(B)←[HAVE]→(Os)→[EDGES].

The verb *have* (= experience) includes *have* (sensations), such as *have pain, have feelings,* or *have* (emotions), such as *have confidence, have fear,* or *have* (cognition) such as *have faith, have understanding.* Experience is extended to sickness, such as *have a cold, have diarrhoea* and to the weather as in *have a good day, have a hurricane.* In all of these examples, the verb *have* may be paraphrased as *experience.* (See §3.1 Experiential state with E-subject.)

(367) I have had (= experienced) worse things than that.   74:17
    [PERSON:I]←(B)←[HAVE = **exp**]→(Os)→[THINGS].

On the negative side, the verbs *lack* and *need* are used to describe lack of possession. The verb *need* is followed by an NP direct object and must be distinguished from the modal *need to* following by an infinitive.

(368) The fish is huge and needs much food.   74:7
    [FISH:#]←(B)←[NEED]→(Os)→[FOOD:@much].

(369) The rope lacked what he had cut away.   101:12
    [LACK] -
    (B)→[ROPE:#]
    (Os)→[[PERSON:#he]←(A)←[CUT AWAY]→(O)→[WHAT]].

4.2. State with Os-subject

Benefactive states with Os-subject are also two-place predicates relating a Benefactive to an Object. The structure of the predication is shown in the following graph which links an ENTITY called the Object, the thing possessed, with a PERSON called the Benefactive.

(370)
$$\boxed{\text{ENTITY}} \leftarrow \textcircled{Os} \leftarrow \boxed{\text{BEN-VERB}} \rightarrow \textcircled{B} \rightarrow \boxed{\text{PERSON}}$$

State benefactive verbs with O-subject may be positive, such as *belong to* and the *be + possessive* construction. Some verbs may be negative, as with the verb *due to*. These verbs contrast with verbs with B-subject.

(371) I /possess /a compass.   B,Os
      [PERSON:I]←(B)←[POSSESS]→(Os)→[COMPASS].

(372) The compass /belongs to /me.   Os,B
      [COMPASS:#]←(Os)←[BELONG TO]→(B)→[PERSON:#me].

(373) The compass /is /mine.   Os,B
      [COMPASS:#]←(Os)←[BE + POSS]→(B)→[PERSON:#mine].

Text analysis of State Benefactive with Os-subject. In the text of the novel, State Benefactive verbs were found with Os-subject. The B case is frequently a deletable indirect object. These included *be + possessive,* such as *be mine,* in which the Benefactive case is a predicate nominal inflected for the genitive case, and *be necessary for,* rank-shifted from the verb *need.*

(374) Tell Pedrico the fish's head is his.   126:10
      [HEAD:#]←(Os)←[BE + POSS]→(B)→[PERSON:#his].

(375) They usually spoke only when it was necessary.   39:13
      [SPEAKING}←(Os)←[BE NECESSARY]→(B)→[NULL].

Benefactives with Os-subject were also found with the positive adjective predicates *be good for, be better for* and with the negative adjective predicate *be bad for.* In this context the predicate is interpreted as "be a benefit to" or "be a detriment to" with a Benefactive indirect object. The Benefactive indirect object is often freely deletable.

(376) The dew was bad for the sail and the lines.   15:11
      [DEW:#]←(Os)←[BE BAD FOR]→(B)→[SAIL:#].

4.3–4.4 Process Benefactive verbs

Process benefactive verbs describe a dynamic possession situation. They require the Benefactive role, for the person acquiring possession, and an Object role expressing the object to be acquired. Process benefactive verbs occur with B-subject or with O-subject.

4.3. Process with B-subject

Benefactive processes are two place predicates relating a Benefactive to an Object. The structure of the predication is shown in the following graph, which links a PERSON called the Benefactive with an ENTITY called the Object, the thing to be acquired.

(377) | PERSON | ← (B) ← | BEN-VERB | → (O) → | ENTITY |

Process benefactive verbs with B-subject may be positive, indicating the acquisition of an object, or negative indicating the loss of an object. The verbs *acquire, attain, find, inherit, lose, receive, win* are process B-O verbs when they express non-intentional acquisition or loss of property, but are interpreted as A,B,O /A=B verbs when the subject controls the activity.

(378) Mary /won /the lottery.   B,O
   = winning without control.
   [MARY]←(B)←[WIN]→(O)→[LOTTERY:#].

(379) Mary /won /the race.   A=B,O
   = winning with control.
   [MARY]←(A=B)←[WIN (A)]→(O)→[RACE:#].

(380) John /found /a penny.   B,O
   = accidental finding.
   [JOHN]←(B)←[FIND] → (O) → [PENNY].

(381) John /found /his car keys.   A=B,O
   = looked for and found.
   [JOHN]←(A=B)←[FIND (A)]→(O)→[KEYS:#his].

Text analysis of Process Benefactive verbs with B-subject. In the text of the novel, Process Benefactive verbs were found with B-subject.

The principal verbs were the nonagentive occurrences of *find* and *lose.* Other verbs included the nonagentive *get* and *gain,* and the verb *attain.*

(382) The old man knew he /had attained /humility.   14:1
    = acquire without control
    [MAN:#]←(B)←[ATTAIN]→(O)→[HUMILITY].

4.4. Process with O-subject

Benefactive processes with O-subject are also two place predicates relating a Benefactive to an Object. The structure of the predication is shown in the following graph which links an ENTITY called the Object, the thing to be acquired, with a PERSON called the Benefactive, who acquires possession.

(383)

$$\boxed{\text{ENTITY}} \quad \leftarrow \quad \text{O} \quad \leftarrow \quad \boxed{\text{BEN-VERB}} \quad \rightarrow \quad \text{B} \quad \rightarrow \quad \boxed{\text{PERSON}}$$

Process benefactive verbs with O-subject are extremely rare in English, but may be found in parallel with certain Benefactive state verbs. The stative structure *be + possessive* is paralleled by the process structure *become + possessive* and the stative *be good for* (= be a benefit to) is paralleled by the process verb *do good for,* as in sentences (384)–(387).

(384) The money is mine.   Os,B
    = State of possession
    [MONEY:#]←(Os)←[BE + **Poss**]→(B)→[PERSON:#mine].

(385) The money became mine.   O,B
    = The process of acquiring possession.
    [MONEY:#]←(O)←[BECOME + **Poss**]→(B)→[PERSON:#mine].

(386) The money is good for me.   Os,B
    = The money is a benefit to me.
    [MONEY:#]←(Os)←[BE GOOD FOR]→(B)→[PERSON:#me].

(387) The money did me good.   O,B
    = The money became a benefit to me.
    [MONEY:#]←(O)←[DO GOOD FOR]→(B)→[PERSON:#me].

Text analysis of Process Benefactive verbs with O-subject. In the text of the novel, Process Benefactive verbs were found with O-subject.

The principal verbs were *do good for,* as described above, and a predicate wishing bad luck to come to some one, listed as *become bad luck to.*

(388) But the gaff /will do /you /no good.   112:4
  [GAFF:#]←(O)←[DO GOOD FOR]→(B)→[PERSON:#you].

(389) Bad luck (come) to your mother.   101:20
  = A wish that bad luck will come.
  [LUCK:bad]←(O)←[COME TO]→(B)→[MOTHER:#your].

4.5–4.7 Action Benefactive verbs

Action benefactive verbs describe a change of possession. They require an Agent role, the person directing the transfer, the Benefactive role, the second party in the transaction, and an Object role expressing the object transferred. Action benefactive verbs occur with A=B coreference, with O-lexicalized, or with all three roles overt.

4.5. Action with A=B coreference

Action benefactive verbs with A=B coreference are two-place predicates with the subject simultaneously an Agent and a Benefactive, and an Object representing the object transferred. The structure of the predication is shown in the following graph, which links a PERSON who is Agent and Benefactive with an ENTITY called the Object.

(390) | PERSON | ← (A=B) ← | BEN-VERB | → (O) → | ENTITY |

Action benefactive verbs with A=B coreference refer to the acquisition of property with the meaning "acquire for oneself." The Agent directing the activity is simultaneously the one benefiting from the transaction. Some of these verbs are Agentive reinterpretations of Process Benefactive verbs, such as *acquire, find, gain, get, keep, receive, take (= accept), win.* Others are more properly Agentive, such as *catch, bring =* earn, *earn, make =* earn, and *save.*

(391) They /caught /three good fish /the first week.   A=B,O
  = acquire for themselves.
  [PERSON:#they]←(A=B)←[CATCH]→(O)→[FISH:@3].

(392) Jordan /makes /a lot of money.   A=B,O
      = acquires for himself.
      [JORDAN]←(A=B)←[MAKE = **earn**]→(O)→[MONEY:@much].

Text analysis of Action Benefactive verbs with A=B coreference.
In the text of the novel, the principal verbs are *catch,* the agentive *find,*
and the verbs, *get* (for self) and *take* (for self). Other verbs found in the
text include *keep, pick up* (scent), *summon* (strength) and agentive *win.*

(393) In the dark he /found /a water bottle.   121:22
      [PERSON:#he]←(A=B)←[FIND (A)]→(O)→[BOTTLE].

(394) I was lucky to /get /this fish instead of the dolphin.   59:8
      [PERSON:#I]←(A=B)←[GET **(for self)**]→(O)→[FISH:#this].

(395) He hasn't eaten since he /took /the bait.   74:6
      [PERSON:#he]←(A=B)←[TAKE **(for self)**]→(O)→[BAIT:#].

4.6. Action with O-lexicalized

Action benefactive verbs with the O case lexicalized are two-place
predicates with the Object case lexicalized into the verb. The structure of
the predication is shown in the following graph, which links a PERSON
who is Agent with a PERSON called the Benefactive.

(396) | PERSON | ← (A) ← | BEN /O-lex | → (B) → | PERSON |

Action benefactive verbs with O-lexicalized have the Object transferred as part of the verb. The lexicon often shows the same form for
noun and verb, as in *blame,tv* and *blame,n.* The lexicalized noun may be
copied into a prepositional phrase. Some of the prominent lexicalizations
are as follows:

blame	= put blame on	*respect*	= give respect to
bribe	= give bribe to	*ruin*	= bring ruin to
feed	= give food to	*serve*	= give service to
help	= give help to	*train*	= give training to

(397) The detective /blamed /the butler.   A,B,*O /O-lex
      = put the blame on.
      [DETECTIVE:#]←(A)←[BLAME **/O-lex**]→(B)→[BUTLER:#].

(398) George /bribed /the guard /with twenty dollars.   A,B,*O /O-lex
    = gave a bribe to
    [GEORGE]←(A)←[BRIBE /O-lex]→(B)→[GUARD:#].

Text analysis of Action Benefactive verbs with O-lexicalized. In the
text of the novel, the principal verbs based on nouns are *feed* = give food
to, *help* = give help to, *pity* = show pity towards, *respect* = show respect
to, *ruin* = bring ruin to, and *serve* = give service to.

(399) They had coffee at a place that served fishermen.   26:2
    = gives service to fishermen.
    [PLACE]←(A)←[SERVE /O-lex]→(B)→[FISHERMEN].

(400) If sharks come, God pity him and me.   68:16
    = give pity to.
    [GOD]←(A)←[PITY /O-lex]→(B)→[PERSONs:#him and me].

(401) We have killed many sharks and ruined many others.   115:13
    = bring ruin to.
    [PERSON:#we]←(A)←[RUIN /O-lex]→(B)→[SHARKS:@many].

4.7. Action with all roles overt

Action benefactive verbs with all roles overt are three-place predicates
requiring an Agent instigating the transfer, a Benefactive as the second
party, and an Object transferred. The structure of the predication is
shown in the following graph, which links an Agent PERSON to a Benefactive PERSON and an ENTITY called the Object.

(402)   [PERSON] ← (A) ← [VERB] → (B) → [PERSON]
                             ↓
                            (O)
                             ↓
                          [ENTITY]

Action benefactive verbs with all roles overt refer to the transfer of
property. The prototype verbs in this class are *buy* and *sell*. Other verbs
of transfer include *beg, borrow, get, give, lend, offer, order, pay, share,
trade*. Fillmore (1977:72) speaks of a commercial event in which there

are many actors. But the choice of verb focuses upon one actor as Agent and gives perspective to the scene. The focus is different for *buy, sell, pay, cost.*

(403) Chris /bought /the car /from Bob.   A,B,O
  = buyer is Agent.
  [CHRIS]←(A)←[BUY]→(O)→[CAR]→(B)→[FROM [BOB]].

(404) Bob /sold /the car /to Chris.   A,B,O
  = seller is Agent.
  [BOB]←(A)←[SELL]→(O)→[CAR]→(B)→[TO [CHRIS]].

(405) Chris /paid /Bob /two thousand dollars.   A,B,O
  = payer is Agent.
  [CHRIS]←(A)←[PAY]→(B)→[BOB]→(O)→[DOLLARS:@2000].

(406) The car /cost /two thousand dollars.   Os,Os
  = focus on cost.
  [CAR:#]←(Os)←[COST]→(Os)→[DOLLARS:@2000].

Reversible roles. The verb *rob* has A-B-O order, with the Benefactive as direct object and the Object stolen deletable. The verb *steal* has A-O-B order with the Object stolen as direct object and the Benefactive freely deletable. The verb *blame* may be used with either A-B-O or A-O-B order.

(407) David /robbed /the bank /(of money).   A,B,O
  [DAVID]←(A)←[ROB]→(B)→[BANK]→(O)→[NULL].

(408) David /stole /the money /(from the bank).   A,O,B
  [DAVID]←(A)←[STEAL]→(O)→[MONEY]→(B)→[NULL].

(409) Helen /blamed /Fred /for the mess.   A,B,O
  [HELEN]←(A)←[BLAME]→(B)→[FRED]→(O)→[FOR [MESS]].

(410) Helen /blamed /the mess /on Fred.   A,O,B
  [HELEN]←(A)←[BLAME]→(O)→[MESS]→(B)→[ON [FRED]].

Action verbs with complements. Some three-place A,B,O predicates take action complements. Chief among these are the predicates *cause* and *let. Causing* is bringing about an event, *letting* is ceasing to prevent an event. Gruber (1976:164) distinguishes these two kinds of Agency by calling the former a Causative Agent (C-Agent) and calling the latter a Permissive Agent (P-Agent). The distinction between causative Agents and permissive Agents is retained in Jackendoff (1976:105).

Permissive Agent. Permissive Agents (P-Agents) occur as subject of the three-place A,B,O verbs *allow, let, permit.* The Benefactive is the indirect object of the main verb, and also serves as the subject of the complement. The Object is the embedded complement. If the embedded sentence is not an action, there is no indirect object and the main verb is a two-place A,O verb. The three-place A,B,O verb is listed as *let (do),* meaning "let some one do the action," while the two-place A,O verb is listed as *let (happen),* meaning "let an event happen."

(411) The plumber /let /the water run down the drain.   A,O
    [LET (happen)] -
       (A)→[PLUMBER:#]
       (O)→[[WATER:#]←(O)←[RUN]→(L)→[DOWN [DRAIN]]].

(412) The class /let /the teacher open the window.   A,B,O
    [LET (do)] -
       (A)→[CLASS:#]
       (B)→[TEACHER:#]
       (O)→[[TEACHER:#]←(A)←[OPEN]→(O)→[WINDOW:#]].

Causative Agent. Causative Agents (C-Agents) occur as subject of the three-place A,B,O verbs *cause, force, get, make.* The Benefactive is the indirect object of the verb. The Object is the embedded complement and must be an action. Whenever the embedded sentence is a process, the main verb is a two-place A,O verb since it has no indirect object. The three-place A,B,O verb is listed as *make (do),* meaning "cause some one to do the action," while the two-place A,O verb is listed as *make (happen),* "cause an event to happen." Some verbs with C-Agents, such as *coerce, induce,* require an animate indirect object and only occur in the *cause (do)* meaning. Negative C-Agents occur with the verbs *keep (from), prevent (from).*

(413) The plumber /made /the water run down the drain.   A,O
    [MAKE (happen)] -
       (A)→[PLUMBER:#]
       (O)→[[WATER:#]←(O)←[RUN]→(L)→[DOWN [DRAIN]]].

(414) The class /made /the teacher open the window.   A,B,O
    [MAKE (do)] -
        (A)→[CLASS:#]
        (B)→[TEACHER:#]
        (O)→[[TEACHER:#]←(A)←[OPEN]→(O)→[WINDOW:#]].

Text analysis of Action Benefactive verbs with O-lexicalized. In the text of the novel, the standard verbs of transfer of property are very prominent, including the verbs *beg, borrow, buy, give, pay, sell, steal,* and *trade.* The verb *help* with a complement is generally a three-place A-B-O verb in which the B-role serves as indirect object of the verb *help* and also serves as subject of the complement verb.

(415) The boy always went down to help him carry the lines.   9:10
    [HELP (do)] -
        (A)→[BOY:#]
        (B)→[PERSON:#him]
        (O)→[[PERSON:#he]←(A)←[CARRY]→(O)→[LINES:#]].

Also prominent are Action verbs with complements including *let (do)* with twenty-five occurrences, *make (do),* and *get (do).* Negative causality is illustrated with the verb *keep (from)* with the meaning of prevent.

(416) I'll try to get him to come out after dolphin.   14:13
    [GET (do)] -
        (A)→[PERSON:#I]
        (B)→[PERSON:#him]
        (O)→[[PERSON:#he]←(A=O)←[COME]→(L)→[OUT]].

(417) I cannot keep the shark from hitting me.   101:18
    [KEEP (from)] -
        (A)→[PERSON:#I]
        (B)→[SHARK:#]
        (O)→[[SHARK:#]←(A)←[HIT]→(O)→[PERSON:#me]].

The verbal form *let's* seems to be a hortatory modal, and does not have either the meaning *let (happen)* or *let (do).* It should be treated as a modal and not listed as a main verb, as in the sentence *Let's go home.*

5
The Locative Domain

The Locative domain consists of those predicates which require the Locative concept, combined with the Object concept, or with the Agent and Object concepts. The presence of the Locative role indicates that the predicate belongs in the Locative domain. Stative and directional locatives are in complementary distribution under a single Locative concept. In a survey of 5,000 clauses in Hemingway's *The Old Man and the Sea*, 1,411 clauses or 29% were in the Locative domain. Of these 286 or 6% were Locative States, 207 or 4% were Locative Process, and 918 or 19% were Locative Actions.

(418) The Locative domain

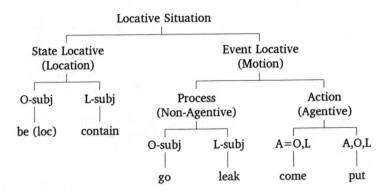

143

State Locative (286 clauses). State Locative verbs express stative location in a place. State locative predications require an Object, the entity being located, and a Location, the place where the entity is located. The Object case is marked with the subscript (s) to show stativity.

State Locative verbs with the Os,L frame regularly choose the located Object as subject and express the Location with an adverb or a prepositional phrase. The linking verb *be* in the structure is interpreted as *be located*. These are all classified as states since they do not take the progressive and express a static situation.

State Locative verbs with the L,Os frame show a rank shift in the subject choice hierarchy. The Locative role, which represents the Location of the object is promoted to subject over the Object role. Since the Object is an entity, and the Locative is a place, there is no problem in determining when this rank shift occurs.

Process Locative (207 clauses). Process locative verbs express motion from one place to another. Process locative predications require an Object, the entity which is moving, and a directional Locative describing the source, goal, or path where the entity is moving.

Process Locative verbs with the O,L frame regularly take the moving Object as subject. The path along which the Object moves is expressed as the Locative. These Process verbs are distinguished from States in their ability to freely take the progressive.

Process Locative verbs with the L,O frame show a rank shift in the subject choice hierarchy. The Locative role, which represents the trajectory of motion, is promoted to subject over the Object role, the moving entity. Rank shift is detected when the Locative role, designating a path, occurs in subject position.

Action Locative (918 clauses). Action Locative verbs express motion from one place to another which is instigated by an Agent. Action locative predications require an Agent, the instigator of the motion, a moving Object, and a Locative, describing the source, goal, or path where the Object is moving. The Agent may be coreferential with the Object or Location, and either Location or Object may be lexicalized into the verb.

Action Locative verbs with the A,*O,L /A=O frame include verbs of self-movement. The subject is both an Agent, acting as instigator of the Action, and a moving Object.

Action Locative verbs with the A,O,*L /A=L frame are relatively rare, but occur when an active Agent is simultaneously a location, as with the verbs *surround, encircle* when they have Agentive subjects.

Action Locative verbs with the A,*O,L /O-lex frame include both put-on verbs such as *bait* = *put bait on* or *butter* = *put butter on* and take-off verbs such as *husk* = *take husk off* or *peel* = *take peel off.* The principal clue is the occurrence of the same lexical item as noun and verb in the lexicon.

Action Locative verbs with the A,O,*L /L-lex frame include verbs interpreted as containers for inanimate objects, such as *bag* = *put in a bag* or *bottle* = *put in a bottle,* and containers for animate beings, such as *jail* = *put in a jail* or *imprison* = *put in a prison.*

Action Locative verbs with all roles overt are move-object verbs with an Agent, the mover, the Object being moved, and a Location which indicates the path along which the Object moves.

Some Action Locative verbs undergo rank shift with the Locative role moved into direct object position and the Object role, when included, as a prepositional phrase, creating an A,L,O frame.

Locative expressions. Locative expressions in English are generally adverbial words, phrases, or clauses. The most general adverbials are *here, there,* or *where.* More concrete expressions occur in prepositional phrases, in which the prepositions may be stative or directional.

Stative prepositions indicate location in a place. Some stative prepositions describe a location absolutely, like *at* (a point), *on* (a line or surface), *in* (a volume or area), as in *I live at 324 on Prospect Street in Georgetown.* Many stative prepositions describe a location relative to another object, like *by, near, next to, with,* or describe location from the perspective of the viewer, like *before, in front of; behind, in back of; above, over, on top of; below, under, underneath.* But whatever the preposition, the prepositional phrase can be replaced by the proforms *here, there,* and hence constitute a stative locative expression. Multiple stative expressions may occur, as in *I sat on a bench in the park under a tree,* but the reference is to a single location, as Fillmore observed (1971a:51). Many phrases may be used to indicate a single stative position, but the verb by its meaning only requires one stative location.

Directional prepositions indicate movement from one place to another. The prepositions may indicate the SOURCE of the motion, like *from, out of, off of,* or the GOAL of the motion, like *to, towards, into, onto,* or the PATH of the motion, like *across, along, through,* or some TRANSIT POINT, like *by, past.* Multiple directional expressions may occur, as in *Over the hills and through the woods to grandmother's house we go,* but these multiple phrases describe a single motion trajectory. Many locative phrases may be used to indicate the trajectory of the motion, but the process or action locative verb by its meaning only requires one indication of the motion trajectory.

Locative phrases occur which are modal locatives and not required by the meaning of the verb. Fillmore (1968:26) refers to these as locatives outside the verb phrase. In general, outer locatives are used to locate events, as in *John washes his car in the garage;* inner locatives are used to locate objects, as in *John keeps his car in the garage.* "The highly restricting L selects verbs like *keep, put,* and *leave,* but not *polish, wash,* and *build;* the weakly restricting L selects *polish, wash,* and *build,* but not *believe, know,* or *want*" (Fillmore 1968:26, footnote 34). In his Case Grammar terms, *keep, put,* and *leave* require an inner locative; *polish, wash,* and *build* accept an outer locative; and *believe, know,* and *want* allow no locative at all.

When stative prepositions like *in, at, on* occur with action or process verbs then there is a contradiction between stativity and motion. This is a clear sign that the locative phrase is an outer locative. In sentences like *John fell in the kitchen,* the phrase *in the kitchen* is the place where the whole event took place. *It was in the kitchen that John fell.* But the real answer to *where did John fall* is the Goal locative *down,* as in *John fell down (in the kitchen).* These outer locative phrases should be divorced from the case frame, and considered as part of the modality. They may be placed as higher predicates with a proposition within their scope.

5.1–5.2 State Locative verbs

State Locative verbs are state verbs in the locative domain which relate an Object to a definite location. The Object case is marked as Os to distinguish it from process O. Depending upon the verb chosen, either the Object or the Location may occur as grammatical subject.

5.1. With O-subject (Os,L)

For State Locative predications with Object as subject, the structure of the predication is shown in the following graph, which links an ENTITY called the Object with a PLACE called the Location.

(419) | ENTITY | ← (Os) ← | LOC-VERB | → (L) → | PLACE |

State Locative verbs with Object (Theme) as subject include: (1) the verb *be* with the meaning *be (located),* (2) the verb *be* combined with a locative past participle, (3) position verbs like *lie, sit, stand,* (4) extension verbs, like *extend,* and *stretch,* including motion verbs expressing extension, like *come, go, rise, run,* and (5) habitation verbs, like *live, inhabit, occupy.*

Be + Locative. In English, the subject located is any entity capable of being located, the verb *be* is interpreted as *be (located),* and the Locative expression is a locative clause, a locative prepositional phrase, or a locative adverb. Locative clauses are relatively rare.

(420) Home /is /where the heart is. Os,L
    [HOME]←(Os)←[BE-LOC]→(L)→[LOC-Clause].

(421) The toys /are /in the box. Os,L
    [TOYS:#]←(Os)←[BE-LOC]→(L)→[in [BOX:#]].

(422) Here /is /your book. Os,L
    [BOOK:#your]←(Os)←[BE-LOC]→(L)→[HERE].

The principal argument for considering *be (located)* as the predicate is the unity of the locative expression. No matter what the expression, it may be replaced by the proforms *here, there, where.* Chafe (1970:159) claimed that the locative preposition was the predicate and that it was followed by a locative noun. But this does not take into account the unity of all locative expressions, demonstrated by the fact that they may be replaced by locative adverbs, nor does it account for locative adverbs which include no locative prepositions.

Text analysis of *be* + locative structure. There are more than 200 examples of the *be* + locative structure in the Hemingway novel. Predominant locative prepositional phrases include the stative prepositions *at* (with 11 occurrences), *on* (with 19 occurrences) and *in* (with 38 occurrences). Prepositions occasionally occur alone as locative adverbs.

(423) The second bait /was /at seventy-five fathoms. 30:22
    [BAIT:#]←(Os)←[BE-LOC]→(L)→[at [FATHOMS:@75]].

(424) The brown blotches of the skin cancer /were /**on** his cheeks. 9:16
    [BLOTCHES:#]←(Os)←[BE-LOC]→(L)→[on [CHEEKS:#his]].

(425) The two sets of knives and forks /were /in his pocket. 20:2
    [SETS:@2]←(Os)←[BE-LOC]→(L)→[in [POCKET:#his]].

Among the locative adverbs are *here* (with 11 occurrences), *there* (with 6 occurrences) and *where* (with 9 occurrences) and *somewhere* (1 occurrence). In the same class are locative prepositions used as adverbs.

(426) I wish /the boy /was /**here**.   50:9
      [BOY:#]←(Os)←[BE-LOC]→(L)→[HERE].

(427) The shark oil /was /**there** /for all the fishermen.   37:16
      [OIL:#]←(Os)←[BE-LOC]→(L)→[THERE].

(428) The bait /was /exactly **where** he wished it to be.   32:15
      [BAIT:#]←(Os)←[BE-LOC]→(L)→[WHERE].

(429) My big fish /must be /**somewhere**.   35:1
      [FISH:#my]←(Os)←[BE-LOC]→(L)[SOMEWHERE].

Comitative expressions, denoting accompaniment, for which Fillmore in 1968 postulated a Comitative case, are subsumed under the Locative case, following Fillmore's later practice. The predominant preposition used for accompaniment is *with* (15 occurrences).

(430) In the first 40 days /a boy /had been /**with** him.   9:3
      [BOY]←(Os)←[BE-LOC]→(L)→[with [PERSON:#him]].

(431) No one /should be /**alone** in their old age.   48:8
      [PERSON: none]←(Os)←[BE-LOC]→(L)→[ALONE].

(432) He had first started to talk aloud /when he /was /**by himself**. 39:7
      [PERSON:#he]←(Os)←[BE-LOC]→(L)→[by [HIMSELF]].

There are at least 48 locative prepositions and adverbs in the novel dominating the occurrence of over 205 predicated locative expressions. The following list includes most of these prepositions and adverbs.

(433) be above - 1   be clear of - 1   be low - 2
      be across - 3   be close - 2   be on - 19
      be against - 1   be close to - 1   be out - 7
      be alone - 6   be down - 10   be out of - 5
      be alongside - 3   be even with - 1   be all over - 1
      be around - 6   be far away - 1   be over - 1
      be at - 9   be far from - 1   be somewhere - 1
      be before - 1   be free from - 1   be there - 5

be behind - 1	be from - 1	be true (course) - 1
be below - 1	be here - 11	be to eastward - 1
be beside - 2	be higher - 3	be under - 4
be between - 1	be home - 1	be up - 6
be back - 6	be in - 38	be up to - 1
be by himself - 2	be in place - 1	be widespread - 1
be by the side of - 1	be inshore - 1	be with - 15
be clear -1	be inside - 3	be where - 9

Be + **participle.** State locative predications also occur which consist of the verb *be* followed by the past participle of action locative verbs. These structures are ambiguous between *be* + adjective structure and true passives. The adjective (Os,L) has the meaning "state as the result of a process." In this structure no Agent is expressed or implied. True passive structures (A,O,L/Passive) consist of the passive form of the action verb and always have an Agent expressed or implied. The meaning must be deduced from the context. In resolving the ambiguity of the short passive, when no by-phrase occurs, the principal test is for agency. Does the question "by whom?" make sense? Present tense forms tend to be stative, past tense forms remain ambiguous. The *be* + adjective structure never takes the progressive; the passive takes the progressive. The *be* + adjective structure allows intensifiers like *very*, the passive structure does not. (See §5.9 Passive Locatives (606)–(610).)

(434) The ship /is anchored /in the harbor.   Os,L
      = in an anchored state.
      [SHIP:#]←(Os)←[BE ANCHORED]→(L)→[in [HARBOR:#]].

(435) The ship /was anchored /in the harbor /last night.   A,O,L /(P)
      = someone anchored it.
      [PERSON]←(A)←[ANCHOR]→(O)→[SHIP:#]→(L)→[in [HARBOR:#]].

Text analysis of BE + participle structure (54). There are over fifty examples of *be* + participle structures in the novel. These structures are stative predications (Os,L) with the meaning "state as the result of a process" and do not imply an Agent. They are to be distinguished from passive structures (A,O,L /Passive) which do imply an Agent.

(436) be anchored (2)   be gone (6)   be replaced
      be braced (2)   be headed   be rigged
      be cleared away   be joined   be set
      be cut off   be lashed (3)   be slanted
      be connected   be left   be spread (3)
      be fast to   be looped   be submerged
      be furled (2)   be made fast   be wrapped

(437) The bird /was gone.   56:10
      [BIRD:#]←(Os)←[BE GONE]→(L)→[NULL].

(438) Now we /are joined /together.   50:18
      [PERSONS:#we]←(Os)←[BE JOINED]→(L)→[TOGETHER].

(439) A paper napkin /was wrapped /around each set.   20:3
      [NAPKIN]←(Os)←[BE WRAPPED]→(L)→[around [SET:@each]].

Position verbs. Position verbs are a proper subset of locative verbs, including *lie, sit,* and *stand.* In English, the position verb indicates the position of the object, and the locative phrase indicates the location of the object. Aristotle distinguished *situs* (position) from *locus* (location). POSITION deals with the relation of the parts of an object to each other, as when the object is said to be *lying, sitting,* or *standing.* LOCATION refers to the location of the whole object in space, as when an object is *in, at, on* a place. Position implies location, so that position verbs rarely occur without a locative phrase. Position verbs may be used with inanimate objects. These verbs are state locatives with the frame Os,L. (For animate subjects, see §5.5.)

(440) The glass /is sitting /on the bar.   Os,L
      *The glass is sitting.
      [GLASS:#]←(Os)←[SIT]→(L)→[on [BAR:#]].

(441) The newspaper /is lying /on the bed.   Os,L
      *The newspaper is lying.
      [NEWSPAPER:#]←(Os)←[LIE]→(L)→[on [BED:#]].

(442) The statue /is standing /in the park.   Os,L
      ?The statue is standing.
      [STATUE:#]←(Os)←[STAND]→(L)→[in [PARK:#]].

It is unusual to use verbs that refer to positions of the human body for inanimate objects. Many other languages do not have this option, and a word-for-word translation of these sentences is unacceptable. Instead these languages would use an expression meaning "be located" and, if necessary, would paraphrase the verb *lie* as "in a prone position," and the verb *stand* as "in an upright position." The verb *sit* has no ready equivalent.

(443) The glass is sitting on the bar.   Os,L
      = position indeterminate.

(444) The newspaper is lying on the bed.   Os,L
      = in prone position.

(445) The statue is standing in the park.   Os,L
      = in upright position.

Position verbs with inanimate subjects may occur with either point or durative adverbials. With point adverbials, they are considered States, but with durative adverbials, they represent a state which lasts through time, and are Process verbs. With no adverbials, these verbs are two ways ambiguous as illustrated in sentences (446)–(448).

(446) a. The glass was sitting on the bar at 5 o'clock.   Os,L
          SIT (X, at L)

      b. The glass was sitting on the bar all day.   O,L
          REMAIN (SITTING (X, at L))

(447) a. The newspaper was lying on the bed when I came.   Os,L
          LIE (X, at L)

      b. The newspaper was lying on the bed for days.   O,L
          REMAIN (LYING (X, at L))

(448) a. The statue was standing in the park yesterday.   Os,L
          STAND (X, at L)

      b. The statue was still standing in the park.   O,L
          REMAIN (STANDING (X, at L)

Stative position verbs seem to take the progressive, despite the fact that they are stative. If the verb is in the progressive it cannot be stative, and if it is stative it cannot take the progressive. When position verbs are used with inanimate objects, nothing is moving and the verb must be considered stative. How then can one explain the presence of the -ing form? It cannot be an adjective, like *interesting* for example, for it fails all the adjective tests. The -ing form cannot be modified by intensifiers like *very*, it cannot follow the verb *seems*, and it cannot be preposed.

(449) *The glass is very sitting on the bar.

(450) *The newspaper seems lying on the bed.

(451) *The standing statue is in the park.

Leech says that these apparently progressive forms are "notoriously problematic" (1969:148). In state predications, the progressive has no distinctive value. Anderson states that this type of clause is notionally stative and that "the interpretation of the *be* + *ing* clause in such instances is rather different" (1971:94). Dowty (1972:96) believes the progressive is more acceptable with moveable objects, with *there* insertion, and in the past tense contexts.

Two facts indicate that the -ing form is not a normal progressive. First, the participle is deletable, leaving a locative predication with no reference to position, as in *the glass is on the bar*. Second, the participle is moveable when modified, as in *the glass is on the bar, sitting upright*. This leads us to believe that the -ing form is a movable participle which is not to be interpreted as a progressive form. This form seems rather to be a floating participle which adds an extra dimension to the predication, but is not a normal progressive.

There are other verbs which follow the pattern of the position verbs and occur with the present participle. These include the verbs *hang, project,* and *rest,* and marginally *fit, intersect, meet, touch.*

(452) The picture /was hanging /on the wall.   Os,L
     [PICTURE:#]←(Os)←[HANG]→(L)→[on [WALL:#]].

(453) A nail /was projecting /from the floor.   Os,L
     [NAIL]←(Os)←[PROJECT]→(L)→[from [FLOOR:#]].

(454) His arm /was resting /on the table.   Os,L
    [ARM:#his]←(Os)←[REST]→(L)→[on [TABLE:#]].

Text analysis of position verbs. There are 28 occurrences of the position verbs *lie* (10), *sit* (13), and *stand* (5) in the novel. Past tense forms are assumed to be durative, lasting through time.

(455) The newspaper /lay /across his knees.   19:2
    = remained lying
    [NEWSPAPER:#]←(O)←[LIE]→(L)→[across [KNEES:#his]].

(456) He saw the tail of the fish /**standing up** /behind the stern. 121:5
    = be standing
    [TAIL:#]←(Os)←[STAND UP]→(L)→[behind [STERN:#]].

Other verbs show the same characteristics as position verbs. For example, the verb *hang* (7 occurrences), the verb *project* (2 occurrences), and the verb *rest* (26 occurrences). The verb *hang* occurs in stative and durative meanings. The verb *rest* occurs in inchoative and durative meanings. In these meanings the verb is not stative and the case frame is O,L.

(457) The sack /**hung** /down over his back.   47:7
    = BE HANGING
    [SACK:#]←(Os)←[HANG]→(L)→[over [BACK:#his]].

(458) The fish /seemed to **hang** /motionless /in the air.   94:9
    = REMAIN (HANG)
    [FISH:#]←(O)←[HANG]→(L)→[in [AIR:#]].

(459) The shaft of the harpoon /**was projecting** /at an angle.   41:16
    = BE PROJECTING (from the fish)   94:16
    [SHAFT:#]←(Os)←[PROJECT]→(L)→[NULL].

(460) He forced the hand down /until it /**rested** /on the wood.   70:10
    = COME ABOUT (REST)
    [HAND:#]←(O)←[REST]→(L)→[on [WOOD:#]].

(461) The filaments would catch on a line /and /**rest** /there.   36:5
    = REMAIN (REST)
    [FILAMENTS:#]←(O)←[REST]→(L)→[THERE].

Extension verbs. Extension verbs are a proper subset of state locative verbs, including *extend, lead, stretch, surround,* and the motion verbs *come, go, run, rise,* when used as verbs of extension. These extension verbs are recognized by the fact that they do not take the progressive and are accompanied by directional not stative locatives. Syntactically, these verbs do not take the progressive, but the present participle may occur when it is well separated from the verb *be.*

Proper verbs of extension. The verbs which directly refer to extension in space are stative and do not take the progressive. The subject is normally inanimate and the verbs are normally intransitive. Extension verbs may take Source and Goal locatives to limit the Path of the extension.

(462) The carpet /extends /from wall to wall.   Os,L
     * The carpet is extending from wall to wall.
     [CARPET:#]←(Os)←[EXTEND]→(L)→[PATH].

(463) Tall trees /surround /the house.   Os,L
     *Tall trees are surrounding the house.
     [TREES:#]←(Os)←[SURROUND]→(L)→[HOUSE:#].

(464) The fog /stretches /from London to Brighton.   Os,L
     *The fog is stretching from London to Brighton.
     [FOG:#]←(Os)←[STRETCH]→(L)→[PATH].

Motion verbs as verbs of extension. The use of motion verbs as stative verbs of extension is proper to the English language. In translating to other languages it is often necessary to change to a verb which means *extend.* These verbs include *come, go, rise,* and *run.*

(465) The drapes /come /to the floor.   Os,L
     *The drapes are coming to the floor.
     The room has drapes coming to the floor.
     [DRAPES:#]←(Os)←[COME (=extend)]→(L)→[to [FLOOR:#]].

(466) Route 95 /goes /through Richmond.   Os,L
     *Route 95 is going through Richmond.
     There is a Route 95 going through Richmond.
     [ROUTE:#]←(Os)←[GO (=extend)]→(L)→[through [RICHMOND]].

(467) The mountains /rise /from the sea.   Os,L
   *The mountains are rising from the sea.
   There are mountains rising from the sea.
   [MOUNTAINS:#]←(Os)←[RISE (=extend)]→(L)→[from [SEA:#]].

(468) My property runs to the river.
   *My property is running to the river.
   I have property running to the river.
   [PROPERTY:#my]←(Os)←[RUN (=extend)]→(L)→[to [RIVER:#]].

Text analysis of extension verbs. There are sixteen extension verbs
in the Hemingway novel. Eight of these are proper extension verbs such
as *band* (1), *cover* (4), *extend* (1), and *stretch* (2). Eight verbs are motion
verbs of extension, like *go* (3), *rise* (3) and *run* (2).

(469) He could see the purple stripes that **banded** the fish.   90:10
   = extend around
   [STRIPES:#]←(Os)←[BAND]→(L)→[FISH:#].

(470) Old newspapers **covered** the springs of the bed.   24:18
   = extend over
   [NEWSPAPERS]←(Os)←[COVER]→(L)→[SPRINGS:#].

(471) The line **extended** out and down into the water.   53: 5
   [LINE:#]←(Os)←[EXTEND]→(L)→[into [WATER:#]].

(472) He could see the line **stretching** ahead.   60:22
   [LINE:#]←(Os)←[STRETCH]→(L)→[AHEAD].

(473) The lines **went** straight down into the water.   32:11
   [LINES:#]←(Os)←[GO (= extend)]→(L)→[into [WATER:#]].

(474) He saw the white peaks of the Islands **rising** from the sea. 25:8
   [PEAKS:#]←(Os)←[RISE (= extend)]→(L)→[from [SEA:#]].

(475) The blotches **ran** well down the sides of his face.   10:1
   [BLOTCHES:#]←(Os)←[RUN (= extend)]→(L)→[down [FACE:#his]].

Habitation verbs. Habitation verbs are used as stative verbs when
they indicate permanent residence. The progressive form seems to indicate temporary residence. These include the verbs *inhabit, live, occupy.*

(476) The aborigines /inhabit /the outback.   Os,L
    = permanent residence
    [ABORIGINES:#]←(Os)←[INHABIT-1]→(L)→[OUTBACK:#].

(477) The aborigines /are inhabiting /the outback.   O,L
    = temporary residence.
    [ABORIGINES:#]←(O)←[INHABIT-2]→(L)→[OUTBACK:#].

(478) Shay /lives /in Hawaii.   Os,L
    = his permanent residence.
    [SHAY]←(Os)←[LIVE-1]→(L)→[in [HAWAII]].

(479) Shay /is living /in Georgetown.   O,L
    = his temporary residence.
    [SHAY]←(Os)←[LIVE-2]→(L)→[in [GEORGETOWN]].

5.2. State with L-subject (L,Os)

For state locative predications with Location as subject, the structure
of the predication is shown in the following graph, which links a PLACE
called the Location with an ENTITY called the Object. This graph is the reverse of the graph with Os-subject.

(480) | PLACE | ← | Ⓛ | ← | LOC-VERB | → | Ⓞⓢ | → | ENTITY |

State locative verbs normally occur with the Object (Theme) as subject and the Location expressed adverbially. The subject choice
hierarchy, listed as A-E-B-O-L, requires that Object be chosen as subject
before Location. But there are exceptions to this hierarchy which require
Location as subject. These exceptions must be marked in the lexicon as
requiring a Locative subject and classified as L,Os in contrast with the
normal Os,L verbs. State Locative verbs with L-subject include the verbs
contain, hold, seat. They express a stative situation and may not take the
progressive inflection. Other verbs which take an L-subject include *have
(located)* and reversible state verbs that take both Os-subject and
L-subject.

(481) The box /contains /the toys.   L,Os
    *The box is containing the toys.
    [BOX:#]←(L)←[CONTAIN]→(Os)→[TOYS:#]

(482) This auditorium /seats /300 people.
   *This auditorium is seating 300 people.
   [AUDITORIUM:#]←(L)←[SEAT]→(Os)→[PEOPLE:*@300]

(483) This bottle /holds /a quart.
   *This bottle is holding a quart.
   [BOTTLE:#]←(L)←[HOLD]→(Os)→[QUART]

The verb HAVE. The verb *have*, in the sense of *have (located)*, is used as the flip version of *be (located)*, reversing Location and Object. With the verb *have (located)*, Fillmore (1968:47) claims that when L is chosen as subject, the subject L loses its preposition, the verb *have* is inserted, and the subject may be repeated as a Locative copy following the direct object and with the proper preposition.

(484) The children /are /with Mary.   Os,L
   [CHILDREN:#]←(Os)←[BE-LOC]→(L)→[with [MARY]].

(485) Mary /has /the children / (with her).   L,Os
   [MARY]←(L)←[HAVE-LOC]→(Os)→[CHILDREN:#].

(486) A scar /is /on his face.   Os,L
   [SCAR]←(Os)←[BE-LOC]→(L)→[on [FACE:#his]].

(487) His face /has /a scar /(on it).   L,Os
   [FACE:#his]←(L)←[HAVE-LOC]→(Os)→[SCAR].

Reversible states. Some verbs allow either the Object or the Location as subject, and must be listed in the lexicon as both Os,L and L,Os. These verbs, first described by Anderson (1971:90) under subjectivization of locatives, include the verbs *abound, be abundant, be strewn.* According to Anderson, such locative clauses naturally do not allow for imperatives and are not used in the progressive, establishing them as States.

(488) Wild life /abounds /in the area.   Os,L
   [WILD LIFE]←(Os)←[ABOUND-1]→(L)→[in [AREA:#]].

(489) The area /abounds /with wild life.   L,Os
   [AREA:#]←(L)←[ABOUND-2]→(Os)→[with [WILD LIFE]].

(490) Litter /is strewn /on the ground.   Os,L
    [LITTER]←(Os)←[BE STREWN-1]→(L)→[on [GROUND:#]].

(491) The ground /is strewn /with litter.   L,Os
    [GROUND:#]←(L)←[BE STREWN-2]→(Os)→[with [LITTER]].

(492) Flowers /are abundant /in the garden.   Os,L
    [FLOWERS]←(Os)←[BE ABUNDANT-1]→(L)→[in [GARDEN:#]].

(493) The garden /is abundant /with flowers.   L,Os
    [GARDEN:#]←(L)←[BE ABUNDANT-2]→(Os)→[with [FLOWERS]].

Text analysis of State Locatives with L-subject. State Locative
clauses in the novel include *have* + L-subject (14), and adjective + L-
subject (6). The verb *have (located)* occurs with L-Subject, often followed
by a Locative copy. The verb *have* occurred in the text in the combinations *have in* (1), *have on* (6), and *have with* (5). Other verbs with
L-subject included *hold (=contain)*.

(494) His fight /**has** /no panic /**in** it.   9:10
    [FIGHT:#his]←(L)←[HAVE-LOC]→(Os)→[PANIC:none].

(495) His hands /**had** /deep-creased scars /(**on** them).   10:2
    [HANDS:#his]←(L)←[HAVE-LOC]→(Os)→[SCARS].

(496) I /had /the boy /(**with** me).   45:7
    [PERSON:#I]←(L)←[HAVE-LOC]→(Os)→[BOY:#].

(497) This skiff /would never **hold** /the marlin.   95:9
    [SKIFF:#]←(L)←[HOLD]→(Os)→[MARLIN:#].

Some of the locative adjectives have a Location noun as subject. Many
are derived from A,*O,L verbs with the O lexicalized into the verb. In
these States, no Agent is expressed or implied.

(498) The old man came in /with /his skiff /**empty**.   9:10
    = The skiff (L) is empty of fish (Os).
    [SKIFF:his]←(L)←[BE EMPTY]→(Os)→[NULL].

(499) The fish /was **barred** /with purple (bars).   93:15
    = The fish (L) is barred with purple bars (Os).
    [FISH:#]←(L)←[BE BARRED]→(Os)→[with [PURPLE]].

(500) The hook /was **covered** /with fresh sardines.   31:3
  = The fish (L) is covered with sardines (Os).
  [FISH:#]←(L)←[BE COVERED]→(Os)→[with [SARDINES]].

(501) **Drained** of blood and awash, he looked the color of silver. 110:5
  = The fish (L) was drained of blood (Os).
  [FISH:#]←(L)←[BE DRAINED OF]→(Os)→[BLOOD].

(502) He ate one of the flying fish, **gutted** and with its head cut off. 80:2
  = The fish (L) was gutted (Os-lexicalized).
  [FISH:#]←(L)←[BE GUTTED /O-lex].

(503) Each sardine /was **hooked** /through both eyes.   31:4
  [SARDINE:#]←(L)←[BE HOOKED /O-lex].

(504) The walls were **painted** bright blue.   69:16
  [WALLS:#]←(L)←[BE PAINTED /O-lex].

5.3–5.4 Process Locative verbs

Process locative verbs are Process verbs in the locative domain which relate a moving object to a definite path. Depending upon the verb chosen, either Object (Theme) or the Location may be chosen as the grammatical subject.

5.3. Process with O-subject (O,L)

For Process locative predications with Object (Theme) as subject, the structure is shown in the following graph, which links an ENTITY called the Object with a PATH called the Location.

(505) | ENTITY | ← | Ⓞ | ← | LOC-VERB | → | Ⓛ | → | PATH |

Process locative verbs with Object as subject are nonagentive motion verbs. These motion verbs include intransitive verbs, like *come, go, move,* which express location in an adverbial phrase and transitive verbs with lexicalized locative prepositions, like *ascend, cross,* and *enter.* Motion verbs require a moving Object and a Location. The moving Object may be an animate being moving unintentionally, a moving inanimate object, or, by extension, more abstract moving entities. The Location refers to the trajectory of the motion. The locative phrase may refer to the SOURCE (*from*), the GOAL (*to, towards*), the full or partial PATH (*through, across*), or a TRANSIT POINT (*by, near, next to*).

Intransitive motion verbs. Fillmore introduces a concept called conflation which is a much broader look at underlying semantic structure, based on the work of Leonard Talmy. In speaking of motion verbs he says, "the verbs *go* and *come* and *move* are just about the only motion verbs in English which have associated with them no understanding of manner, means, or medium" (1971b:41), as opposed to verbs which incorporate other elements, such as *float, ride, swim* (1971b:48). Yoshiko Ikegami (1969) takes a similar approach, analyzing motion verbs in terms of basic motion predicates, with added features of manner, means, or medium. According to Ikegami (1969:28) the motion verbs which are most unmarked are the verbs *come, go,* and *move.*

(506) This train /goes /to Chicago.   O,L
    [TRAIN:#]←(O)←[GO]→(L)→[TO [CHICAGO]].

(507) The car /entered /the highway.   O,L
    [CAR:#]←(O)←[ENTER]→(L)→[HIGHWAY:#].

Some verbs are ambiguous between simple Process and Process Locative. The verb *float,* with the meaning *be-suspended-in-a-medium,* is a simple Process with the case frame O, but with the meaning *go-by-floating* this same verb is a Process Locative, with the case frame O,L. This difference was illustrated by Fillmore (1971b:48).

(508) Ivory soap is 99% pure. It /floats.   O
    [IVORY SOAP]←(O)←[FLOAT].

(509) The bottle /floated /into the cove.   O,L
    [BOTTLE:#]←(O)←[GO-BY-FLOATING]→(L)→[into [COVE:#]].

Lexicalized prepositions. Some verbs, like *set* (sun), *rise, sink,* have lexicalized locative prepositions. The verb *set* (sun) means "go down," the verb *rise* means "go up," the verb *sink* means "go down." These verbs may occur with overt prepositional phrases to give a more precise description of the motion path.

(510) The ship /sank slowly /beneath the waves.   O,*L
      = The ship went down.
      [SHIP:#]←(O)←[SINK]→(L)→[beneath [WAVES:#]].

(511) The sun /set /behind the hills.   O,*L
      = The sun went down.
      [SUN:#]←(O)←[SET]→(L)→[behind [HILLS:#]].

(512) The balloon /rose slowly /into the sky.   O,*L
      = The balloon went up.
      [BALLOON:#]←(O)←[RISE]→(L)→[into [SKY:#]].

Text analysis of Process verbs with O-subject (171). Process Locative clauses with an O-subject include over 170 occurrences in the Hemingway novel, showing a wide variety, with motion verbs *come* (21), *go* (21), *move* (11), and *sail* (10) predominant. Other verbs are here listed in (513).

(513)

back - 2	knife - 1	settle - 1
break (through) - 1	lash - 1	shift - 1
bulge - 1	lift - 1	sink - 2
burn out (=move) - 1	pass - 4	slice - 1
cut - 1	pivot - 1	slide - 2
dip - 2	plow - 1	slip - 5
disperse - 1	pour - 1	spill - 1
draw up - 1	pull - 1	spread - 3
drift - 4	race - 2	swing - 3
drive - 1	ride - 2	trail - 1
fall - 7	rise - 10	trickle - 1
feed - 1	run - 5	unroll - 1
float - 4	rush - 2	wallow - 1
jump - 2	set - 3	weave - 1

(514) He saw /the native boats /**come** riding /through the surf.   25:1
      [BOATS:#]←(O)←[COME]→(L)→[through [SURF:#]].   28:6

(515) He let /the line /**go** /over the side.   34:5
      [LINE:#]←(O)←[GO]→(L)→[over [SIDE:#]].

(516) The skiff /**was moving** /steadily /to the Northwest.   45:18
      [SKIFF:#]←(O)←[MOVE]→(L)→[to [NORTHEAST:#]].

Verbs other than *come, go,* and *move* incorporate other elements, such as manner, means, or medium. The verb *sail* means 'go-by-sailing', the verb *drift* means 'go-by-drifting', the verb *fall* means 'go down', the verb *pass* means 'go past', the verb *rise* means 'go-up'.

(517) The skiff /**was sailing** /well.   98:14
     [SKIFF:#]←(O)←[SAIL]→(L)→[NULL].

(518) He let /the lines /**drift** /with the current.   32:16
     [LINES:#]←(O)←[DRIFT]→(L)→[with [CURRENT:#]].

(519) The marlin /**fell** /into the water /with a crash.   90:10
     [MARLIN:#]←(O)←[FALL]→(L)→[into [WATER:#]].

(520) An airplane /**passed** /overhead /on its way to Miami.   71:8
     [AIRPLANE]←(O)←[PASS]→(L)→[OVERHEAD].

(521) The sun /**rose** /thinly /from the sea.   32:4
     [SUN:#]←(O)←[RISE]→(L)→[from [SEA:#]].

(522) The blood /**ran** /down his cheek.   52:7
     [BLOOD:#]←(O)←[RUN]→(L)→[down [CHEEK:#his]].

(523) The line /**was slipping** /lightly /through his fingers.   43:8
     [LINE:#]←(O)←[SLIP]→(L)→[through [FINGERS:#his]].

(524) The huge tail lifted and /**swung** /with the tide.   126:18
     [TAIL:#]←(O)←[SWING]→(L)→[with [TIDE:#]].

5.4. With L-subject (L,O)

For Process locative predications with Location as subject, the structure is shown in the following graph, which links a PATH called the Location with an ENTITY called the Object.

(525) | PATH | ← | (L) | ← | LOC-VERB | → | (O) | → | ENTITY |

Some verbs allow either the Object (Theme) or the Locative as subject. Fillmore (1968:48) cites the verb *swarm.* But there is also a large class of verbs that deal with liquid motion, which take either noun as subject. The structure of the predication is represented by either of the two locative graphs.

(526) Bees /are swarming /in the garden.   O,L
    [BEES]←(O) →[SWARM-1]→(L)→[in [GARDEN:#]].

(527) The garden /is swarming /with bees.   L,O
    [GARDEN:#]←(L)→[SWARM-2]→(O)→[with [BEES]].

Liquid verbs. Liquid verbs are a subset of process locative verbs in which the Object is fluid or gaseous, and the Location is a container. Liquid verbs have the following characteristics: (1) they are process verbs, and freely take the progressive; (2) they are motion verbs, and usually take directional prepositions, such as *to, from, into, out of;* (3) they have no underlying state verb from which they may be derived; and (4) they are not used in an Agentive construction, except when used with non-liquid subjects.

Many of these liquid verbs allow either the Object noun or the Locative noun as subject. When the Locative is chosen as subject, the Object is often redundant and is deleted. This class of verbs are verbs of motion with the meaning "go from" and include the verbs *drip, exude, flow, gush, issue, leak, run, spurt, trickle.*

(528) Water /is dripping /from the faucet.   O,L
    [WATER]←(O) →[DRIP-1]→(L)→[from [FAUCET:#]].

(529) The faucet /is dripping /(water).   L,O
    [FAUCET:#]←(L)→[DRIP-2]→(O)→[WATER]

(530) Blood /was issuing /from the wound.   O,L
    [BLOOD]←(O)→[ISSUE-1]→(L)→[from [WOUND:#]].

(531) The wound /was issuing /blood.   L,O
    [WOUND:#]←(L)→[ISSUE-2]→(O)→[BLOOD]

(532) Zerex /is leaking /from the radiator.   O,L
    [ZEREX]←(O)→[LEAK-1]→(L)→[from [RADIATOR:#]].

(533) The radiator /is leaking /(Zerex).   L,O
    [RADIATOR:#]←(L)→[LEAK-2]→(O)→[ZEREX].

(534) Blood /ran /in the streets.   O,L
    [BLOOD]←(L)→[RUN-1]→(O)→[in [STREETS:#]].

(535) The streets /ran /with blood.   L,O
    [STREETS:#]←(O)→[RUN-2]→(L)→[with [BLOOD]].

Text analysis of Process verbs with L-subject (6). Process Locative clauses in the novel with L-subject include 6 clauses with the verbs
bleed (3), *cloud over* (1), *fill* (1), and *take = bear.* The verb *bleed = issue
blood* has the object noun *blood* lexicalized; the verb *cloud = fill with
clouds* has the object noun *cloud* lexicalized. The verb *fill,iv* is distinct
from the agentive transitive verb *fill,tv,* and the verb *take,tv* (strain) in a
special meaning means to accept the strain.

(536) His hand /**was bleeding.**   56:2
    = His hand (L) issued blood (O)
    [HAND:#his]←(L)→[**BLEED /O-lex**].

(537) And now /my fish /**bleeds** /again.   103:3
    = My fish (L) issues blood (O)
    [FISH:#my]←(L)→[**BLEED /O-lex**].

(538) The sky /**was clouding** over /to the east.   80:11
    = The sky (L) was filling with clouds (O).
    [SKY:#]←(L)→[**CLOUD /O-lex**].

(539) The sail /**filled** /(with air).   109:24
    = the sail (L) became filled with air (O).
    [SAIL:#]←(L)→[**FILL**]→(O)→[NULL].

(540) The boat /**took** /the strain.   74:3
    = The boat (L) accepted the strain (O).
    [BOAT:#]←(L)→[**TAKE**]→(O)→[STRAIN:#].

5.5–5.10 Action Locative verbs

Action locative verbs are Action verbs in the locative domain which
relate an Agent to an Object moving in a definite path. The Agent is
coreferential with the Object when the Agent is moving itself. The Object
or Locative may be lexicalized into the verb, or all roles may be overt.

5.5. Action with A=O coreference (A,*O,L /A=O)

For Action Locative verbs with Agent and Object coreferential, the structure of the predication is shown in the following graph, which links a PERSON who is both Agent and moving Object with a PATH called the Location.

(541) | PERSON | ← (A=O) ← | LOC-VERB | → (L) → | PATH |

The Agent is coreferential with the Object when the Agent is moving itself. The noun is Agent as instigator of the action, but is also the moving Object. Self-movement verbs contrast with those A,O,L verbs in which the Agent moves an Object distinct from himself.

(542) John /came /from Chicago.   A,*O,L /A=O
      [JOHN]←(A=O)←[COME]→(L)→[from CHICAGO].

(543) Harry /removed /the book /from the table.   A,O,L
      [HARRY]←(A)←[REMOVE]→(O)→[BOOK:#]→(L)→[from [TABLE:#]].

Self-movement verbs. Nowhere is coreference more necessary than with self-movement verbs. Agents can move objects, but Agents can also move themselves. They are Agents because they instigate the action, but they are also the Object that is being moved. Fillmore (1968) had no coreference, but Fillmore (1971b) introduces roles that are coreferential. Chafe (1970) had no coreference, but Anderson (1971) uses coreferential roles. Gruber (1976), working with an obligatory Theme role, favored coreference from the start. Jackendoff's motive for rejecting Fillmore's 1968 Case Grammar was because it lacked coreference, and he chose Gruber's thematic relations. "In Gruber's system of thematic relations, noun phrases can function in more than one thematic role within the same sentence" (1972:34). This coreference is demonstrated in the following examples from Jackendoff (1972:34).

(544) Max /rolled /down the hill.   O,L
      = The action was not intended.
      [MAX]←(O)←[ROLL-1]→(L)→[down [HILL:#]].

(545) Max /rolled /down the hill.   A,*O,L /A=O
      = Max intentionally rolled down the hill.
      [MAX]←(A=O)←[ROLL-2]→(L)→[down [HILL:#]].

Motion verbs require a moving Object and a motion trajectory called its Location. (See §5.3 Process with O-subject.) Self-movement verbs are motion verbs in which an Agent is in control of the motion and is at the same time the moving object. Consequently, all motion verbs can receive an Agentive re-interpretation (a term coined by Rudanko, 1989) whenever the subject of the motion verb is animate and in control of its own activity.

(546) Bill /went /to the hospital.   O,L
He was unconscious after the accident.
[BILL]←(O)←[GO-1]→(L)→[to [HOSPITAL:#]].

(547) Bill /went /to the hospital.   A,*O,L /A=O
He went to visit his wife.
[BILL]←(A=O)←[GO-2]→(L)→[to [HOSPITAL:#]].

Fillmore suggests that motion verbs, such as *walk, swim, run, drive* may refer to "types of activities, described in terms of their duration, or types of movements, describable in terms of their paths" (1971b:41). Activities would then be described as Basic Action verbs with no Locative (A,*O /A=O), and movement verbs, interpreted as *go-by-walking, go-by-swimming*, would be described as Action Locatives (A,*O,L /A=O).

(548) Harry /swam /from noon until two o'clock.   A,*O /A=O
= activity verb, no Location
[HARRY]←(A=O)←[SWIM-1].

(549) Harry /swam /from the dock to the shore.   A,*O,L /A=O
= motion verb, with Location
[HARRY]←(A=O)←[SWIM-2]→(L)→[PATH].

Self-movement verbs, like Process locative verbs, are generally intransitive, but they may become transitive, with a locative noun as direct object, when a preposition indicating Source, Goal, or Path is incorporated into the verb. The verb *go* is intransitive, but the verb *enter* = *go into* is transitive.

(550) Richard /went /into the room.   A,*O,L /A=O
= intransitive motion, with locative adverbial
[RICHARD]←(A=O)←[GO]→(L)→[into [ROOM:#]].

(551) Richard /entered /the room.   A,*O,L /A=O
  = transitive motion, with locative object noun
  [RICHARD]←(A=O)←[ENTER]→(L)→[ROOM:#].

Text analysis of Action verbs with A=O coreference (393). Almost half of the Action Locative verbs are verbs in which the Agent is coreferential with the moving object. Most of these are motion verbs in which an Agent is added to the motion verb to indicate self-movement. The subject is the one acting, but the subject is also the object that is moving. These action locatives are different from State extension locatives (§5.1) and Process Locatives (§5.3).

The majority of motion verbs with A=O coreference are self-movement verbs. These verbs are two-place intransitive predicates. The most dominant self-movement verbs are the general motion verbs *come* (65), *go* (65), and *move* (13). Other self-movement verbs have direction or manner incorporated into the verb. General movement verbs occur 143 times.

(552) He saw the old man **come** in each day.   9:9
  [MAN:#]←(A=O)←[COME]→(L)→[IN].

(553) The boy **had gone** at their orders in another boat.   9:7
  [BOY:#]←(A=O)←[GO]→(L)→[in [BOAT:other]].

(554) Along the road in the dark barefoot men **were moving.**   26:15
  [MEN:#]←(A=O)←[MOVE]→(L)→[NULL].

(555) Movement with direction (96 occurrences)

circle - 17	leap - 3	reach,tv (=arrive) - 4
climb - 3	leave - 4	return - 1
close - 4	make (= reach) - 4	rise - 8
cross - 1	make (circle) - 2	settle - 2
crowd - 1	make (drop) - 1	sink - 1
drop - 4	make (turn) - 4	slant - 1
re-enter - 1	pass - 2	soar - 1
follow - 2	plunge - 1	sound - 1
head for - 3	put to sea - 1	turn - 13
hit (=reach) - 1	reach,iv - 2	work (back) - 3

(556) Movement with manner (90 occurrences)

burst - 1	jump - 24	stagger - 1
congregate - 1	lunge - 1	step out - 1
cut (=move) - 2	quarter - 1	swim - 16
dart - 1	roll - 2	swing - 2
dip - 3	row - 4	take cover - 1
dive - 1	sail - 4	teeter - 1
drive, iv - 1	slide - 3	walk - 6
fly - 3	slip - 1	work one's way - 5
jerk - 3	spurt - 1	

Some intransitive self-movement verbs become transitive with a locative direct object when the preposition is incorporated into the verb. The dominant transitive verbs were *climb* = *go up, follow* = *go after, leave* = *go away.*

(557) They **climbed** the bank from where the skiff was hauled up. 10:9
[PERSONS:#they]←(A=O)←[CLIMB]→(L)→[BANK:#].

(558) The bird **followed** the flying fish.   34:12
[BIRD:#]←(A=O)←[FOLLOW]→(L)→[FISH:#].

(559) You did not **leave** me because you doubted.   10:21
[PERSON:#you]←(A=O)←[LEAVE]→(L)→[PERSON:#me].

Active position verbs. Active position verbs contrast with stative position verbs. (See §5.1 State locative with Os-subject.) When position verbs are used with animate subjects, the presumption is that the animate subject is an Agent in control of his own activity. This Agent is also the Object assuming a position or remaining in a position. When the animate subject is not in control of the activity, these verbs are State Locative verbs with the frame Os,L but when the subject acts intentionally, they are Action Locative verbs with the frame A,O,L /A=O. Position verbs include *lie, sit, rest,* and *stand.*

When the animate subject is not in control of the activity, position verbs are ambiguous between a stative and a durative interpretation, as if the subject were inanimate. With point adverbials the predication is stative, but with durative adverbials the predication is a durative process.

(560) Father /was sitting /in his favorite chair,   Os,L
and he was sound asleep.
= BE LOCATED (X, at L)
[FATHER]←(Os)←[SIT-1]→(L)→[in [CHAIR:#his]].

(561) Father /was sitting /in his favorite chair /for an hour,
and he was sound asleep.   O,L
= REMAIN (BE LOCATED (X, at L))
[FATHER]←(O)←[SIT-2]→(L)→[in [CHAIR:#his]].

When the animate subject is in control of his activity there are two
further meanings. The subject may cause himself to get into a position,
or the subject may cause himself to remain in a position. The former is a
causative Action Locative, the latter a durative Action Locative. Both of
these meanings have the case frame A=O,L.

(562) The boys were standing on the corner,   A,*O,L /A=O
watching all the girls go by.
= CAUSE (boys, REMAIN (STAND (boys, at L)))
[BOYS:#]←(A=O)←[STAND-1]→(L)→[on [CORNER:#]].

(563) Veronica /sat down /on the porch.   A,*O,L /A=O
= CAUSE (X, (COME ABOUT (SIT (X, at L))))
[VERONICA]←(A=O)←[SIT]→(L)→[on [PORCH:#]].

Text analysis of active position verbs (55). When position verbs
occur with an animate subject, the presumption is that the subject is an
Agent in control of his actions. The Agent either causes himself to assume a position, or causes himself to remain in a position. The
nondurative active meaning is often emphasized with adverbials in the
common expressions *sit down, lie down, stand up.* The added adverbials
are normally a positive sign of the *assume position* meaning, but they occur occasionally with the stative meaning. When the adverbials do not
occur the meaning remains ambiguous. The dominant verbs were *lean*
(13), *lie* (7), *rest* (9), *sit* (10), and *stand* (4).

(564) He **leaned** back and cut the line.   51:6
[PERSON:#he]←(A=O)←[LEAN]→(L)→[BACK].

(565) Then he **lay down** on the bed.   121:23
[PERSON:#he]←(A=O)←[LAY DOWN]→(L)→[on [BED:#]].

(566) He **lay** in the stern and steered.   116:12
  [PERSON:#he]←(A=O)←[REMAIN LYING]→(L)→[in [STERN:#]].

(567) The bird **rested** on the line.   54:22
  [BIRD:#]←(A=O)←[REST]→(L)→[on [LINE:#]].

(568) He had to **sit down** five times.   121:19
  [PERSON:he]←(A=O)←[SIT DOWN]→(L)→[NULL].

(569) The betters **sat** on high chairs against the wall.   69:16
  [BETTERS:#]←(A=O)←[REMAIN SIT]→(L)→[on [CHAIRS]].

(570) He put the mast down and **stood up.**   121:17
  [PERSON:#he]←(A=O)←[STAND UP]→(L)→[NULL].

5.6. Action with A=L coreference (A=L,O)

For Action Locative verbs with Agent and Locative coreferential, the structure of the predication is shown in the following graph, which links a PERSON who is both Agent and Locative with an ENTITY called the Object.

(571) | PERSON | ← (A=L) ← | LOC-VERB | → (O) → | ENTITY |

The Agent is coreferential with the Locative when the Agent is considered to also be the containing entity, as with the verb *contain.* This type of construction is illustrated by John Anderson (1971:99), but is relatively rare. This type of verb was not found in the Hemingway text.

(572) The bottle /contains /one gallon.   L,Os
  [BOTTLE:#]←(L)←[CONTAIN-1]→(Os)→[GALLON:@1].

(573) The regiment /contained /the attack.   A,O,*L / A=L
  [REGIMENT:#]←(A=L)←[CONTAIN-2]→(O)→[ATTACK:#].

5.7. Action with O-lexicalized (A,*O,L)

For Action Locative predications with Object lexicalized, the structure of the predication is shown in the following graph, which links a PERSON called the Agent with a PLACE called the Location. The Object case is contained in the verb.

(574)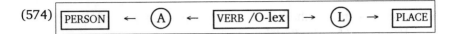

One indication of this lexicalization is the frequent occurrence in the lexicon of noun and verb with the same spelling, as in *powder,tv* and *powder,n.* The verb, as in *Lucy powdered her nose,* means *put powder on.* If the noun is modified, the lexicalized noun can be forced to the surface as in the sentence *Lucy powered her nose with white powder.* A wide range of verbs include a lexicalized Object. They include PUT-ON and TAKE-OFF types.

PUT-ON **verbs.** Action Locative verbs with O-lexicalized of the PUT-ON variety are fairly common. Typical of this type are the verbs *powder* = put powder on, and *water* = put water on.

(575) Lucy /powdered /her nose /(with white powder).   A,*O,L /O-lex
[LUCY]←(A)←[POWDER /O-lex]→(L)→[NOSE:#her].

(576) Michael /watered /the lawn /(with tap water).   A,*O,L /O-lex
[MICHAEL]←(A)←[WATER /O-lex]→(L)→[LAWN:#].

The list in (577) is illustrative and shows the wide range of lexicalized objects, particularly in the household. These verbs are often linked to specific Locative words which describe the Location where the Object is placed.

(577) bait (hook)   grease (machine)   spice (curry)
butter (bread)   hook (fish)   shoe (horse)
bridle (horse)   ice (cake)   stain (cloth)
board up (house)   knife (enemy)   stamp (letter)
color (picture)   noose (calf)   stuff (pillow)
cover (trash can)   oil (machinery)   sugar (coffee)
clothe (self)   paint (wall)   sweeten (coffee)
dust (crops)   pepper (meat)   tape (package)
dress (person)   plaster (wall)   swamp (boat)
feather (nest)   poison (food)   varnish (chair)
frame (picture)   roof (house)   water (lawn)
frost (cake)   saddle (horse)   wax (floor)
gaff (fish)   salt (meat)   wrap (package)

TAKE-OFF **verbs.** Action Locative verbs with O-lexicalized of the TAKE-OFF variety are also common. Typical are the verbs *skin* and *peel.*

(578) Roger /skinned /the lion /(of its shaggy mane).   A,*O,L /O=lex
[ROGER]←(A)←[SKIN /O-lex]→(L)→[LION:#].

(579) The chimp /peeled /the banana.   A,*O,L /O=lex
[CHIMP:#]←(A)←[PEEL /O-lex]→(L)→[BANANA:#].

The list in (580) is illustrative, again with verbs used within the household. These verbs are often linked to specific Locative words which describe the Location from which the lexicalized Object is properly extracted.

(580) bail (boat)   dust (house)   scalp (person)
      behead (person)   gut (fish)   shear (sheep)
      bleed (meat)   husk (corn)   shell (peas)
      clear (everything)   peel (banana)   shuck (corn)
      core (apple)   pluck (chicken)   skin (lion)
      declaw (lobster)   scale (fish)   undress (person)

Text analysis of Action Locative verbs with O-lexicalized (35). There are 35 examples of lexicalized objects in the Hemingway novel. Many verbs deal specifically with fishing, such as the verbs *bait* (4), *gut* (3), *hook* (11), *skin* (3).

(581) He **baited** the line with one of the sardines.   34:4
      = He put bait on the line.
      [PERSON:#he]←(A)←[BAIT /O-lex]→(L)→[LINE:#].

(582) I must **gut** the dolphin.   76:4
      = I must remove the guts from the dolphin.
      [PERSON:#I]←(A)←[GUT /O-lex]→(L)→[DOLPHIN:#].

(583) He **had hooked** one of a pair of marlin.   49:9
      = He put the hook into the marlin.
      [PERSON:#he]←(A)←[HOOK /O-lex]→(L)→[MARLIN:#].

(584) The old man **skinned** one side of the fish.   78:21
      = The old man removed the skin from the fish.
      [MAN:#]←(A)←[SKIN /O-lex]→(L)→[FISH:#].

5.8. Action with L-lexicalized (A,O,*L /L-lex)

For Action Locative predications with Locative lexicalized, the structure of the predication is shown in the following graph, which links a PERSON called the Agent with an ENTITY called the Object. The Locative case is contained in the verb.

(585) | PERSON | ← Ⓐ ← | VERB /L-lex | → Ⓞ → | ENTITY |

Container nouns, such as *bag, bottle, box, can, file, package, pocket* are used as verbs, with an inanimate Object noun as direct object. The Locative is also lexicalized with animate Objects, as in *cage, jail, imprison.*

(586) Harry /bottled /the beer /(in green bottles).   A,O,*L /L-lex
       [HARRY]←(A)←[BOTTLE/L-lex]→(O)→[BEER:#].

(587) The sheriff /jailed /Robin Hood /(in a dirty jail).   A,O,*L /L-lex
       [SHERIFF:#]←(A)←[JAIL/L-lex]→(O)→[ROBIN HOOD].

Text analysis of Action Locative verbs with L-lexicalized (21). Most of verbs with L=lexicalized deal with the details of sailing, such as *furl (sail), ship (oars), step (mast).* Other verbs occur, such as *put on* and *take off (clothes).*

(588) He **furled** the sail.   121:1
       = He wrapped the sail around the mast.
       [PERSON:#he]←(A)←[FURL/L-lex]→(O)→[SAIL:#].

(589) He **shipped** his oars.   34:2
       = He put the oars into the boat.
       [PERSON:#he]←(A)←[SHIP/L-lex]→(O)→[OARS:#].

(590) Then he **stepped** the mast.   97:18
       = He put the mast in a hole in the deck.
       [PERSON:#he]←(A)←[STEP/L-lex]→(O)→[MAST:#].

(591) The old man **took off** his trousers.   24:14
       [PERSON:#he]←(A)←[TAKE OFF /L-lex]→(O)→[TROUSERS:#his].

(592) The old man took his trousers and **put** them **on**.   24:14
       [PERSON:#he]←(A)←[PUT ON /L-lex]→(O)→[TROUSERS:#his].

5.9. Action with all roles overt (A,O,L)

For Action Locative predications with all roles overt, the structure of the predication is shown in the following graph, which links a PERSON called the Agent with an ENTITY called the Object and with a PLACE called the Location.

(593) $\boxed{\text{PERSON}}$ ← Ⓐ ← $\boxed{\text{VERB}}$ → Ⓞ → $\boxed{\text{ENTITY}}$

                                   ↓

                                   Ⓛ

                                   ↓

                               $\boxed{\text{PLACE}}$

Action Locative verbs are generally transitive verbs. These transitive verbs include move-object verbs, placement verbs, attachment verbs, and locative alternation verbs which allow reversal of Object and Locative.

Move-object verbs. Move-object verbs have an Agent causing the movement, an Object that is being moved, and the Source, Goal, or Path of the motion. Principal verbs in this category include *bring, carry, move, push, pull, take, throw*. The Locative phrase may be deleted, but is understood as part of the semantics of the verb.

(594) Helen /took /a book /from the library.   A,O,L
     [HELEN]←(A)←[TAKE]→(O)→[BOOK]→(L)→[from [LIBRARY:#]].

(595) David /carries /his lunch /to school.   A,O,L
     [DAVID]←(A)←[CARRY]→(O)→[LUNCH:#his]→(L)→[to [SCHOOL]].

(596) Abe /pushed /the piano /into a corner.   A,O,L
     [ABE]←(A)←[PUSH]→(O)→[PIANO:#]→(L)→[into [CORNER]].

Text analysis of Action Locative with all roles overt (394). In the Hemingway novel there are almost 400 examples of action locatives with all three roles overt. The majority of these verbs move an object from one place to another. These include *bring* (32), *hold* (37), *pull* (31), *take* (27). Other verbs incorporate the manner or means of motion.

Verbs dealing with the movement of objects include general verbs of movement. These verbs are transitive. The Object is the object moved and the Locative phrase indicates the path of the motion.

(597) The old man **brought** the newspaper out from under the bed. 17:4
[MAN:#]←(A)←[BRING]→(O)→[NEWSPAPER]→(L)→[from[BED:#]].

(598) The ice truck **carried** the fish to the market in Havana.   11:16
[TRUCK:#]←(A)←[CARRY]→(O)→[FISH:#]→(L)→[to [MARKET:#]].

(599) The breeze **moved** the lamps.   69:20
[BREEZE:#]←(A)←[MOVE]→(O)→[LAMPS:#]→(L)→[NULL].

(600) Then we'll **take** the stuff home.   11:4
[PERSONS:#we]←(A)←[TAKE]→(O)→[STUFF]→(L)→[HOME].

These basic movement verbs are supplemented with movement verbs incorporating direction. Movement with direction occurred 30 times as listed in (601).

(601) hoist - 2   raise - 5   take up - 1
      lift - 5   scoop up - 1   turn - 3
      pass - 4   sink - 1   withdraw - 2
      pick up - 7   spread - 3

The movement verbs are also supplemented with movement verbs incorporating manner. Movement with manner occurred seventy-six times as listed in (602).

(602) drive - 8   ram - 1   slip - 2
      haul - 1   roll - 1   swing - 6
      kick - 1   sail - 4   throw - 5
      pull - 31   shift - 5   toss - 1
      push - 6   slide - 2   tow - 2

A small number of Action Locative verbs are causatively derived from process verbs. These include *drift,tv* (1) = let drift, *drop,tv* (3) = let drop, and *leave,tv* (5) = let remain.

(603) They spoke about the depths they had **drifted** their lines at. 11:10
[PERSONS:#they]←(A)←[DRIFT]→(O)→[LINES]→(L)→[at [DEPTHS]].

(604) He **dropped** the guts and the gills over the stern.   78:18
[PERSON:#he]←(A)←[DROP]→(O)→[GUTS]→(L)→[over [STERN:#]].

(605) The boy **left** him there.   19:05
[BOY:#]←(A)←[LEAVE]→(O)→[PERSON:#him]→(L)→[THERE].

The passive of action locatives, marked A,O,L/Passive, are to be distinguished from stative locatives, marked Os,L (see §5.1). The passives
by their meaning imply an Agent.

(606) The fish **were brought** alongside.   15:9
    = Someone brought the fish alongside
    [PERSON]←(A)←[BRING]→(O)→[FISH:#]→(L)→[ALONGSIDE].

(607) The sharks **were hoisted** on a block and tackle.   11:18
    = Someone hoisted the sharks on a block and tackle.
    [PERSON]←(A)←[HOIST]→(O)→[SHARKS]→(L)→[on [BLOCK]].

(608) Maybe this fish **has been hooked** before.   42:21
    = Some one has hooked this fish before
    [PERSON]←(A)←[HOOK /O-lex]→(L)→[FISH:#].

(609) He allowed himself to **be pulled** forward.   74:2
    = Something pull the old man forward.
    [SOMETHING]←(A)←[PULL]→(O)→[MAN:#]→(L)→[FORWARD].

(610) The ice house was where the baits **were stored**.   27:13
    = Someone stored the baits in the ice house.
    [PERSON]←(A)←[STORE]→(O)→[BAITS:#]→(L)→[in [HOUSE:#]].

Placement verbs. Placement verbs involve an Agent, an Object, and
a Location. The Agent causes the Object to be or remain in a definite
place. They generally occur with stative, not directional prepositions.

(611) Mary /put /the book /on the shelf.
    [MARY]←(A)←[PUT]→(O)→[BOOK:#]→(L)→[on [SHELF:#]].

Within the set of placement verbs are transitive position verbs, some
of which require a change in morphological form, *sit* may become *set, lie*
must change to *lay* (contrast §5.5 Action with A=O coreference).

(612) Tom /set (sits) /the glass /on the bar.   A,O,L
      [TOM]←(A)←[SET]→(O)→[GLASS:#]→(L)→[on [BAR:#]].

(613) Dick /lay /the newspaper /on the bed.   A,O,L
      [DICK]←(A)←[LAY]→(O)→[NEWSPAPER:#]→(L)→[on [BED:#]].

(614) Harry /stood /the statue /on the shelf.   A,O,L
      [HARRY]←(A)←[STAND]→(O)→[STATUE:#]→(L)→[on [SHELF:#]].

Text analysis of placement verbs. Another set of A,O,L verbs deals
with placement rather than motion. They are transitive verbs with stative
prepositions. Active position verbs are included in this class. The dominant placement verbs are *hold* (37) and *put* (30).

(615) brace - 5   lean, tv - 4   rub - 3
      confide (= put) - 1 meet - 1   set, tv - 1
      cramp (= put) - 1   place - 2   settle - 5
      draw (= pull) - 4   point to - 1   soak - 3
      force - 2   put - 30   splash - 1
      hold - 37   reach - 3   steer - 10
      jerk - 1   replace - 1   wipe - 3
      lay, tv - 4   rest, tv - 1   wrap - 1

Attachment verbs. A small set of A,O,L verbs are verbs of attachment or detachment with the meaning "fasten X to Y" or "separate X
from Y." The dominant verbs of this type are *fit, fix, fasten, tie* and *break
off, free from, tear off, untie*.

(616) Ben /fixed /a reflector/ on his bike.   A,O,L
      [BEN]←(A)←[FIX]→(O)→[REFLECTOR]→(L)→[on [BIKE:#his]].

(617) Charles /freed /the boat /from the dock.
      [CHARLES]←(A)←[FREE]→(O)→[BOAT#]→(L)→[from [DOCK:#]].

Text analysis of attachment (30) and detachment (23) verbs. A
small subset of A,O,L verbs are verbs of attachment/detachment with the
meaning "fasten X to Y" or "separate X from Y." The dominant attachment verbs are *lash* (8), *make fast* (12), and *tie* (3). The dominant
detachment verbs are *cut off* (11), *tear off* (2), *untie* (2).

(618) I'll **lash** the two oars together across the stern.   73:15
[PERSON:#I]←(A)←[LASH]→(O)→[OARS:@2]→(L)→[TOGETHER].

(619) He **made** the line **fast** to a ring bolt in the stern.   34:04
[PERSON:#he]←(A)←[FASTEN]→(O)→[LINE:#]→(L)→[to [BOLT]].

(620) He **tied** the sack around his neck.   47:6
[PERSON:#he]←(A)←[TIE]→(O)→[SACK:#]→(L)→[around[NECK]].

(621) He **cut** strips of meat from the back of the head.   57:21
[PERSON:#he]←(A)←[CUT]→(O)→[MEAT]→(L)→[from [HEAD:#]].

(622) The sharks were **tearing off** the pieces of meat.   118:14
[SHARKS:#]←(A)←[TEAR OFF]→(O)→[MEAT]→(L)→[NULL].

(623) He **untied** the harpoon rope from the bitt.   96:13
[PERSON:#he]←(A)←[UNTIE]→(O)→[ROPE:#]→(L)→[from[BITT]].

Locative alternation verbs. In an article entitled *What to do with Theta-Roles,* Rappaport and Levin (1988:18) discuss locative alternation verbs, characterized as Agent-Object-Location verbs, in which Object and Location roles occur in different positions, forming two structures which are near paraphrases of each other. These locative alternation verbs are illustrated in the following sentences.

(624) a.   Jack /sprayed /paint /on the wall.   A,O,L
         b.   Jack /sprayed /the wall /with paint.   A,L,O

(625) a.   Bill /loaded /cartons /onto the truck.   A,O,L
         b.   Bill /loaded /the truck /with cartons.   A,L,O

According to this article, "an adequate lexical semantic representation of these verbs must meet the following requirements: (a) the near paraphrase relation between the two variants must be captured, (b) the linking of the arguments (to syntax) should be predictable in terms of their theta-roles, and (c) the affected (holistic) interpretation of the goal (Locative) as direct argument (direct object) must be accounted for" (1988:19). According to this article, it is difficult to satisfy these three requirements using only case roles.

Responding to (a), the near-paraphrase relationship is indicated by the fact that the verb is the same and the list of cases is the same. Responding to (b), the linking of the arguments to syntax is accomplished

by arranging the cases in hierarchical order. If the theta-roles are listed
as A-O-L and A-L-O respectively, then the Agent is automatically chosen
as subject, the second case is listed as direct object, and the third case is
in a prepositional phrase. Responding to (c), the Locative role, in direct
object position, is interpreted as the whole location. This interpretation
coincides with the verb *fill* which always takes a Locative direct object,
and which is always interpreted as the whole location. A lexical redundancy rule can specify that three-place predicates with Locatives in
direct object position are interpreted holistically, but verbs with the Object (Theme) in that position are not.

The account of locative alternation verbs with Goal locatives, such as
spray and *load*, can also be applied to verbs with Source locatives, such
as *clear* and *empty*, as in Rappaport and Levin (1988:22).

(626) a. Doug /cleared /dishes /from the table.   A,O,L
     b. Doug /cleared /the table /of dishes.   A,L,O

(627) a. Mary /emptied /water /from the tub.   A,O,L
     b. Mary /emptied /the tub /of water.   A,L,O

Locative alternation verbs have a long history in Case Grammar literature, in which they were often referred to as *spray-paint* verbs, with the
Object (Theme) and Locative cases alternating in the direct object position. These verbs were first noted by Fillmore (1968:48) with the
following examples.

(628) a. John /smeared /paint /on the wall.   A,O,L
     b. John /smeared /the wall /with paint.   A,L,O

(629) a. John /planted /peas and corn /in his garden.   A,O,L
     b. John /planted /his garden /with peas and corn.   A,L,O

Fillmore suggested (1968:48, footnote 49) that the relation between
the two variants might be captured by a grammatical transformation
with semantic import. He is not explicit about the semantic difference,
but seems to be aware of it. The list of locative alternation verbs was
later expanded (Fillmore 1969:321) to include verbs suggested by Bruce
Fraser.

Paul Mellema (1974) suggests that Fillmore is unaware of the semantic distinction between the holistic and partitive locative variants, and
therefore, Case Grammar fails to distinguish the variants. But Fillmore's
footnote seems to indicate that he was aware of the semantic change.

John Anderson (1971:94), in dealing with the objectivization of locatives, claimed that in one locative variant the Locative is objectivized and the Object (Theme), displaced as object, is marked with the preposition *with*. Citing Fillmore (1968:48), Anderson attributes minor semantic differences to a difference in focus. Anderson has the following examples.

(630) a. John /planted /apple trees /in the garden.   A,O,L
      b. John /planted /the garden /with apple trees.   A,L,O

(631) a. John /strewed /litter /on the ground.   A,O,L
      b. John /strewed /the ground /with litter.   A,L,O

In conclusion, the verb *pour* has only the A-O-L order, and the meaning is partitive. The verb *fill* has only A-L-O order, and the meaning is holistic. Other verbs allow both the A-O-L order with partitive meaning and A-L-O order with holistic meaning. These locative alternation verbs include verbs with Goal Locatives like *plant, smear, spray, stack, strew, stuff,* and verbs with Source Locatives like *clear,* and *empty.*

(632) Cynthia /poured /(some) wine /into the glass.   A,O,L
      [CYNTHIA]←(A)←[POUR]→(O)→[WINE]→(L)→[into [GLASS:#]].

(633) Cynthia /filled /the (whole) glass /with wine.   A,L,O
      [CYNTHIA]←(A)←[FILL]→(L)→[GLASS:#]→(O)→[with [WINE]].

(634) John /sprayed /(some) paint /on the wall.   A,O,L
      [JOHN]←(A)←[SPRAY-1]→(O)→[PAINT]→(L)→[on [WALL:#]].

(635) John /sprayed /the (whole) wall /with paint.   A,L,O
      [JOHN]←(A)←[SPRAY-2]→(L)→[WALL:#]→(O)→[with [PAINT]].

Some active locative verbs show a similar alternation in nonactive forms. The verb *strew,tv* has both A-O-L and A-L-O order, and the adjective, *be strewn,* has both Os-L and L-Os order. The verb *empty,tv* has both A-O-L and A-L-O order, and the Process verb *empty,iv* has both O-L and L-O order.

(636) The ground /was strewn /with litter.   Os,L
      [GROUND:#]←(L)←[BE STREWN-1]→(Os)→[with [LITTER]].

(637) Litter /was strewn /on the ground.   L,Os
        [LITTER]←(Os)←[BE STREWN-2]→(L)→[on [GROUND:#]].

(638) Ben /strewed /litter /on the ground.   A,O,L
        [BEN]←(A)←[STREW-1]→(O)→[LITTER]→(L)→[on [GROUND:#]].

(639) Ben /strewed /the ground /with litter.   A,L,O
        [BEN]←(A)←[STREW-2]→(L)→[GROUND:#]→(L)→[with [LITTER]].

(640) Water /emptied /from the tub.   O,L
        [WATER]←(O)←[EMPTY-1]→(L)→[from [TUB:#]].

(641) The tub /emptied /(of water).   L,O
        [TUB:#]←(L)←[EMPTY-2]→(O)→[NULL].

(642) Mame /emptied /water /from the tub.   A,O,L
        [MAME]←(A)←[EMPTY-3]→(O)→[WATER]→(L)→[from [TUB:#]].

(643) Mame /emptied /the tub /of water.   A,L,O
        [MAME]←(A)←[EMPTY-4]→(L)→[TUB:#]→(O)→[of [WATER]].

Text analysis of locative alternation verbs. A special set of A,O,L
verbs allow the reversal of the Object and Locative cases. With A,O,L order, like *pour* (1), they have partitive meaning, but with A,L,O order, like
fill (2), they have holistic meaning.

(644) He has **filled** the sacks along his back with air.   83:20
        [PERSON:#he]←(A)←[FILL]→(L)→[SACKS:#]→(O)→[with [AIR]].

(645) He **poured** some of the coffee into a glass.   124:1
        [PERSON:#he]←(A)←[POUR]→(O)→[COFFEE]→(L)→[into [GLASS]].

5.10. Double Agent verbs

For Action Locative predications with two Agents, the structure of the
predication is shown in the following graph, which links a PERSON called
the Agent with a SITUATION which involves another moving ENTITY and a
PATH called the Location.

(646)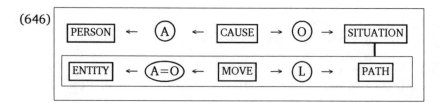

A small subclass of transitive verbs requires two occurrences of the Agent role. These verbs are normally intransitive verbs of the A-O, or A-O-L type. When they are used transitively, a second Agent is added to the structure. The locative verbs include *march,tv,* and *walk,tv.* No examples of this unusual construction were found in the Hemingway text.

(647) Mary /walked /the dog /along the canal.   A + A=O,L
      = CAUSE (Mary, WALK (dog, along the canal))
      [CAUSE] -
        (A)→[MARY]
        (O)→[[DOG:#]←(A=O)←[WALK]→(L)→[along [CANAL:#]].

(648) The guard /marched /the men /around the yard.   A + A=O,L
      = CAUSE (guard, MARCH (men, around the yard))
      [CAUSE] -
        (A)→[GUARD:#]
        (O)→[[MEN:#]←(A=O)←[MARCH]→(L)→[around [YARD:#]].

6
The Modality

According to John Sowa (1984:175), "Fillmore followed modal logic in separating the propositional part of a sentence from the modality." In Fillmore (1968:23) the proposition is "a tenseless set of relationships involving verbs and nouns," the modality "includes such modalities on the sentence-as-a-whole as negation, tense, mood, and aspect." These logical elements were developed in the work of John Ross (1969), James McCawley (1973), and others in the context of what was then known as Generative Semantics. Their goal was to construct underlying logical structures which would include all logical elements which added to the literal meaning of the sentence. Their logical structures included tense, aspect, modal verbs, and negation as logical predicates in the structure.

6.1. Auxiliaries as main verbs

In traditional grammar the modality is studied within the context of the verb phrase. In English this includes a sequence of verb forms called auxiliary verbs in combination with the main verb. These auxiliaries include tense, the modal verbs, the *have* of the perfect and the *be* of the progressive. In standard transformational theory the auxiliary is considered to be a single constituent represented by the formula:

(649) Aux = Tense (Modal) (Perfect) (Progressive)   Chomsky (1965:43)

183

John Ross (1969) proposed that all auxiliaries are main verbs in logical structure. Within this theory each auxiliary verb is a main verb with the rest of the sentence as its complement. James McCawley (1973:259) adds the suggestion that "tenses are not features but are themselves underlying verbs." This theory could then represent all elements of the auxiliary as logical predicates. In sentence (650) PRES becomes a tense marking on *may,* PERF becomes *have* with *-en* on the next lower predicate, PROG becomes *be* with *-ing* on the next lower predicate in the derivation of surface structure.

(650) Ben may have been drinking tea.

    [PRES] -
       [MAY] -
          [PERF] -
             [PROG] -
               [[BEN]←(A)←[DRINK]→(O)→[tea]].

6.2. Neutralization of the perfect

The theory of tenses was further developed by McCawley (1973:259) by adding a proposal of Ronald Hoffman (1966). Hoffman noted that for nonfinite verbs "the distinction between simple past, present perfect, and past perfect is neutralized in favor of *have.*" Finite verb forms have one present tense and three past tenses; nonfinite verb forms have one present tense and one past tense. The infinitive, for example, has only two forms, the present infinitive *to be,* and the past infinitive, *to have been.* The gerund also has only two forms, *being* and *having been.* Hoffman concluded that with past nonfinite forms only the context could determine whether the underlying form is derived from the past, the present perfect, or the past perfect tense.

(651) a. Present tense becomes nonfinite present:
        The house seems to be empty.
    b. Past tense becomes nonfinite past:
        The house seems to have been empty (yesterday).
    c. Present perfect tense becomes nonfinite past:
        The house seems to have been empty (for years).
    d. Past perfect tense becomes nonfinite past:
        The house seems to have been empty (when I came).

The first assumption from neutralization is that even nonfinite clauses have tense. The second assumption is that perfect is a tense and not an aspect marking. Comrie (1976:6) holds that the English perfect is not an aspect. Tense is deictic and locates the state or event relative to the act of speaking; aspect is nondeictic and refers to the way of viewing the internal temporal consistency of the state or event (Comrie 1976:3). Since the perfect refers the state or event to two points in time it is considered a compound expression of tense. In logical structure perfect tenses are represented by two tense predicates. Present perfect is PRES PAST; past perfect is PAST PAST.

McCawley suggests a series of tense replacement rules which apply to all tenses in logical structure where "the tense morpheme would not undergo subject-verb agreement" (McCawley 1973:261). PRES becomes zero, PAST becomes *have* + *en*, *have* becomes zero before another *have*. Whenever *have* occurs, the suffix -*en* is added to the next lower predicate.

(652) a. The house seems to have been empty yesterday.
        = PAST + be empty
        = have + been empty

    b. The house seems to have been empty for years.
        = PRES + PAST + be empty
        = 0 + have + been empty

    c. The house seems to have been empty when I came.
        = PAST + PAST + be empty
        = have + have + been empty
        = 0 + have + been empty

6.3–6.5 Tense and aspect

Universal semantic tense deals with present, past, and future. In English present and past tenses are indicated by morphological marking, but future tense is indicated mainly by the modals *shall* and *will.*

(653) The tense system of English

		−Progressive		+Progressive
−Perf	1	Simple Pres He sings	7	Pres Prog He is singing
	2	Simple Past He sang	8	Past Prog He was singing
	3	Simple Future He will sing	9	Future Prog He will be singing
+Perf	4	Pres Perf He has sung	10	Pres Perf Prog He has been singing
	5	Past Perf He had sung	11	Past Perf Prog He had been singing
	6	Future Perf He will have sung	12	Future Perf Prog He will have been singing

McCawley used Present, Past, and Future as monadic predicates with propositions within their scope. John Sowa suggests that PAST is a higher relation. "PAST is a monadic relation that links to a PROPOSITION, that was true at some time preceding the present" (1984:418).

(654) Julian /watched /a football game. (1984:175)
        (PAST)→[[JULIAN]←(AGNT)←[WATCH]→(OBJ)→[GAME]]

But the question arises: Are these tenses RELATIONS, enclosed in circles, or CONCEPTS, enclosed in boxes? Generative semantics, by treating tenses as higher predicates, suggests that tenses are concepts.

(655) Julian /watched /a football game.
        [PAST] -
        [[JULIAN]←(A)←[WATCH]→(O)→[GAME]].

6.3. Nonprogressive tenses (States and events)

The nonprogressive tenses are (1) Present, (2) Past, (3) Future, (4) Present Perfect, (5) Past Perfect, and (6) Future Perfect. The logical structure of the nonprogressive tenses is formed with the predicates PRES for present time, PAST for past time and for perfect aspect, and FUTURE for future time.

1. Present	PRES	4. Present Perfect	PRES PAST
2. Past	PAST	5. Past Perfect	PAST PAST
3. Future	FUTURE	6. Future Perfect	FUTURE PAST

Present tense. Present State, also called the "unrestrictive present" (Leech 1971:138), describes a State having indefinite duration. The meaning is *State-now*. Present Event, also called the "instantaneous present" (Leech 1971:138), describes an Event taking place at the moment of speaking. The meaning is *Event-now*. Meanings are represented on a time line where the left-to-right direction of the line represents the time from past THEN to present NOW to future LATER. This representation is adapted from Leech (1971:42). The present tense is represented on a time line as NOW, referring to the moment of speaking. The logical structure of the definite present tense is represented as PRES.

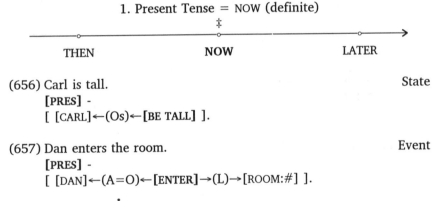

1. Present Tense = NOW (definite)

THEN   NOW   LATER

(656) Carl is tall.   State
　　　[PRES] -
　　　[[CARL]←(Os)←[BE TALL]].

(657) Dan enters the room.   Event
　　　[PRES] -
　　　[[DAN]←(A=O)←[ENTER]→(L)→[ROOM:#]].

Past tense. Past State, also called the 'definite past' (Leech 1971:142), describes a State which existed at some definite past moment relative to the moment of speaking. The meaning is ***State-then***. Past Event, also called the 'definite past' (Leech 1971:142), describes an Event which took place at some definite past moment relative to the moment of speaking. The meaning is *Event-then*. The Past tense is represented on a time line as THEN, a definite point prior to the present NOW. The logical structure of the definite past tense is represented as PAST.

2. Past Tense = THEN (definite)

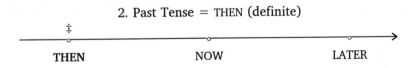

THEN   NOW   LATER

(658) Charles was tall.   State
      [PAST] -
      [[CHARLES]←(Os)←[BE TALL]].

(659) Dan entered the room.   Event
      [PAST] -
      [[DAN]←(A=O)←[ENTER]→(L)→[ROOM:#]].

Future tense. Future State is used where some State in the future is predicted (Leech 1971:53) and usually occurs with definite time adverbials. The meaning is *State-future*. Future Event is an Event taking place at some future time (Leech 1971:53). The meaning is *Event-future*. Time adverbials are not required. The future tense is represented on a time line as LATER. The logical structure is represented as FUTURE.

3. Future Tense = LATER

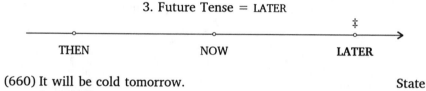

(660) It will be cold tomorrow.   State
      [FUTURE] -
      [[WEATHER:it]←(Os)←[BE COLD]].

(661) Carl will leave (tomorrow).   Event
      [FUTURE] -
      [[CARL]←(A=O)←[LEAVE]→(L)→[NULL]].

Present Perfect. Present Perfect State, also called the 'indefinite past' (Leech, 1971:30), describes a State in past time with present relevance, a state lasting up to the present time. It implies a continuing state. The meaning is *State-before-now*. Present Perfect Event describes an Event occurring at least once before now, at an indefinite time in the past, with effects continuing into the present. It may be accompanied by durative adverbials but not by point time adverbials. The meaning is *Event-before-now*. The present perfect is represented on a time line as BEFORE NOW. The logical structure is represented as PRES PAST. Empty addresses (deletable roles) which are required by the meaning of the main verb are marked NULL.

4. Present Perfect = Before NOW

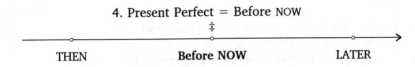

THEN	**Before NOW**	LATER

(662) The house has been empty for years.   State
    [PRES] -
      [PAST] -
      [[HOUSE:#]←(L)←[BE EMPTY]→(Os)→[NULL]].

(663) The postman hasn't come yet.   Event
    [PRES] -
      [PAST] -
      [[POSTMAN:#]←(A=O)←[COME]→(L)→[NULL]].

Past Perfect. Past Perfect State describes a State which existed at some definite or indefinite time period before a fixed point in past time (Leech 1971:42). The meaning is *State-before-then.* Past Perfect Event is an indefinite past-in-past (Leech, 1971:42) and describes an Event which occurred at some definite or indefinite time before a fixed point in past time. Past perfect tense takes both point and durative time adverbials. The meaning is *Event-before-then.* The past perfect is represented on a time line as BEFORE THEN. The logical structure is represented as PAST PAST.

5. Past Perfect = Before THEN

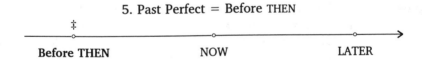

Before THEN	NOW	LATER

(664) The house had been empty before he arrived.   State
    [PAST] -
      [PAST] -
      [[HOUSE:#]←(L)←[BE EMPTY]→(Os)→[NULL]].

(665) The postman hadn't come yet.   Event
    [PAST] -
      [PAST] -
      [[POSTMAN:#]←(A=O)←[COME]→(L)→[NULL]].

Future Perfect. Future Perfect State, indicates a State which is in the past relative to some future time point (Leech 1971:54). The meaning is

State-before-future. Future Perfect Event describes an Event which is in the past relative to some future time point (Leech 1971:54). The meaning is *Event-before-future.* The future perfect is represented on a time line as BEFORE LATER. The logical structure is represented as FUTURE PAST.

6. Future Perfect = Before LATER

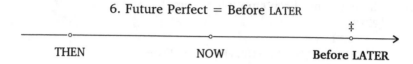

THEN   NOW   Before LATER

(666) Tomorrow Dan will have been sick two weeks.   State
    [FUTURE] -
      [PAST] -
      [[DAN]←(Os)←[BE SICK]].

(667) By tomorrow Edward will have finished the book.   Event
    [FUTURE] -
      [PAST] -
      [[EDWARD]←(A)←[FINISH]→(O)→[BOOK:#]].

6.4. Progressive tenses (Events only)

The progressive tenses are (1) Present Progressive, (2) Past Progressive, (3) Future Progressive, (4) Present Perfect Progressive, (5) Past Perfect Progressive, and (6) Future Perfect Progressive. The effect of the progressive is to establish a 'temporal frame' (Leech, 1971:17) around the time point which stretches the time span of Event verbs, resulting in the tense expressing limited duration. The logical structure is formed with the predicates PRES for present time, PAST for past time and perfect aspect, FUTURE for future time, and PROG for progressive.

1. Present progressive	PRES PROG
2. Past progressive	PAST PROG
3. Future progressive	FUTURE PROG
4. Present perfect progressive	PRES PAST PROG
5. Past perfect progressive	PAST PAST PROG
6. Future perfect progressive	FUTURE PAST PROG

Present Progressive. The Present Progressive describes an Event of limited duration continuing through the present moment (Leech 1971:14). The meaning is *Event-going-on-now.* Since events are normally conceived of as having duration, this is the normal way of describing present events. The present progressive contrasts with the simple present which views the event as taking place instantaneously. The time line drawing shows a situation which is GOING ON NOW. The logical structure is represented as PRES PROG.

1. Present Progressive = Going on NOW

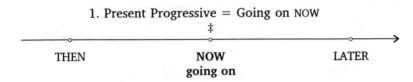

THEN   NOW   LATER
                      going on

(668) The king is entering the room.   Event
   ≠The king enters the room.
   [PRES] -
     [PROG] -
       [[KING:#]←(A=O)←[ENTER]→(L)→[ROOM:#]].

Past Progressive. The Past Progressive describes an Event of limited duration continuing through a definite point in past time (Leech 1971:16). The meaning is *Event-going-on-then.* The Past Progressive describes an Event not necessarily complete and contrasts with the simple Past. The time line drawing shows a situation GOING ON THEN at some definite point in past time. The logical structure is represented as PAST PROG.

2. Past Progressive = Going on THEN

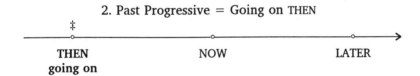

THEN   NOW   LATER
going on

(669) Joan was writing a letter.   Event
   ≠Joan wrote a letter.
   [PAST] -
     [PROG] -
       [[JOAN]←(A)←[WRITE]→(O)→[LETTER]].

Future Progressive. The Future Progressive describes temporary situations going on at some future time (Leech 1971:62). The meaning is *Event-going-on-in-the-future.* The normal progressive meaning of continuous, temporary, incomplete is combined with the future tense meaning. In contrast, the simple future merely states a future event. The time line

shows an event GOING ON LATER at some definite future time. The logical
structure is represented as FUTURE PROG.

3. Future Progressive = Going on LATER

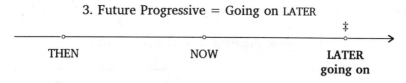

THEN	NOW	LATER
		going on

(670) The train will be arriving in a few minutes.   Event
≠The train will arrive in a few minutes
[FUTURE] -
  [PROG] -
  [[TRAIN:#]←(O)←[ARRIVE]→(L)→[NULL]].

Present Perfect Progressive. The Present Perfect Progressive describes an event of limited duration, not necessarily complete, going on
at some indefinite time prior to the present (Leech 1971:44). The meaning is *Event-going-on-before-now*. The present perfect progressive contrasts
with the present perfect by emphasizing the temporary nature of the
event. The time line shows an event which is GOING ON at some indefinite
time period before the present moment, BEFORE NOW. The logical structure is represented as PRES PAST PROG.

4. Present Perfect Progressive = Going on before NOW

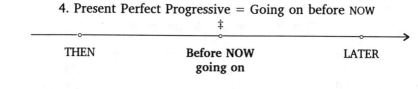

THEN	Before NOW	LATER
	going on	

(671) Who has been eating my porridge?   Event
≠Who has eaten my porridge?
[PRES] -
  [PAST] -
    [PROG] -
    [[WHO]←(A)←[EAT]→(O)→[PORRIDGE:#my]].

Past Perfect Progressive. The Past Perfect Progressive describes an
event of limited duration, which is not necessarily complete, going on at
a definite or indefinite time prior to a fixed moment in past time (Leech
1971:47). The meaning is *Event-going-on-before-then*. It contrasts with the

Past Perfect by emphasizing the temporary and incomplete. It may take durative or point time adverbials. The logical structure is PAST PAST PROG.

5. Past Perfect Progressive = Going on before THEN

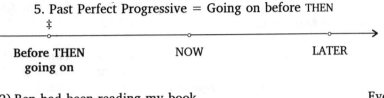

Before THEN   NOW   LATER
going on

(672) Ben had been reading my book.   Event
≠Ben had read my book.
[PAST] -
   [PAST] -
      [PROG] -
      [[BEN]←(A)←[READ]→(O)→[BOOK:#my]].

Future Perfect Progressive. This tense describes progressive situations going on at some time which is past relative to some defined future moment (Leech 1971:54). The meaning is *Event-going-on-before-future*. The nonprogressive form sums up the event as a single whole, whereas the progressive form sees the event from within as an ongoing event relative to some future time. The time line shows a situation going on at some moment before some future time. The logical structure is FUTURE PAST PROG.

6. Future Perfect Progressive = Going on before LATER

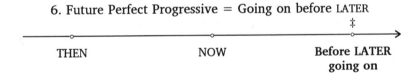

THEN   NOW   Before LATER
                                      going on

(673) By tomorrow Frank will have been working three weeks.   Event
≠By tomorrow he will have worked three weeks.
[FUTURE] -
   [PAST] -
      [PROG] -
      [[FRANK]←(A)←[WORK /O-lex]].

6.5. Habitual tenses (Events only)

Habitual aspect is used "to describe a situation which is characteristic of an extended period of time" (Comrie 1976:27). Habitual tenses include

(1) Present, (2) Past, (3) Present Perfect, and (4) Past Perfect. Habitual aspect has zero surface representation in the present but may be realized by
used to in the past. The logical structure of the habitual tense may be distinguished from the simple tenses by adding the abstract predicate HABIT-
UAL above the main verb.

Present Habitual. The Present Habitual describes a general state of
affairs continuing through the present moment and consisting of repeated events. The meaning is *repeated-Events-now*. Habitual is used to
express habitual, customary, or iterative events. When the verb is transitive, the object tends to be a plural noun (Leech 1971:6). Without surface
adverbials, the habitual present is ambiguous. The logical structure is
PRES HABITUAL.

1. Present Habitual = Habitual NOW

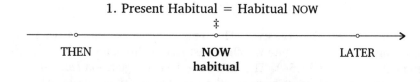

| THEN | **NOW**
habitual | LATER |

(674) Harry walks to school (usually).   Event
    [PRES] -
      [HABITUAL] -
      [[HARRY]←(A=O)←[WALK]→(L)→[TO [SCHOOL]]].

Present Progressive is also used with habitual meaning. Progressive aspect refers to repeated events. The meaning is "habit in existence over a
limited period" (Leech 1971:28). The present habitual is never used with
States.

(675) Harry is walking to school these days.   Event
    [PRES] -
      [PROG]
        [HABITUAL] -
        [[HARRY]←(A=O)←[WALK]→(L)→[TO [SCHOOL]]].

Past Habitual. Past Habitual describes a series of events leading up
to, but excluding, the present moment (Leech 1971:143). The meaning is
repeated-events-then. Past may be represented by the quasi-auxiliary *used
to*.

2. Past Habitual = Habitual THEN

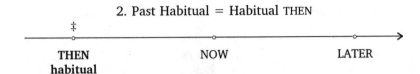

(676) Harry walked to school (in those days).   Event
= Harry used to walk to school.
[PAST] -
 [HABITUAL] -
  [[HARRY]←(A=O)←[WALK]→(L)→[TO [SCHOOL]]].

Habitual Past is restricted to events, but the form *used to* is used of states as well as events. Comrie (1976:27) considers these past states as habitual since they are characteristic of a period of time.

(677) George used to believe in ghosts.   State
= George habitually believed in ghosts.
[PAST] -
 [HABITUAL] -
  [[GEORGE]←(E)←[BELIEVE IN]→(Os)→[GHOSTS]].

Past Progressive is also used with habitual meaning. The meaning of limited duration is applied to individual events that are characteristic of the period. Progressive means "repetition of events of limited duration" (Leech 1971:28).

(678) Trains were arriving late every day.   Event
[PAST] -
 [PROG] -
  [HABITUAL] -
   [[TRAINS]←(O)←[ARRIVE]→(L)→[NULL]].

Present Perfect Habitual. Present Perfect Habitual describes a habit in past time leading up to the present moment. The meaning is *habit-up-to-now*. Durational adverbs are usually required (Leech 1971:34). The logical structure is represented as PRES PAST HABITUAL.

3. Present Perfect Habitual = Habit up to NOW

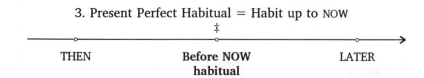

(679) Mary has sung in the choir for years.   Event
       ≠Mary has sung in the choir.
       [PRES] -
          [PAST] -
             [HABITUAL] -
             [[MARY]←(A)←[SING]→(O)→[NULL]].

Present Perfect Progressive is also used with habitual meaning. This meaning is clear with transitive verbs when they govern plural objects, indicating a series of events going on in a period leading up to the present.

(680) Helen has been writing letters.   Event
       ≠Helen has been writing a letter.
       [PRES] -
          [PAST] -
             [PROG] -
                [HABITUAL] -
                [[HELEN]←(A)←[WRITE]→(O)→[LETTERS]].

Past Perfect Habitual. This habitual describes habitual activity in a time period which is before a fixed point in past time (Leech 1971:33). The meaning is *habit-up-to-then.* The implication is that the habit came to an end. The Past Perfect is often replaced by the simple past or past with *used to.* The time line shows a habitual structure in a time frame which exists before some definite past moment, BEFORE THEN. The logical structure is represented as PAST PAST HABITUAL.

4. Past Perfect Habitual = Habit up to THEN

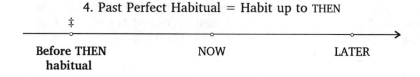

(681) David had always worked there.							Event
= David no longer works there.
[PAST] -
  [PAST] -
    [HABITUAL] -
     [[DAVID]←(A)←[WORK /O-lex]].

Past Perfect Progressive can also be used with habitual meaning. The progressive adds the notion of limited duration, and the Past Perfect Habitual implies the situation that was an ongoing characteristic has come to an end. The logical structure is represented as PAST PAST PROG HABITUAL.

(682) David had always been working there.						Event
= David is no longer working there.
[PAST] -
  [PAST] -
    [PROG] -
     [HABITUAL] -
      [[DAVID]←(A)←[WORK /O-lex]].

Comrie (1976:29) describes past habituals as having an implicature rather than an implication. An implicature is an implication that can be canceled by an explicit denial. The speaker is deliberately misleading if he utters an implicature without an explicit denial. The implicature in the Present Perfect Habitual is that the event described is on-going.

(683) Jim has been teaching there.							Event
= Jim is still teaching there.
[PRES] -
  [PAST] -
    [HABITUAL] -
     [[JIM]←(A)←[TEACH]→(O)→[NULL]→(E)→[NULL]].

6.6–6.11 Modal verbs

Chomsky used five modals, *can, may, must, shall, will* in their present and past forms. Generative semantics considered these modals as main verbs with propositions within their scope. Modal verbs may be classified according to their meanings into epistemic and root modals.

Epistemic modals modify a sentence and deal with the truth value of the proposition; root modals relate an agent to an activity and deal with permission, obligation, and ability. The range of meanings of *can, may, should, ought to, must, have to,* is given in (684).

(684) Epistemic and root modals

Modal verb meanings	Possibility and necessity	Permission and obligation	Ability (know how)
CAN	CAN = be possible	CAN = be permitted	CAN = be able to
MAY	MAY = be possible	MAY = be permitted	
SHOULD	SHOULD = be probable	SHOULD = be obliged	
OUGHT TO	OUGHT TO = be probable	OUGHT TO = be obliged	
MUST	MUST = be certain	MUST = be obliged	
HAVE TO	HAVE TO = be certain	HAVE TO = be obliged	

6.6. Epistemic modals

Epistemic modals deal with possibility and necessity. The epistemic modal is a one-place intransitive predicate with a sentence as its subject. To analyze sentences which contain epistemic modals, extract the modal verb from the sentence and replace it with paraphrases such as *It is possible that, It is probable that, It is certain that* prefixed to the remaining sentence. If the paraphrase matches the intended meaning of the sentence then the modal is an epistemic modal. Sowa describes epistemic modalities, possibility and necessity, as "alethic modalities or modes of truth" (1984:175). Sowa suggests that possibility and necessity are relations, not concepts. "Possible (PSBL) is a monadic relation that links to a [PROPOSITION] which is possibly true" (1984:418). "Necessary (NECS) is a monadic relation that links to a [PROPOSITION], which is necessarily true" (1984:417).

(685) It is possible /for Julian to fly to Mars.   (1984:175)
       (PSBL)→[[JULIAN]←(AGNT)←[FLY]→(DEST)→[MARS]].

Generative semantics treated possibility and necessity modes as monadic predicates. As predicates, they are concepts, not relations. These concepts are arrayed in a Tense-Modal-Aspect layer with the content layer containing the proposition within their scope.

(686) It is possible /for Julian to fly to Mars.   (1984:175)
    [PRES] -
      [BE POSSIBLE] -
      [[JULIAN]←(A=O)←[FLY]→(L)→[TO [MARS]]].

CAN = be possible. Epistemic *can* is frequently used in negatives and questions. It is used with state and process verbs, but rarely with action verbs. It is used with stative *be*, in *be* + adjective, *be* + predicate noun, *be* + locative structures. It is used with passive *be*, with progressive *be*, and with the perfect *have*. Inanimate subjects with *can* generally indicate that *can* is epistemic.

(687) John can be lying.
    = It is possible that John is lying.
    [PRES] -
      [CAN = be possible] -
        [PROG] -
        [[JOHN]←(A=O)←[LIE]].

Epistemic *can* has some special uses in generic statements = it is sometimes true that, and in polite suggestions = I suggest to you that.

(688) Good teachers can make mistakes.
    [PRES] -
      [CAN = be sometimes true that] -
      [[TEACHERS]←(A)←[MAKE]→(O)→[mistakes]].

(689) Joseph can come tomorrow.
    [PRES] -
      [CAN = I suggest to you that] -
      [[JOSEPH]←(A=O)←[COME]→(L)→[NULL]].

MAY = be possible. Epistemic *may* is used in statements but never in questions. This epistemic modal is used like epistemic *can* to express possibility. Epistemic *can* expresses a theoretical possibility, whereas epistemic *may* expresses a more factual possibility.

(690) John may be lying.
    = It is possible that John is lying.
    [PRES] -
      [CAN = be possible] -
        [PROG] -
        [[JOHN]←(A=O)←[LIE]].

SHOULD = **be probable.** The modal *should* has uses not related to the future modal *shall,* but parallel to the modal *ought to.* The modal *should* in these contexts is used in the epistemic sense of probability.

(691) Frank should be home by now.
    = It is probable that Frank is home.
    [PRES] -
      [SHOULD = be probable] -
      [[FRANK]←(Os)←[BE-LOC]→(L)→[HOME]].

OUGHT TO = **be probable.** The probability modal *ought to* in many contexts may be substituted for the modal *should.* The modal *ought to* in its probability sense indicates a stronger probability than the modal *should.*

(692) Frank ought to be home by now.
    = It is highly probable that Frank is home.
    [PRES] -
      [OUGHT TO = be probable] -
      [[FRANK]←(Os)←[BE-LOC]→(L)→[HOME]].

MUST = **be certain.** Epistemic *must* indicates a factual necessity or a sound assumption. It is used in the same contexts as *can* and *may* but expresses certainty.

(693) There must be some mistake.
    = It is certain that there is some mistake.
    [PRES] -
      [MUST = be necessary] -
      [[MISTAKE]←(Os)←[BE = exist]].

HAVE TO = **be certain.** Epistemic *have to* is used to express theoretical necessity, a no-other-choice situation. It is often used in the same contexts as *can, may,* or *must.* In the past tense the modal becomes *had to.*

(694) There has to be some mistake.
     = It is certain that there is some mistake.
     [PRES] -
      [MUST = **be necessary**] -
      [[MISTAKE]←(Os)←[BE = **exist**]].

6.7. Root modals

Root modals deal with permission and obligation. The root modal is a three-place transitive predicate with an agent as subject, a receiver as indirect object, and an action sentence as its direct object. The noun which is subject of the modal is also the subject of the action sentence. To analyze sentences which contain root modals, extract the modal verb and the NP subject from the sentence, and replace it with paraphrases such as *NP is permitted to, NP is obliged to,* prefixed to the remainder of the embedded sentence. If the paraphrase matches the intended meaning of the sentence then the modal involved is a root modal and the logical structure contains a three-place transitive predicate. The surface structure of the deontic modals, however, is always a two-place predicate with the authority granting permission or imposing the obligation understood.

According to Sowa, "deontic logic introduces modes for permission and obligation to support the English modals *may* and *ought*" (1984:176). These deontic modes are not described in Sowa's conceptual catalog. In generative semantics these deontic root modals are described as triadic predicates linking an authority, who gives a permission, with a person, who receives the permission, to a proposition, which describes what is permitted. Multi-place predicates have to be concepts, not relations.

CAN = **be permitted.** Root modal *can* of permission is usually interchangeable with *may.* This root modal is used with action verbs with agentive subjects. The authority granting permission is indeterminate with *can,* whereas with *may* the speaker grants the permission.

(695) You can smoke in the lounge.
     = You are permitted to smoke in the lounge.
     [PRES] -
      [CAN = **be permitted**] -
       (A)→[NULL]
       (B)→[PERSON:#you]
       (O)→[[PERSON:#you]←(A)←[SMOKE]→(O)→[NULL]].

MAY = **be permitted.** The modal *may* of permission is usually inter-changeable with *can.* The modal *may* refers generally to speaker authority but *can* leaves the authority indeterminate. Since *may* (permission) acts the same as *can (permission),* these two modals will react in a similar way when they are used with negation.

(696) You may smoke in the lounge.
        = You are permitted to smoke in the lounge.
        [PRES] -
            [MAY = **be permitted**] -
                (A)→[NULL]
                (B)→[PERSON:#you]
                (O)→[[PERSON:#you]←(A)←[SMOKE]→(O)→[NULL]].

SHOULD = **be obliged.** The root modal *should* expresses an obligation by some indeterminate authority. This modal is not a past tense form of the future modal *shall.* The modals *should, ought to* in their root sense of obligation assert a weaker obligation than the modals *must, have to.*

(697) You should leave now.
        = You are obliged to leave now.
        [PRES] -
            [SHOULD = **be obliged**] -
                (A)→[NULL]
                (B)→[PERSON:#you]
                (O)→[[PERSON:#you]←(A=O)←[LEAVE]→(L)→[NULL]].

OUGHT TO = **be obliged.** The root modal *ought to* expresses an obli-gation by some indeterminate authority. It is used in the same contexts as *should* of obligation. The root modals *should, ought to* both express a relationship between a person capable of accepting an obligation and the action which the subject is obliged to perform.

(698) Carl ought to pay for it.
        = Carl is obliged to pay for it.
        [PRES] -
            [OUGHT TO = **be obliged**] -
                (A) → [NULL]
                (B) → [CARL]
                (O) → [[CARL]←(A)←[PAY FOR]→(O)→[ENTITY:It]].

MUST = **be obliged.** The root modal *must* generally expresses obligation by speaker authority. It is used in the same contexts as *can* and *may*
which express permission.

(699) I must go now.
  = I am obliged to go now.
  [PRES] -
    [MUST = **be obliged**] -
      (A)→[NULL]
      (B)→[PERSON:#I]
      (O)→[[PERSON:#I]←(A=O)←[GO]→(L)→[NULL]].

HAVE TO = **be obliged.** The root modal *have to* expresses an obligation from any authority. It is limited to action verbs with animate
subjects which accept authority. In the past it becomes *had to.*

(700) He has to refuse the offer.
  = He is obliged to refuse the offer.
  [PRES] -
    [HAVE TO = **be obliged**] -
      (A)→[NULL]
      (B)→[PERSON:#he]
      (O)→[[PERSON:#he]←(A)←[REFUSE]→(O)→[OFFER:#]].

6.8. Ability modal

The modal *can* = *be able to* is a root modal of ability. This modal is
used with action verbs with animate or inanimate potent subjects. The
ability modal *can* is not treated in Sowa. In generative semantics the modal *can* expressing ability is a dyadic predicate relating a person, who
has the ability, with an action.

(701) John can lift 100 pounds.
  = John is able to lift 100 pounds.
  [PRES] -
    [CAN = **be able to**] -
      (A)→[JOHN]
      (O)→[[JOHN]←(A)←[LIFT]→(O)→[POUNDS:@100]].

Special uses of *can* of ability include the expression of permanent ability, a substitute progressive for state perception verbs, and the actual
realization of state cognitive verbs.

(702) Ted can speak French.
   = permanent ability
   [PRES] -
     [CAN = **be able to**] -
       (A)→[TED]
       (O)→[[TED]←(A)←[**SPEAK**]→(O)→[FRENCH]].

(703) Harry can see the house.
   = Harry does see.
   [PRES] -
     [CAN = **be able to**] -
       (A)→[HARRY]
       (O)→[[HARRY]←(E)←[**SEE**]→(Os)→[HOUSE:#]].

(704) Abe can't remember his name.
   = Abe doesn't remember his name.
   [PRES] -
     [NOT] -
       [CAN = **be able to**] -
         (A)→[ABE]
         (O)→[[ABE]←(A=E)←[**REMEMBER**]→(O)→[NAME:#his]].

6.9. Epistemic modals with tense

Modal verbs have present and past tense forms. The past forms corresponding to *can and may* are *could* and *might. Should, ought to,* and *must* have no past tense form. The past tense form of *have to* is *had to.* The past form modals *could* and *might* have past time meanings in past discourse contexts, with past time adverbials, and after past tense verbs of saying or thinking. But past tense forms also have present meanings when used in present time contexts.

COULD = **be/was possible.** Epistemic *could* is used for both present and past possibility, but the combination *could have* applies only to the past. When used with present meaning *could* may be replaced by *can.* In logical structure the tense marker indicates present or past meaning.

(705) There can /**could** be trouble.
   = present possibility
   [PRES] -
     [COULD = **be possible**] -
       [[TROUBLE]←(O)←[BE = **occur**]].

(706) Ocean voyages **could** be dangerous in those days.
   = past possibility
   [PAST] -
      [COULD = **was possible**] -
         [[VOYAGES]←(Os)←[BE DANGEROUS]].

(707) The fish **could have** been a shark.
   = past possibility
   [PAST] -
      [COULD = **was possible**] -
         [PAST] -
            [[FISH:#]←(Os)←[BE-IDENT]→(Os)→[SHARK]].

MIGHT = **be/was possible.** Epistemic *might* is used for both present and past possibility, but the combination *might have* applies only to the past. When used with present meaning *might* may be replaced by *may*.

(708) Oscar may /**might** be the winner.
   = present possibility
   [PRES] -
      [MIGHT = **be possible**] -
         [[OSCAR]←(Os)←[BE-IDENT]→(Os)→[WINNER:#]].

(709) In that era taxes **might** be avoided.
   = past possibility
   [PAST] -
      [MIGHT = **was possible**] -
         [[NULL]←(A)←[AVOID]→(O)→[TAXES]].

(710) Jean **might have** been mistaken.
   = past possibility
   [PAST] -
      [MIGHT = **was possible**] -
         [PAST] -
            [[JEAN]←(Os)←[BE MISTAKEN]].

6.10. Root modals with tense

Root modals also have present and past forms. Present forms have present meaning, but past forms have present and past meanings. Past root modals *could* and *might* are used for both present and past permission, with past permission rare. Past modal *could* is used for present and past ability, with past ability frequent.

COULD = **be /was permitted.** Root modal *could* is used for both present and past permission, with past permission rare. The combination *could have* is always past. With present meaning *could* may be replaced by *can.*

(711) Can /**could** Fred use the car?
    = present permission
    [PRES] -
       [COULD = **be permitted**] -
         [[FRED]←(A)←[USE]→(O)→[CAR:#]].

(712) In college students **could** stay out late.
    = past permission
    [PAST] -
       [COULD = **was permitted**] -
         [[STUDENTS]←(A=O)←[STAY]→(L)→[OUT]].

(713) Janet **could have** taken that course.
    = past permission
    [PAST] -
       [COULD = **was permitted**] -
         [PAST] -
           [[JANET]←(A)←[TAKE]→(O)→[COURSE:#]].

MIGHT = **be /was permitted.** Root modal *might* is used for both present and past permission, with past permission rare. The combination *might have* applies only to the past. When used with present meaning *might* may be replaced by *may.*

(714) Students may /**might** smoke in the lounge.
    = present permission
    [PRES] -
       [MIGHT = **be permitted**] -
         [[STUDENTS]←(A)←[SMOKE]→(O)→[NULL]].

(715) After the war ended the prisoners **might** leave camp.
= past permission
[PAST] -
   [MIGHT = **was permitted**] -
      [[PRISONERS:#]←(A=O)←[LEAVE]→(L)→[CAMP]].

(716) Robert **might have** written a thesis.
= past permission
[PAST] -
   [MIGHT = **was permitted**] -
      [PAST] -
         [[ROBERT]←(A)←[WRITE]→(O)→[THESIS]].

6.11. Ability modal with tense

Ability modal *could* = *be able to* is used for both present and past ability. When used with present meaning *could* may be replaced by *can.* Past ability requires a well-defined past context, but the combination *could have* applies only to the past.

(717) The fish can /**could** break the line.
= present ability
[PRES] -
   [COULD = **be able**] -
      [[FISH:#]←(A)←[BREAK]→(O)→[LINE:#]].

(718) When Jake was younger he **could** lift 150 pounds.
= past ability
[PAST] -
   [COULD = **was able**] -
      [[JAKE]←(A)←[LIFT/**L-Lex**]→(O)→[POUNDS:@100]].

(719) Julie **could have** danced all night.
= past ability
[PAST] -
   [COULD = **was able**] -
      [PAST] -
         [[JULIE]←(A)←[DANCE]→(O)→[NULL]].

6.12–6.13 Negation

Sentence negation in Chomsky (1965) was accomplished with a NEG marker, which represented not only the negative *not* but also various negative adverbials such as *hardly, scarcely.* McCawley (1973:280) claimed that this negative is not an adverb but a one-place logical predicate with the proposition within its scope.

6.12. Negation of propositions

Sowa's conceptual graphs use a system with (NEG) marking the negative. This negative is defined as a relation, not a concept, linking to a proposition. "Negation (NEG) is a monadic relation that links to a [PROPOSITION], which is asserted to be false" (1984:418).

(720) Ostriches /don't /fly.
     (NEG)→[[Ostriches]←(AGNT)←[FLY]].

In generative semantics, *not* was considered a monadic predicate with a proposition within its scope. Since *not* is a predicate, it is a concept and not a relation. This negative is placed directly above the proposition and below any tense or aspect markers.

(721) Ostriches /don't /fly.
    [PRES = **generic**] -
      [NOT] -
       [[Ostriches]←(A=O)←[FLY]].

6.13. Negation with modals

Structures with modal verbs are two verb structures which contain a modal verb and a main verb. When a negative is added to this structure the negative modifies either the modal verb or the main verb. In EXTERNAL NEGATION the negative is outside the scope of the modal and negates the modal; in INTERNAL NEGATION the negative is inside the scope of the modal and negates the main verb. In logical structure the negative is placed above the modal verb when the negation is external and below the modal verb when the negation is internal. The type of negation is constant for each meaning of a modal.

The SCOPE LINEARITY PRINCIPLE predicts that each predicate in surface structure has everything to its right within its scope. According to this principle, if the negative precedes the modal in surface structure the negation is external, but if the modal precedes the negative in surface structure the negation is internal. In the negation of modals, the exceptions to this principle are *can* in all its meanings and *may* of permission.

Epistemic modals and negation. Epistemic modals show external and internal negation. Epistemic *cannot* = not possible. Contrary to the scope linearity principle the negation is external. The negation is internal for epistemic *may not* = possible not, *must not* = necessary not, *should not* = probably not, *ought not* = probably not, and *must not* = certainly not. The negation is external for epistemic *not have to* = not certain.

(722) George can't be lying.   External negation
    = It is not possible that George is lying.
    [PRES] -
      [NOT] -
        [CAN = **be possible**] -
        [[GEORGE]←(A)←[LIE /O-lex]].

(723) George may not be lying.   Internal negation
    = It is possible that John is not lying.
    [PRES] -
      [MAY = **be possible**] -
        [NOT] -
        [[GEORGE]←(A)←[LIE /O-lex]].

Since epistemic *may* has internal negation, the contradictory statement must be formed by using the corresponding modal with external negation. Given the sentence *George may be lying* the contradictory is not *George may not be lying* (= possible not), but *George can't be lying* (= not possible). Change *may not* to *cannot*. This is called the M-modal shift.

(724) George must not be lying.   Internal negation
    = It is certain that George is not lying.
    [PRES] -
      [MUST = **be necessary**] -
        [NOT] -
        [[GEORGE]←(A)←[LIE /O-lex]].

Since epistemic *must* has internal negation, the contradictory statement must be formed by using the corresponding modal with external negation. Given the sentence *George must be lying*, the contradictory is not

George must not be lying (= necessary not), but *George doesn't have to be lying* (= not necessary). Change *must not* to *doesn't have to*. This is also an M-modal shift.

(725) George doesn't have to be lying.   External negation
      = It is not necessary that George is lying.
      [PRES] -
        [NOT] -
          [HAVE TO = **be necessary**] -
          [[GEORGE]←(A)←[LIE /**O-lex**]].

Root modals and negation. Root modals show external and internal negation. Contrary to the scope linearity principle root *cannot* = not permitted and root *may not* = not permitted. Root *must not, should not,* and *ought not* = obliged not, and *not have to* = not obliged, as expected.

(726) You can't smoke in the library.   External negation
      = You are not permitted to smoke in the library.
      [PRES] -
        [NOT] -
          [CAN = **be permitted**] -
          [[PERSON:#you]←(A)←[SMOKE]→(O)→[NULL]].

(727) You may not smoke in the library.   External negation
      = You are not permitted to smoke here.
      [PRES] -
        [NOT] -
          [MAY = **be permitted**] -
          [[PERSON:#you]←(A)←[SMOKE]→(O)→[NULL]].

(728) You must not read the book.   Internal negation
      = You are obliged not to read the book.
      [PRES] -
        [MUST = **be obliged**] -
          [NOT] -
          [[PERSON:#you]←(A)←[READ]→(O)→[BOOK:#]].

(729) You don't have to read the book.   External negation
    = You are not obliged to read the book.
    [PRES] -
      [NOT] -
        [HAVE TO = **be obliged**] -
        [[PERSON:#you]←(A)←[READ]→(O)→[BOOK:#]].

The modal *must* has internal negation, but the modal *have to* has external negation. Given the sentence *You must read the book,* the contradictory is not *You must not read the book,* but *You don't have to read the book* (= not obliged). To form the contradictory, change *must not* to *don't have to.*

Ability modal and negation. The ability modal *cannot* = not able to, contrary to the scope linearity principle. Therefore, the modal *can* in all its uses has external negation. The modal *cannot* always means *not can.*

(730) Jake can't lift 100 pounds.   External negation
    = He is not able to lift 100 pounds.
    [PRES] -
      [NOT] -
        [CAN = **be able**] -
        [[JAKE]←(A)←[LIFT/L-lex]→(O)→[ENTITY:@100 lbs]].

6.14–6.19 Logical structure

The logical structure of a sentence should contain all of the elements in the total literal meaning of the sentence. In his 1975 article, Ronald Langacker proposes that this structure be broken down into three layers: the performative layer, the tense-aspect-modal layer, and the propositional layer. The performative layer, as the highest layer, distinguishes statements, questions, and commands; the tense-aspect-modal layer describes these predicates as higher than the proposition; and the propositional layer describes the basic predicate-argument structure.

6.14. Performative layer

In his 1962 work Austin distinguishes performative sentences from constative sentences. Performatives are verbs that do what they say, such as *I warn, I promise.* Austin also suggests that all sentences are implicitly performatives since every speech act has an illocutionary force, whatever is accomplished in speaking. John Ross, in his 1970 article, asserts that every sentence contains a performative verb as the highest verb in logical structure. Higher verbs of saying, asking, or ordering distinguish the sentences as statements, questions, or commands. These verbs are assumed to be present nonprogressive, with first-person subject and second-person indirect object. The proposition then becomes the direct object of the performative.

Semantically, the advantage of using the higher performative is that every sentence becomes a speech act with its own illocutionary force. Syntactically, the performative distinguishes statements, questions, and commands; direct and indirect discourse are represented by the same logical structure; the understood subject of imperatives is explained as identical to a higher indirect object; and certain adverbs, *frankly, briefly* may modify the performative rather than the main verb. In the sentence *Frankly, my dear, I don't give a damn,* the adverb *frankly* does not modify anything in the surface structure, but modifies the implicit performative verb: *I say to you frankly that...* If the performative is not expanded, the sentence may be prefixed with Statement (STMT).

6.15. Tense-Aspect-Modal layer

The elements of tense, aspect, and the modals verbs are grouped in the middle layer of the logical structure. Tense is represented by PRES, PAST, or FUTURE as one-place predicates with the main proposition within their scope. Aspect is represented by PROG for progressive, or a second occurrence of PAST as the perfect aspect. The modal verbs include epistemic, deontic, and ability modals.

Elements of this layer are grouped as Tense above Aspect above Modal verbs. All elements of this layer are predicate concepts, not relations. The tenses bear the tense (TNS) relation to the verb, the aspects bear the Aspect (ASP) relation to the verb, and the modal verbs expresses the modality (MODAL) relation to the main verb. Epistemic modals are one-place predicates with a proposition in their scope. Corresponding deontic modals of permission or obligation are three-place predicates with an implied Agent giving the permission or imposing the obligation, a Benefactive which occurs as subject of the modal, and an Object which is permitted or imposed. The ability modals *can, could* are two-place predicates expressing an Agent who has the ability and an Object referring to the ability.

6.16. Propositional layer

The propositional layer includes the basic predicate-argument structure, along with nonessential adjuncts which may occur in the sentence. The basic predicate-argument structure involves only the five essential cases: Agent, Experiencer, Benefactive, Object, and Locative. The Object case is universally present in every predication, and sentences are embedded only under the Object case. Negative propositions are described by placing the *not* predicate above the main verb in logical structure.

Sentence adjuncts are those adverbial elements not required by the meaning of the verb. They are listed as modal cases, part of the modality, not part of the proposition. Principal adjuncts include modal Time (Tm), modal location (Lm), and modal Benefactive (Bm). Each of these may also occur as essential cases. Other sentence adjuncts, usually represented by clauses are cause (Cs), purpose (Ps), and result (Rs). These are peripheral elements which may occur with virtually any predicate.

(731) Tom /fell /down /in the kitchen.
  = It was in the kitchen that Tom fell down.
  [PAST] -
    [FALL] -
      (O)→[TOM]
      (L)→[DOWN]
      (Lm)→[in [KITCHEN:#]].

The verb *fall* is a motion verb that requires, as part of its meaning, a source, goal, or path locative. Since the preposition in the phrase *in the kitchen* expresses stative location, it does not fill the requirement that motion verbs require directional adverbs, and is therefore a modal locative. Modal locatives are marked as (Lm), essential locatives as (L).

Time and place expressions can occur with virtually any predicate, but time expressions are complements only when they are predicate adverbials, or with special verbs such as *last* or *spend (time)*.

(732) George ate dinner at five o'clock.
  = It was at five o'clock that George ate dinner.
  [PAST] -
    [EAT] -
      (A)→[GEORGE]
      (O)→[DINNER]
      (Tm)→[at [FIVE O'CLOCK]].

6.17. Noun phrase modification

Nouns have premodifiers listed as determiners (Det), quantifiers (Qn) and attributive adjectives (Att). They also have postmodifiers, such as prepositional phrases and relative clauses. The determiner, in conceptual graph notation, is the definite marker # in a type: referent notation. All other premodifiers and postmodifiers are represented by the conceptual relation modifier (Mod).

6.18. Parsing with Case Grammar

A sample Case Grammar parse can reveal the logical structure of the sentence. This parse indicates the elements of the performative layer, the tense-aspect-modal layer, and the propositional layer. The performative layer indicates whether the sentence is a statement, a question, or a command. The tense-aspect-modal layer indicates the tense, represented as PRES or PAST, and the aspect, represented by PERF or PROG. Modal verbs are listed as higher predicates. The parse distinguishes essential elements required by the case frame of the verb from optional adjuncts which may be used with virtually any predicate.

(733) As the sun *set* he *remembered*, to *give* himself more confidence,
the time in the tavern at Casablanca when he had *played* the
hand game with the great negro from Cienfuegos who *was* the
strongest man on the docks.

```
[STMT -
  [REMEMBER -
    (TNS)→[PAST]
    (A=E)→[PERSON:#he x]
    (O)→[TIME:#]
      (Mod)→[in [TAVERN:#] ]
        (Mod)→[at [CASABLANCA] ]
      (Mod)→[PLAY -
        (TNS)→[PAST]
        (ASP)→[PERFECT]
        (A)→[PERSON:#he x]
        (O)→[GAME:#]
          (Mod)→[HAND]
        (Acc)→[with [NEGRO:# y]
          (Mod)→[GREAT]
          (Mod)→[from [CIENFUEGOS] ]
          (Mod)→[BE-IDENT -
            (TNS)→[PAST]
            (Os)→[PERSON:#who y]
            (Os)→[PERSON:man:# y]
              (Mod)→[STRONGEST]
              (Mod)→[on [DOCKS:#] ]
        (Tm)→[WHEN]
    (Tm)→[SET -
      (TNS)→[PAST]
      (O)→[SUN:#]
      (L)→[L-lex]
    (Purpose)→[GIVE -
      (TNS)→(PRES)
      (A)→[PERSON:#he x]
      (B)→[PERSON:#himself]
      (O)→[CONFIDENCE]
        (Mod)→[MORE].
```

The performative is suggested by the concept [STMT] which can be expanded to *I say to you that...* which involves an Agent speaking subject,

an Experiencer as listening indirect object, and the main proposition as direct object. The main verb is *remember*, with the tense marked as *past*. The lexicon chooses *remember* = *deliberate recall*, with the case frame A=E,O. The subject (A=E) is *he*, the object (O) is *time*. The verb has a time adjunct (Tm) *as the sun set*, and a purpose adjunct (Ps) *to give himself more confidence*. These phrases are nonessential adjuncts.

In the time adjunct the verb *set* = *go down* is a one-place process predicate (O,*L) in the past tense with subject *sun* (O) and the Locative (L) lexicalized. In the purpose adjunct the verb *give* is a three-place predicate in the present tense, with subject *he* (A), indirect object *himself* (B), and direct object *confidence* (O), modified by *more*.

The direct object *time* of the main verb has prepositional and relative clause modifiers. The prepositional phrase *in the tavern* is listed with *in* as a governing preposition and *tavern* as its object. The prepositional phrase *at Casablanca* is construed as modifying the noun *tavern*. The relative clause *when he had played the hand game...* has a main verb *play* which is an A,O verb with the tense marked as past perfect. The subject is *he* (A), and the object is *game* (O) with modifier *hand*. This relative clause has an accompaniment adjunct *with the negro* and a temporal adjunct *when*, which by relative clause formation was moved to first position in the clause. The noun *negro* has a premodifier *great*, a postmodifier prepositional phrase *from Cienfuegos*, and a postmodifier relative clause. The relative clause has the main verb *be*, an identity predicate with the frame Os,Os marked for past tense. The subject is *who* and the object is *man*. The predicate noun *man* has a premodifier *strongest* and a postmodifer prepositional phrase *on the docks*.

(734) They *had gone* one day and one night with their elbows *(being)*
on a chalk line on the table and their forearms *(being)* straight up
and their hands *(being) gripped* tight.

```
[STMT -
    (TNS)→PAST
    (ASP)→PERF
    [GO = last -
        (A=O)→[PERSONS:#they x and y]
        (T)→[AND -
            [DAY:@ one]
            [NIGHT:@ one] ]
        (Mn)→[with -
            [AND -
                [BE-LOC -
                    (O)→[ELBOWS:#their x and y]
                    (L)→[on [LINE] ]
                        (Mod)→[CHALK]
                        (Mod)→[on [TABLE:#] ] ]
                [BE-LOC -
                    (O)→[FOREARMS:#their x and y]
                    (L)→[UP]
                        (Mod)→[STRAIGHT] ]
                [BE GRIPPED -
                    (O)→[HANDS:#their x and y]
                    (Mn)→[TIGHT] ] ] ] ]
```

The performative is suggested by the concept [STMT]. The main verb is
go = last, with the tense marked as *past* and the aspect as *perfect.* The
main verb is interpreted as intentional, with the case frame A=O,T. The
subject (A=O) is *they,* the object (T) is *one day and one night.* The verb
has a triple set of manner (Mn) clauses introduced by the preposition
with.

In the main clause, coordination is represented by the multi-place
predicate *and* joining *one day* and *one night.* In the manner adjunct, the
multi-place predicate *and* joins the three clauses *be on, be up,* and *be
gripped.* The first manner clause locates elbows *on a line,* with modifiers
chalk and *on the table.* The second manner clause locates forearms as *up,*
with modifier *straight.* The third manner clause describes hands as
gripped, with modifier *tight.*

(735) Each one *was trying* to *force* the other's hand down into the table.

    [STMT -
        (TNS)→[PAST]
        (ASP)→[PROG]
        [TRY -
            (A)→[EACH ONE x and y]
            (O)→[FORCE -
                (A)→[EACH ONE]
                (O)→[HAND:#other's x and y]
                (L)→[onto [TABLE:#]]
                (Mod)→[DOWN]]]

The performative is suggested by the concept [STMT]. The main verb is *try*, with the tense marked as *past* and the aspect as *progressive*. The case frame of the main verb is A,O. The subject (A) is *each one*, the object (O) is an infinitive complement. The infinitive *force* is a three-place A,O,L predicate meaning *move-something-to-a-place-by-force*. The PRO-subject (A) of the verb is *each one*, the object (O) is *the other's hand*, and the locative (L) is *down onto the table*. The goal locative *onto the table* is modified by the general directional locative *down*.

Preposition attachment. The default attachment for prepositional phrases is to the immediately preceding noun. When two prepositional phrases follow a noun, the second prepositional phrase by default is attached to the noun in the first prepositional phrase. In sentence (734), *on a chalk line on the table,* the phrase *on the table* modifies the noun *line.* However, this default attachment may be overruled by the semantics of the situation. In *the house on the hill with two baths,* our world knowledge tells us that *hills* do not have baths, but *houses* do. Therefore, the second prepositional phrase must modify *house* and not *hill.* The structure NP PP1 PP2 necessarily involves ambiguity. Although the first prepositional phrase (PP1) normally modifies the immediately preceding noun, the second prepositional phrase (PP2) may modify either the immediately preceding noun (which is the default attachment), or it may modify the head noun, as demanded by the semantics of the situation.

Anaphoric resolution. The scenario for sentences (733)–(735) is that of a hand-wrestling match, identified as *the hand game* in sentence (733). Our world knowledge of this game is that it is a contest between two individuals, a one-on-one competition. In sentence (733) the two contestants are identified as *the old man,* (marked x), and *the negro from*

Cienfuegos, (marked y). In sentence (734) *they* (marked x and y) refers to the two contestants as does the modifier *their* in *their elbows, their forearms,* and *their hands.* In sentence (735), the subject *each one* (marked x and y) refers to the two contestants as does the modifier *the other's* in the object phrase *the other's hand.* Thus, the referents of all the pronouns in sentences (734) and (735) are resolved when put in the context of our world knowledge of a hand-wrestling match.

6.19. Knowledge representation

Our knowledge, in its most visible form, is represented by our natural language. But knowledge representation in natural language processing refers to that representation that breaks down natural language into underlying logical units. The most basic elements of knowledge are represented in the predicate-argument structure that underlies the natural language proposition. Other elements include the tense, mode, and aspect that supplement the predicate-argument structure. This breakdown of natural language sentences into underlying logical elements is necessary if a computer is to be able to recognize and respond to natural language input.

The meaning of a sentence includes both its literal and its conveyed meaning. The performative, tense-aspect-mode, and underlying predicate-argument structure represent the literal meaning of the sentence. Conveyed meaning, however, depends upon world knowledge and indicates what the sentence means when given in a particular context. The focus in the current work has been on literal meaning, since literal meaning must be determined before conveyed meaning is determined by context.

Although the description of the tenses and aspects relies heavily on the work of Leech (1971) and Comrie (1976) for the meaning of various tenses and aspects, the representation of tense and aspect as they appear in logical structure has followed the work of the generative semanticists, such as Ross (1969), McCawley (1973), and Langacker (1975).

7
Verb Ontology

The Case Grammar matrix model was developed in chapter one, based upon the models described by Fillmore (1968, 1978), Chafe (1970), and Anderson (1971). This revised matrix model consists of twelve cells which represent twelve major verb classes. A verbal hierarchy was established by separating verbs into four semantic domains. The Basic domain was treated in chapter 2, the Experiential domain in chapter 3, the Benefactive domain in chapter 4, and the Locative domain in chapter 5. The modality elements, consisting of tense, aspect, and modal verbs, were considered in chapter 6. Within each domain verbs were hierarchized according to verb type, as State, Process, or Action verbs, producing three major verb classes within each of the four domains. Over 500 examples of verb classification in terms of Case Grammar and conceptual graphs were used to illustrate these verb classes.

The present chapter illustrates the organization of the lexicon by reviewing all the verb classes in each semantic domain along with the characteristics of each class and the subclasses which illustrate that class. This organization shows a set of syntactically relevant, semantically coherent classes (see Levin 1993:22) based on domain and verb type. The key notion in the establishment of a verbal hierarchy is the notion of verbal domain.

The domains are based upon the presence or absence of certain case roles in the case frames. The Basic domain is the default category which contains only Agents and Objects. The Experiential domain includes all verbs which require the Experiencer role and is the domain of sensation,

emotion, cognition, and communication. The Benefactive domain includes all verbs which require the Benefactive role and is the domain of
possession and transfer of property. The Locative domain includes all
verbs which require the Locative role and is the domain of physical location and motion.

Within each domain verbs are classified as State, Process, or Action
verbs, based upon their syntactic environments. State verbs express a
stative situation in which nothing is moving. They contain a stative Object in their case frame and never occur with the progressive or
imperative. Process verbs describe nonagentive events which are ongoing. Process verbs have a moving object but no Agent, and may occur
with the progressive but not the imperative. Action verbs describe agentive events in which some Agent is involved in some activity. They occur
with the progressive and the imperative. Finally, within each of the
twelve verb classes there are subclasses based upon the number of arguments required by the predicate, or the position of arguments within the
structure. Each verb class is defined according to its characteristic
features.

The analysis of the complete text of Ernest Hemingway's novel *The Old
Man and the Sea* yielded 5,028 clauses. Of these, 103 clauses had no verb
so the number of verb occurrences was 4,925. The percentages of occurrence of each of the 12 basic verb classes is given in (736). The few verbs
in the Time domain were grouped with the locatives for all percentages.

(736) Verb occurrences = 4,925

Verb type	Basic	Exp	Ben	Loc
4,925	1,833	1,380	301	1,411
100%	37%	28%	6%	29%
1 State	Os	E,Os	B,Os	Os,L
1,846	750	727	93	286
38%	15%	15%	2%	6%
2 Process	O	E,O	B,O	O,L
626	241	148	20	207
12%	5%	3%	0%	4%
3 Action	A,O	A,E,O	A,B,O	A,O,L
2,453	842	505	188	918
50%	17%	10%	4%	19%

After analysis, the 4,925 verb occurrences were reduced to 1,161 lexical entries. The percentage of lexical entries within each of the 12 basic verb classes is given in (737). In the Experiential domain, the high frequency of some of the Experiential verbs resulted in a low number of lexical entries. In the locative domain, the inclusion of all be + *locative* structures under a single lexical entry reduced the number of locative lexical entries. Although the frequency counts are valid for this novel, they represent only frequency within imaginative narrative prose, not necessarily other types of discourse.

(737) Lexical entries = 1,161

Verb type	Basic	Exp	Ben	Loc
1,161	540	198	72	351
100%	46%	19%	6%	30%
1 State	Os	E,Os	B,Os	Os,L
368	206	98	14	50
32%	18%	9%	1%	4%
2 Process	O	E,O	B,O	O,L
217	96	42	6	73
18%	8%	4%	0%	6%
3 Action	A,O	A,E,O	A,B,O	A,O,L
576	238	58	52	228
50%	20%	5%	5%	20%

7.1–7.3 The Basic domain

The Basic domain includes all those verbs which by their meaning require only Agents and Objects. (See (89) in chapter 2.) The relative frequency of occurrence in the Hemingway novel was 366/1000 or 37%.

7.1. Class 1: Basic State

Basic State verbs have two subclasses. The first class is intransitive and requires only one argument, the second class is transitive and requires two arguments. Within each subclass there are both adjectival and verbal predicates. The relative frequency of occurrence was 150/1000 or 15%.

Class 1a: The Os frame. Basic States with single Os include most predicate adjectives, but exclude Action adjectives and Experiential adjectives. Basic States with single Os also include a few intransitive verbs. The semantic structure of the Os frame is represented by the following conceptual graph.

(738) | ENTITY | ← (Os) ← | STATE-VERB |

(739) English verb types with Os frames (see §2.1 for examples):

Descriptive adjectives	*be tall, be heavy*
Weather adjectives	*be hot(w), be windy(w)*
Epistemic adjectives	*be true, be certain to*
Apparent passives	*be broken, be patched*
Existence verbs	*be (=exist), exist*
Raising verbs	*tend, happen*

Class 1a verbs are one-place intransitive States. As State verbs they represent a static situation in which nothing is moving. Their single argument is an Object marked for stativity. State is a universal semantic category. All languages have descriptive techniques which describe a static state of affairs. This semantic category is distinct from the syntactic categories used to express stativity in various languages. In English, state verbs allow neither the progressive nor the imperative as their syntactic context. In addition, many languages do not use the copula *be*. Sentences such as *the man is tall* are simply translated *man tall*. The case frame Os is listed with the adjective predicate in the lexicon. All of the verb types used to illustrate the Os case frame in English do not necessarily apply to all languages.

Class 1b: The Os,Os frame. Basic States with double Os include all predicate noun structures, adjectives that institute a comparison between two objects, and a few transitive verbs. The semantic structure of the Os,Os frame is represented by the following conceptual graph.

(740) | ENTITY | ← (Os) ← | STATE-VERB | → (Os) → | ENTITY |

(741) English verb types with Os,Os frames (see §2.4 for examples):

Predicate nouns   *be* + noun
Comparative adjectives   *be like, be better than, be equal to*
Transitive verbs   *cost, mean, weigh*

Class 1b verbs are two-place transitive States. As State verbs they represent a static situation in which nothing is moving. These predicates require two Objects marked for stativity. The two-place State verb occurs in most languages with the use of predicate nouns. Sentences such as *the man is a teacher* are translated *man teacher.* Predicate noun constructions in these languages cause a problem, since there is no verbal element to which the case frame can be assigned. One solution to this problem is to assign the case frame Os,Os to the N-N structure (see also State Locatives).

7.2. Class 2: Basic Process

Basic Process verbs have two subclasses. The first class is intransitive and requires only one Object argument; the second class is transitive and requires two Object arguments (see §§2.3–2.4 for explanation). The relative frequency of occurrence was 48/1000 or 5%.

Class 2a: The O frame. Basic Process with single O include occurrence verbs, involuntary animate process, inanimate process, and the intransitive forms of inceptive, durative, and terminative aspectual verbs. It also includes inchoatives derived from States, middle verbs derived from Actions, and *become* + *adjective* structures. The semantic structure of the O frame is represented by the following conceptual graph.

(742) | ENTITY | ← (O) ← | PROCESS-VERB |

(743) English verb types with O frames (see §2.3 for examples):

Occurrence verbs   *be (=occur), occur, happen*
Animate process verbs   *cough, die, sleep*
Inanimate process verbs   *break,iv, cook,iv, grow,iv*
Haunted house verbs   *creak, howl, slam*
Aspectual verbs, intransitive   *begin,iv, keep,iv, stop,iv*
Inchoative verbs   *widen,iv, thicken,iv*
Middle verbs   *cut,iv, polish,iv, wash,iv*
Become + adjective structure   *become, get, turn*

Class 2a verbs are one-place intransitive Process. Their single argument is an Object unmarked for stativity. As Process they represent either a nonagentive event in which there is movement, or a static situation which lasts through time. Most languages can represent nonagentive events. But in English Process verbs are distinguished by the fact that they occur in syntactic context with the progressive, but not the imperative. Most languages will not have all the verb types that occur in English.

Class 2b: The O,O frame. Basic Process with double Objects include predicate noun structures with the verbs *become, get,* and *turn.* Also included in this class are a few predicates with an embedded clause as subject which is the cause of the Process. The semantic structure of the O,O frame is represented by the following conceptual graph.

(744) | ENTITY | ← (O) ← | PROCESS-VERB | → (O) → | ENTITY |

(745) English verb types with O,O frames (see §2.4 for examples):

Become + noun structure	*become, turn into*
Causative predicates	*cause, make*

Class 2b verbs are two-place transitive Process verbs. They are distinguished by two Object arguments unmarked for stativity. As Process verbs they represent a nonagentive event. In English, these two-place Process verbs allow the progressive but not the imperative. This class is relatively rare. Many languages have the ability to represent expressions such as *man become teacher,* probably with some equivalent of the verb *become.*

7.3. Class 3: Basic Action

Basic Action verbs require both an Agent and an Object. These include Action verbs with A=O coreference, Action verbs with O-lexicalized, verbs with Agent and Object overt, and Action verbs with double Object (see §§2.5–2.9 for explanation). This is one of the most frequently occurring classes in English, and probably in other languages as well. The relative frequency of occurrence was 168/1000 or 17%.

Class 3a: The A,*O /A=O frame. Basic Actions with A=O coreference are States or Processes which undergo agentive reinterpretation (see

§2.1 for agentive reinterpretation). They include State adjectives used as Actions, and Process verbs with a voluntary Agent as subject. The semantic structure of the A,*O /A=O frame is represented by the following conceptual graph.

(746)

```
┌─────────────────────────────────────────────────────┐
│ ┌────────┐      ┌─────┐        ┌──────────────┐     │
│ │ PERSON │  ←   │ A=O │   ←    │ ACTION-VERB  │     │
│ └────────┘      └─────┘        └──────────────┘     │
└─────────────────────────────────────────────────────┘
```

(747) English verb types with A,*O /A=O frames (see §2.5 for examples):

Action adjectives	*be kind (+agt), be polite (+agt)*
Animate process	*cough (+agt), sneeze (+agt)*

Class 3a verbs are one-place intransitive Action verbs. As Actions they represent an agentive event. The subject is simultaneously the Object affected and the Agent directing the activity. In English they allow both the progressive and the imperative. Most languages will contain verbs that are sometimes interpreted agentively and sometimes nonagentively.

Class 3b: The A,*O /O-lex frame. Actions with the Object lexicalized include intransitive predicates, interpreted as *do* verbs with a nominal object corresponding to the activity. Motion verbs which are interpreted as activities rather than movement verbs belong to this class. The verb *walk* in *walk to the store* means *go-by-walking,* but in *walk a mile* it expresses an activity. The semantic structure of the A,*O /O-lex frame is represented by the following conceptual graph.

(748)

```
┌─────────────────────────────────────────────────────┐
│ ┌────────┐      ┌───┐        ┌──────────────────┐   │
│ │ PERSON │  ←   │ A │   ←    │ ACTION-VERB /O-lex│  │
│ └────────┘      └───┘        └──────────────────┘   │
└─────────────────────────────────────────────────────┘
```

(749) English verb types with A,*O /O-lex frames (see §2.6 for examples):

Lexicalized Object verbs	*fish, gamble, work*
Motion verbs, as activities	*drive, ride, walk*

Class 3b verbs are one-place intransitive action verbs. As Actions they represent an agentive situation, but the activity itself is lexicalized into the verb. In English, they allow both the progressive and the imperative. Some languages have parallel expressions with the verb *do,* such as *do work* for the verb *work.*

Class 3c: The A,O frame. Basic Actions with both roles overt include a few transitive action adjectives, and many transitive verbs, including deletable object verbs, transitive verbs with overt objects, transitive aspectual verbs, and causative verbs with a Process complement. Verbs in the hammer-flat structure are interpreted as cause-by-hammering, with the means used incorporated in the verb. There are Action verbs derived from States, and Action verbs derived from Process. The chart in (139), chapter 2, illustrates transitive and intransitive forms of the inceptive, durative, and terminative aspectuals. The semantic structure of the A,O frame is represented by the following conceptual graph.

(750)

(751) English verb types with A,O frames (see §2.7 for examples):

Action adjectives, transitive	*be careful with*
Deletable object verbs	*eat, shave*
Transitive verbs	*kill, read, write*
Aspectual verbs, transitive	*begin,tv, keep,tv, stop,tv*
Causative + Process	*let (happen), make (happen)*
Hammer-flat structure	*hammer, sweep*
Action derived from State	*widen,tv, thicken,tv*
Action derived from Process	*break,tv, cook,tv, grow,tv*
Causative + Action	*have (=cause)*

Class 3c verbs are two-place transitive Action verbs. As Actions they represent an agentive situation. As transitive verbs, they are capable of taking an object, even though the object may at times be deleted. As two-place predicates they are different from the one-place intransitive Action predicates. In English they allow both the progressive and the imperative. This verb type is one of the most frequently occurring types.

Class 3d: The A,O,O frame. Basic Actions with double Object include verbs with an Agent subject and a double object. In the passive they become two-place stative predicates. The semantic structure of the A,O,O frame is represented by the following conceptual graph.

(752) PERSON ← (A) ← ACT → (O) → ENTITY

↓

(O)

↓

ENTITY

(753) English verb types with the A,O,O frame (see §2.8 for examples):

Double object verbs   *call, elect, name*

Class 3d verbs are three-place transitive Action verbs. As Actions they represent an agentive situation and are identified by their double Object. In English they allow both the progressive and the imperative.

7.4–7.6 The Experiential Domain

The Experiential domain includes all those verbs which require an Experiencer as part of their meaning. These include verbs of sensation, emotion, cognition, and communication. (See (208) in chapter 3.) The relative frequency of occurrence in the novel was 276/1000 or 28%.

7.4. Class 4: State Experiential

State Experiential verbs are two-place State predicates which require an Experiencer and a stative Object. There are two subtypes, one with the Experiencer role as subject and one with the Object role as subject (see §§3.1–3.3 for explanation). The relative frequency was 145/1000 or 15%.

Class 4a: The E,Os frame. State Experientials with E-subject include adjectives and verbs denoting sensation, emotion, and cognition. The subject Experiencer is often coreferential with the Object when the predicate is an adjective. These adjective predicates are listed as E,Os /E=O in the lexicon. The chart in (213) of chapter 3 illustrates verbs representing the five senses of sight, hearing, smell, taste, and touch with O-subject, E-subject, and A-subject as they are expressed in English. Although most languages will have verbs with E-subject or with A-subject, the special structure in English of sense verbs with O-subject are not common to other languages. The semantic structure of the E,Os frame is represented by the following conceptual graph.

(754) | PERSON | ← (E) ← | EXP-VERB | → (Os) → | ENTITY |

(755) English verb types with E,Os frames (see §3.1 for examples):

Sensation adjectives	*be (=feel) cold, be hungry,*
Sensation verbs	*hear, see, smell, taste*
Emotive adjectives	*be fond of, be afraid of*
Emotive verbs	*desire, like, want*
Cognitive adjectives	*be aware of, be sure that*
Cognitive verbs	*know, forget, think*
Psych movement adjectives	*be bored with, be interested in*
Impression verbs	*consider, regard*
Experiential have	*have (=experience)*

Class 4a verbs are two-place State Experiential verbs. As State verbs they represent a stative situation. As Experiential verbs they deal with sensation, emotion, and cognition. The direct object is the content of the experience. In English they take neither the progressive nor the imperative.

Class 4b: The Os,E frame. State Experientials with Os-subject include adjectives and verbs with the Experiencer either expressed or implied as indirect object. The adjectives include emotive adjectives, psych movement adjectives, and tough movement adjectives. The verbs include sensation verbs, cognitive verbs, and impression verbs with Experiencer as object. The diagram in (280) illustrates subject-raising. The semantic structure of the Os,E frame is represented by the following conceptual graph.

(756) | ENTITY | ← (Os) ← | EXP-VERB | → (E) → | PERSON |

(757) Verb types with Os,E frames (see §3.2 for examples):

Sensation verbs, with adjective	*look, smell, sound, taste*
Emotive adjectives	*be comfortable, be pleasant*
Psych movement adjectives	*be boring to, be interesting to*
Tough movement adjectives	*be easy for, be difficult for*
Cognitive verbs	*appear, seem*
Impression verbs	*strike, impress*

Class 4b verbs are two-place transitive State Experiential verbs but with the stimulus as subject and the Experiencer as direct or indirect object. In English they take neither the progressive nor the imperative.

7.5. Class 5: Process Experiential

Process Experientials are two-place predicates which require an Object and an Experiencer with either the Experiencer or the Object as subject (see §§3.4–3.5 for explanation). Relative frequency was 29/1000 or 3%.

Class 5a: The E,O frame. Process Experientials with E-subject include a few emotive verbs and a few cognitive verbs which are nonagentive, such as *learn = inadvertently come to learn,* and *understand = come to understand* as in *I am understanding more each day.* The semantic structure of the E,O frame is represented by the following conceptual graph.

(758) PERSON ← (E) ← EXP-VERB → (O) → ENTITY

(759) English verb types with E,O frames (see §3.4 for examples):

Emotive verbs	*enjoy, feel, hope*
Cognitive verbs	*learn (-agt), understand*

Class 5a verbs are two-place transitive Process verbs with the Experiencer as subject and the content of the experience as object. In English they take the progressive but not the imperative.

Class 5b: The O,E frame. Process Experientials with O-subject are made up of the psych movement verbs. Forty psych movement verbs are listed in (307) with two adjectival derivatives with both E-subject and O-subject. It is improbable that this type of adjectival derivative will occur in other languages. The semantic structure of the O,E frame is represented by the following conceptual graph.

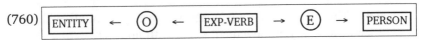
(760) ENTITY ← (O) ← EXP-VERB → (E) → PERSON

(761) English verb types with O,E frames (see §3.5 for examples):

Psych movement verbs   *annoy, bore, interest*

Class 5b verbs are two-place transitive Process verbs with the Object stimulus as subject and the Experiencer as direct object. As Process verbs they take the progressive but not the imperative in English.

7.6. Class 6: Action Experiential

Action Experiential verbs require an Agent, an Experiencer, and an Object. The Agent may be coreferential with the Experiencer or the Object, or the Object may be lexicalized into the verb (see §§3.6–3.9 for explanation). The relative frequency was 101/1000 or 10%.

Class 6a: The A,*E,O /A=E frame. Action Experientials with A=E coreference consist of Action verbs derived from State or Process verbs with Experiencer as subject. These include active sense verbs. It also includes cognitive verbs used in their active intentional sense. The semantic structure of the A,*E,O /A=E frame is represented by the following conceptual graph.

(762)

| PERSON | ← | (A=E) | ← | EXP-VERB | → | (O) | → | ENTITY |

(763) English verb types with A,*E,O /A=E frames (see §3.6 for examples):

Sensation verbs, active form   *listen to, look at*
Sensation verbs, as actions   *feel (+agt), smell (+agt)*
Cognitive verbs, as actions   *forget (+agt), think of (+agt)*

Class 6a verbs are two-place transitive Action verbs in which the subject of the verb is simultaneously an Agent and an Experiencer. As Actions they allow both the progressive and imperative in English. As Experiential verbs they deal with active sensation, emotion, and cognition.

Class 6b: The A,E,*O /A=O frame. Action Experientials with A=O coreference include psych movement verbs with an Agent acting deliberately. The subject is both Agent and stimulus and the Experiencer is the direct object. The semantic structure of the A,E,*O /A=O frame is represented by the following conceptual graph.

(764)

$$\boxed{\text{PERSON}} \leftarrow \overbrace{(A=O)} \leftarrow \boxed{\text{EXP-VERB}} \rightarrow (E) \rightarrow \boxed{\text{PERSON}}$$

(765) English verb types with A,E,*O /A=O frames (see §3.7 for examples):

Psych movement verbs, active   *annoy (+agt), interest (+agt)*

Class 6b verbs are two-place transitive Action verbs in which the subject of the verb is simultaneously an Agent and an Object, and the Experiencer is direct object. The subject is an Agent stimulus acting intentionally and the direct object is the Experiencer. In English these verbs allow both the progressive and the imperative.

Class 6c: The A,E,*O /O-lex frame. Action Experientials with Object lexicalized include verbs of communication derived from a noun with the Object of communication lexicalized into the verb. This type of Object lexicalization probably is language specific. The semantic structure of the A,E,*O /O-lex frame is represented by the following conceptual graph.

(766)

$$\boxed{\text{PERSON}} \leftarrow (A) \leftarrow \boxed{\text{VERB /O-lex}} \rightarrow (E) \rightarrow \boxed{\text{PERSON}}$$

(767) English verb types with A,E,*O /O-lex frames (see §3.8 for examples):

Communication verbs, O-lex   *answer, praise, thank*

Class 6c verbs are two-place transitive Action verbs with Agent as subject, Experiencer as object, and the Object noun lexicalized into the verb. As Action verbs they take the progressive and the imperative in English. These two-place surface predicates may become three-place surface predicates when the lexicalized noun is overtly expressed.

Class 6d: The A,E,O frame. Action Experientials with all roles overt include all verbs of communication with an overt Experiencer and Object, either or both of which may be deletable. These verbs require an Agent speaker, an Experiencer hearer, and the Object, what is said. This subclass also includes a few causatives. The semantic structure of the A,E,O frame is represented by the following conceptual graph.

(768) $\boxed{\text{PERSON}}$ ← (A) ← $\boxed{\text{VERB}}$ → (E) → $\boxed{\text{PERSON}}$

↓

(O)

↓

$\boxed{\text{ENTITY}}$

(769) English verb types with A,E,O frames (see §3.9 for examples):

Communication verbs	*say, speak, tell*
Causatives	*teach, show*

Class 6d verbs are three-place ditransitive Action verbs. In English they take the progressive and the imperative. The focus of the verbs of communication, such as *say, tell,* and *speak* depends upon the order and deletability of their Object and Experiential arguments.

7.7–7.9 The Benefactive domain

The Benefactive domain includes all those verbs which require a Benefactive as part of their meaning. (See (344) in chapter 4.) The frequency of occurrence in the Hemingway novel was 60/1000 or 6%.

7.7. Class 7: State Benefactive

State Benefactive verbs are two-place predicates which require a stative Object and a Benefactive. Either the Benefactive or Object may be subject (see §§4.1–4.2 for explanation). Relative frequency was 2/1000 or 2%.

Class 7a: The B,Os frame. State Benefactives with B-subject include positive verbs of possession as well as negative verbs indicating lack of possession. With both positive and negative verbs the Benefactive is subject. The semantic structure of the B,Os frame is represented by the following conceptual graph.

(770) $\boxed{\text{PERSON}}$ ← (B) ← $\boxed{\text{BEN-VERB}}$ → (Os) → $\boxed{\text{ENTITY}}$

(771) English verb types with B,Os frames (see §4.1 for examples):

    Possession verbs, positive   *have, own, possess*
    Possession verbs, negative   *lack, need, require*

    Class 7a verbs are two-place State Benefactive verbs. As States they represent a stative situation. The possessor is subject and the object possessed is object. Most languages will have the means to express possession, or lack of it, as a State Benefactive expression. In English these verbs may take neither the progressive nor the imperative.

    Class 7b: The Os,B frame. State Benefactives with Os-subject include positive verbs of possession. It also includes negative verbs of possession. In both cases the subject is the Object, not the Benefactive. The semantic structure of the Os,B frame is represented by the following conceptual graph.

(772) 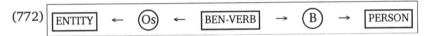

(773) English verb types with Os,B frames (see §4.2 for examples):

    Possession verbs, positive   *belong to, be + possessor*
    Possession verbs, negative   *be bad for, be necessary for*

    Class 7b verbs are two-place State Benefactive verbs. As State verbs they represent a stative situation. The possessor is the object. In English these verbs take neither progressive nor imperative.

7.8. Class 8: Process Benefactive

    Process Benefactive verbs are two-place predicates which require an Object and a Benefactive. Either the Benefactive or the Object may be subject (see §§4.3–4.4 for explanation). Their relative frequency is negligible, including only 4/1000 occurrences.

    Class 8a: The B,O frame. Process Benefactives with B-subject include verbs of nonagentive acquisition or loss of property. The Benefactive is subject and the Object is direct object. The semantic structure of the B,O frame is represented by the following conceptual graph.

(774) | PERSON | ← (B) ← | BEN-VERB | → (O) → | ENTITY |

(775) English verb types with B,O frames (see §4.3 for examples):

Acquisition, nonagentive	*find (−agt), receive (−agt)*
Acquisition, negative	*lose (−agt)*

Class 8a verbs are two-place Process Benefactive verbs. As Process verbs they represent a moving event. The subject is the person unintentionally acquiring or losing possession of an object. In English they take the progressive but not the imperative.

Class 8b: The O,B frame. Process Benefactives with O-subject include verbs of nonagentive acquisition or loss of property in which the object mentioned is the subject. The semantic structure of the O,B frame is represented by the following conceptual graph.

(776) | ENTITY | ← (O) ← | BEN-VERB | → (B) → | PERSON |

(777) English verb types with O,B frames (see §4.4 for examples):

Acquisition, nonagentive	*benefit, become + possessor*
Acquisition structure	*do good for*

Class 8b verbs are two-place Process Benefactive verbs. As Process verbs they represent a moving event. The object acquired or lost is subject. In English they take the progressive but not the imperative.

7.9. Class 9: Action Benefactive

Action Benefactive verbs are three-place predicates which require an Agent, Benefactive, and Object. The Agent may be coreferential with Benefactive, or the Object may be lexicalized into the verb (see §§4.5–4.7 for explanation). Relative frequency was 38/1000 or 4%.

Class 9a: The A,*B,O /A=B frame. Action Benefactives with A=B coreference include active acquisition verbs derived from Process verbs which may reflect positive or negative acquisition. The class also includes verbs of acquisition for self. There is a semantic distinction between *find accidentally* (nonagentive) and *search for and find* (Agentive). This distinction is probably found in other languages. The semantic structure of the A,*B,O /A=B frame is represented by the following conceptual graph.

(778) | PERSON | ← (A=B) ← | BEN-VERB | → (O) → | ENTITY |

(779) English verb types with A,*B,O /A=B frames (see §4.5 for examples):

Acquisition, agentive	find (+agt), receive (+agt)
Acquisition, negative	lose (+agt)
Self-acquisition	catch, earn, make (=earn)

Class 9a verbs are two-place Action Benefactive verbs. As Action verbs they represent an agentive event. The subject is both Agent and Benefactive. In English they take the progressive and the imperative.

Class 9b: The A,B,*O /O-lex frame. Action Benefactives with Object lexicalized include Action Benefactive verbs which incorporate the Object into the verb. This type of Object lexicalization is language specific. These verbs have an Agent subject and a Benefactive object. The semantic structure of the A,B,*O /O-lex frame is represented by the following conceptual graph.

(780) | PERSON | ← (A) ← | VERB /O-lex | → (B) → | PERSON |

(781) English verb types with A,B,*O /O-lex frames (see §4.6 for examples):

Acquisition, O-lexicalized   bribe, feed, help

Class 9b verbs are two-place Action Benefactive verbs. As Action verbs they represent an agentive event. The Object noun is lexicalized into the verb. The Benefactive noun becomes the direct object. In English they take both progressive and imperative.

Class 9c: The A,B,O frame. Action Benefactives with all roles overt include a wide range of verbs of change of possession which may be positive or negative. In English, some verbs of this class allow an A,O,B order with the Benefactive as the direct object and the Object in a prepositional phrase. The semantic structure of the A,B,O frame is represented in the following conceptual graph.

(782)

(783) English verb types with A,B,O frames (see §4.7 for examples):

Acquisition, positive   *beg, buy, get, steal*
Acquisition, negative   *give, sell*
Causative + Action   *let (do), make (do)*
With reversible roles   *blame, rob*

Class 9c verbs are three-place Action Benefactive verbs. As Action verbs they represent an agentive mobile situation and take both progressive and imperative. They require an Agent subject, a Benefactive as the second party in the transaction, and the Object which is transferred.

7.10–7.12 The Locative domain

The Locative domain includes all those verbs which require a Locative role as part of their meaning. The frequency of occurrence was 282/1000 occurrences or 28%.

7.10. Class 10: State Locative

State Locative verbs are two-place predicates which require a stative Object and a Location. Either the Object or the Locative may be subject (see §§5.1–5.2 for explanation). Their relative frequency was 57/1000 or 6%.

Class 10a: The Os,L frame. State Locatives with Os-subject include all be + locative structures, apparent passives, position verbs, proper extension verbs, verbs of motion used as verbs of extension, as well as habitation verbs. Many languages do not allow position verbs such as *lie,* *sit,* and *stand* to occur with inanimate subjects. Also, the use of motion verbs to express extension seems to be a unique property of English. In English State Locative predications are listed as *be + Locative* in the lexicon, with the Locative position filled by any Locative adverbial. In languages which do not use the copula *be* in their State Locative predications, stative location is expressed by the juxtaposition of subject nominal and locative phrase. There is no verb, so the case frame must be assigned to the Noun-Locative structure. The semantic structure of the Os,L frame is represented by the following conceptual graph.

(784) | ENTITY $\leftarrow$ (Os) $\leftarrow$ LOC-VERB $\rightarrow$ (L) $\rightarrow$ PLACE |

(785) English verb types with Os,L frames (see §4.1 for examples):

be + locative phrase	*be (=be located)*
Apparent passives	*be anchored, be situated*
Position verbs	*lie, sit, stand*
Extension verbs, proper	*extend, stretch, surround*
Extension verbs, motion	*come, go, rise, run*
Habitation verbs	*live, inhabit*

Class 10a verbs are two-place State Locative verbs. As State verbs they represent a stative situation. The Object located is the subject and the Location is generally contained in a stative locative phrase. In English they take neither the progressive nor the imperative.

Class 10b: The L,Os frame. State Locatives with L-subject are a flip version of class 10a. This class is distinguished by its Location subject. With some verbs in English, either the Location or the Object may be subject. These reversible role verbs may not occur in other languages. The semantic structure of the L,Os frame is represented by the following conceptual graph.

(786) | PLACE $\leftarrow$ (L) $\leftarrow$ LOC-VERB $\rightarrow$ (Os) $\rightarrow$ ENTITY |

(787) English verb types with L,Os frames (see §4.2 for examples):

Locative have	*have (= have located)*
Locative subject	*contain, hold, seat*
With reversible roles	*abound, be strewn*

Class 10b verbs are two-place State Locative verbs. They represent a stative situation. The subject is a Location and the Object located is post-verbal. In English they take neither progressive nor imperative.

7.11. Class 11: Process Locatives

Process Locative verbs are two-place predicates which require an Object and a Locative. Object or Locative may be subject (see §§5.3–5.4 for explanation). Relative frequency was 41/1000 or 4%.

Class 11a: The O,L frame. Process Locatives with O-subject consist of motion verbs with inanimate or nonagentive animate subjects. The moving Object is the subject and the Locative phrase follows the verb. Motion verbs with inanimate subjects are common to most languages. The degree to which the manner of motion or the direction of the motion are incorporated into the movement verb depends upon the language described. The semantic structure of the O,L frame is represented by the following conceptual graph.

(788)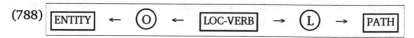

(789) English verb types with O,L frames (see §5.3 for examples):

Motion, nonagentive	*come, go, move*
Motion, with direction	*dip, fall, lift*
Motion, with manner	*drift, float, race*
With lexicalized prepositions	*enter, rise, sink*

Class 11a verbs are two-place Process Locative verbs. As Process verbs they represent a nonagentive event. The moving Object is the subject, and the Locative indicates the source, goal, or path of the motion. In English they take the progressive but not the imperative.

Class 11b: The L,O frame. Process Locatives with L-subject in English consist largely of verbs of liquid motion. Most of these verbs have reversible roles and may occur with either the Locative or the Object as subject. Although most languages will have verbs to express liquid motion, they may occur with a Locative subject, or with the liquid subject, but probably not with the reversible role character of the English verbs. The semantic structure of the L,O frame is represented by the following conceptual graph.

(790) | PATH ← (L) ← LOC-VERB → (O) → ENTITY |

(791) English verb types with L,O frames (see §5.4 for examples):

    Liquid verbs   *bleed, drip, leak, run*

Class 11b verbs are two-place Process Locative verbs. As Process verbs they represent a nonagentive event. The Location is subject but many of these verbs also occur with the Object as subject. In English they take the progressive but not the imperative.

7.12. Class 12: Action Locative

Action Locative verbs are three-place predicates which require an Agent, an Object, and a location. They occur with A=O or A=L coreference. Either Object or Locative may be lexicalized into the verb (see §§5.5–5.10 for explanation). Relative frequency is 184/1000 or 18%.

Class 12a: The A,*O,L /A=O frame. Action Locatives which have A=O coreference consist of self-movement verbs in which the subject is both Agent and moving Object and active position verbs when they occur with agentive animate subjects. Self-movement verbs are common to most languages. All languages will have common verbs similar to *come, go,* and *move.* This type is one of the most productive language types. The semantic structure of the A,*O,L /A=O frame is represented by the following conceptual graph.

(792) | PERSON ← (A=O) ← LOC-VERB → (L) → PATH |

(793) English verb types with A,O,L /A=O frames (see §5.5 for examples):

    Self-movement verbs   *come, go, move, roll*
    Active position verbs   *lie, sit, stand*

Class 12a verbs are two-place Action Locative verbs. As Action verbs they represent an agentive event. The accompanying Locative is directional. In English they take both the progressive and imperative. In other languages, position verbs occur only in their active sense and do not occur with inanimate subjects.

Class 12b: The A,O,*L /A=L frame. Action Locatives in English with A=L coreference consist of a very limited number of verbs in which the subject may be both Agent and Locative. These verbs are an agentive reinterpretation of Stative locatives with L-subject. These verbs are rare in English and probably nonexistent in most languages. The semantic structure of the A,O,*L /A=L frame is represented by the following conceptual graph.

(794) | PERSON | ← (A=L) ← | LOC-VERB | → (O) → | ENTITY |

(795) English verb types with A,O,*L /A=L frames (see §5.6 for examples):

Locative Agent   *contain, surround*

Class 12b verbs are two-place Action Locative verbs. As Action verbs they represent an agentive event. The subject is both Agent and Location. In English they take both the progressive and imperative.

Class 12c: The A,*O,L /O-lex frame. Action Locatives with Object lexicalized include *put-on* verbs which have the meaning of putting an object on or in a location and *take-off* verbs which have the meaning of removing an object from a location. The object noun may be forced to appear in the surface structure if the noun is modified. Object lexicalization is language specific. The semantic structure of the A,*O,L /O-lex frame is represented by the following conceptual graph.

(796) | PERSON | ← (A) ← | VERB /O-lex | → (L) → | PLACE |

(797) English verb types with A,*O,L /O-lex frames (see §5.7 for examples):

Put-on verbs   *butter, powder, water*
Take-off verbs   *core, peel, skin*

Class 12c verbs are two-place transitive Action verbs with an Agent as subject, a Locative as direct object, and with an Object noun which is lexicalized into the verb. As Action verbs, they represent an agentive event. In English they take both the progressive and the imperative.

Class 12d: The A,O,*L /L-lex frame. Action Locatives with Locative lexicalized include verbs which incorporate the container noun into the verb. The object located may be inanimate or the object located may be animate. The Locative container may be forced to the surface if the container noun is modified. Locative lexicalization is language specific. The semantic structure of the A,O,*L /L-lex frame is represented by the following conceptual graph.

(798) PERSON ← (A) ← VERB /L-lex → (O) → ENTITY

(799) English verb types with A,O,*L /L-lex frames (see §5.8 for examples):

Container, for inanimates	*bottle, file, pocket*
Container, for animates	*cage, imprison, jail*

Class 12d verbs are two-place transitive Action verbs with Agent as subject, Object as direct object, but with the Locative noun lexicalized into the verb. As Action verbs, they represent an agentive event. In English they take both the progressive and the imperative.

Class 12e: The A,O,L frame. Action Locatives with all roles overt include all move-object verbs and require an Agent, an Object that is moved, and a Locative expressing Source, Goal, or Path of the motion. This class also includes placement verbs, transitive position verbs, and attachment verbs. Special verbs in this class are the Locative alternation verbs in English which occur with either the Object or the Locative as direct object of the verb. The verb *fill* has no A,O,L alternate; the verb *pour* has no A,L,O alternate. This type of alternation is not common to all languages. The semantic structure of the A,O,L frame is represented by the following conceptual graph.

(800) [PERSON] ← (A) ← [VERB] → (O) → [ENTITY]

↓

(L)

↓

[PLACE]

(801) English verb types with A,O,L frames (see §5.9 for examples):

Move-object verbs	*bring, carry, take*
Move-object, with direction	*lift, pass, turn*
Move-object, with manner	*pull, shift, throw*
Placement verbs	*place, put, situate*
Position verbs, transitive	*set, lay, stand*
Attachment verbs	*fasten, free, tie*
Locative alternation verbs	*load, spray, stuff*

Class 12e verbs are three-place transitive Action verbs with Agent, a moving Object, and a Location. As Action verbs, they represent an agentive event. The Agent is subject, and either Object or Locative is the direct object. In English they take both the progressive and the imperative.

7.13. Conclusion

This work began with the assumption that the Case Grammar model, as suggested by Fillmore, provided a model of semantic analysis that would be useful in both the analysis of text and the development of an extensive verb ontology in the lexicon.

Text analysis. The unit of information is the clause, reduced to a kernel sentence, not the word, not the phrase. It is only when something is predicated of a subject that information is conveyed. Underlying the clause, or simple kernel sentence, is a proposition. This proposition is defined in terms of predicate-argument structure, in which the arguments are required by the meaning of the predicate. Case Grammar adds labels to the arguments required by the predicate, labels that are useful in distinguishing different types of verbs, and consequently form the basis for a credible verb ontology. Verbs are classified according to case frames, which may be conveniently written as conceptual graphs as suggested by

John Sowa (1984). Text analysis of the Hemingway novel yielded 4,925 basic propositions.

The lexicon. The verbs found in the text are assigned case frames and listed in the lexicon. But the order is not haphazard. Verbs are first hierarchically sorted according to domain, as Basic, Experiential, Benefactive, or Locative. Within each domain verbs are sorted according to verb type as State, Process, or Action. Within each verb type there are subtypes based upon the number or the position of the arguments. The hierarchical order is similar to a thesaurus, in which verbs are collected into semantic domains. The lexicon constructed for the Hemingway novel indicated that in narrative prose style roughly 25% of the verbs belonged to the physical location domain, 25% belonged to the Experiential domain, 10% to the Benefactive domain, and 40% to the Basic domain.

Cautions. In using the Case Grammar model, several cautions must be observed regarding the list of cases, the distinction between essential and nonessential cases, and the use of covert roles. To be effective, the list of cases must be well-defined and used consistently throughout the text analysis. In the analysis of the Hemingway novel only five cases were used: Agent, Experiencer, Benefactive, Object, and Locative. Occasionally a Time case was required. There must be a clear distinction between essential cases, which are required by the meaning of the verb, and modal cases, which are mainly adverbial adjuncts. Only essential cases are used for verb description, modal cases are named in text analysis, but not used in verb description. Finally, there is a difference between the cases required by the verb and the cases that appear in surface structure. Sometimes all the required cases appear with the verb, at other times there are cases missing from surface structure, due to deletion, deep coreference, or lexicalization of one of the cases into the verb.

Verb sense. It is obvious from even a casual perusal of a standard dictionary that verbs have many senses. In the Case Grammar analysis each sense of each verb is treated as a separate item, with its own case frame and often with its own recognizable syntactic features. There is much work still to be done on verb sense discrimination, which can be supplied with the use of a dictionary, thesaurus, and text searches for the verb's meaning in particular contexts. The dictionary will list all the meanings, but not in any organized way. The thesaurus will list the meanings according to semantic domains, providing an initial verbal hierarchy, and text searches will reveal the frequency of these various meanings in context. The meanings can then be organized according to case frames, along with the syntactic environment in which they occur, and the frequency of occurrence of each verb sense.

Natural language processing. Leading computational linguists, such as Terry Winograd (1983), John Sowa (1984) and James Allen (1987) have recommended some form of Case Grammar as useful for natural language processing. Although most computational linguists recognize the value of predicate-argument structure, many shy away from labelled structures because they cannot agree on a basic list of cases. Without the case labelling all verbs with logical subject and logical object look the same, and there is no verbal hierarchy with its clear divisions into verbal domain and verb type. While lists of cases may differ in number or kind, the analysis is only fruitful when one set of cases is extensively applied to text analysis. Within the twelve cells of the Case Grammar Matrix Model and the various subtypes within each cell, all the verbs of the English language should be accommodated. If the verbs in a computational lexicon are arranged according to this verbal hierarchy, each individual verb in each of its several senses would be listed along with its obvious relationship to other verbs in the lexicon. This organization should go a long way towards developing a system for natural language understanding.

Case Grammar cannot be expected to solve all the problems of natural language processing, but it can provide, along with supplemental information on tense, aspect, and modality, a solid semantic base for further investigation. It can provide clear predicate-argument structures and a well-organized verb ontology. It cannot solve pragmatic problems of meaning in context, or discourse analysis problems dealing with world knowledge. But in the linguistic hierarchy of phonology, morphology, syntax, semantics, pragmatics, and discourse, Case Grammar seems to be the most useful tool for analysis up to the semantic level. It was designed for text and lexicon. It serves both purposes quite well.

Alphabetical Lexicon

The alphabetical lexicon is a list of predicates illustrated in the text in alphabetical order. Predicates are listed with their case frames. Examples of 450 predicates can be found in the case lexicon.

A (11)	
abound in	Os,L
abound with	L,Os
amuse (−agt)	O,E
amuse (+agt)	A=O,E
anchor	A,O,L
annoy (−agt)	O,E
arrive (−agt)	O,L
ask	A,E,O
attain (−agt)	B,O
attract (−agt)	O,E
avoid	A,O

B (120)	
bait	A,*O,L/O-lex
band	Os,L
be (= exist)	Os
be (=occur)	O
be (=remain)	O
be + clause	Os,Os
be + noun	Os,Os
be + poss	Os,B

be abundant in	Os,L
be abundant with	L,Os
be afraid	E,Os
be against	B,Os
be alone	Os,L
be amused	E,Os
be amusing	Os,E
be anchored	Os,L
be annoyed	E,Os
be annoying	Os,E
be appreciative	E,Os
be armed	B,Os
be at	Os,L
be aware	E,Os
be bad	Os
be bad for	Os,B
be barred	L,Os
be better than	Os,Os
be blue	Os
be bored	E,Os
be boring	Os,E
be broken	Os
be by himself	Os,L

247

be called	Os,Os	be mistaken	Os
be calm	Os	be necessary	Os,B
be careful with	A,O	be on	Os,L
be cautious (A)	A=O	be painted	L,Os
be certain	Os	be patched	Os
be clean	Os	be pleasant	Os,E
be cold	Os	be pleased	E,Os
be cold (w)	Os	be polite	Os
be cold (E)	E,Os	be polite (A)	A=O
be comfortable	Os,E	be possible	Os
be covered	L,Os	be sad (E)	E,Os
be dangerous	Os	be sick	Os
be dead	Os	be silver	Os
be desirous	E,Os	be situated	Os,L
be difficult	Os,E	be somewhere	Os,L
be drained	L,Os	be strewn on	Os,L
be eager	E,Os	be strewn with	L,Os
be easy for	Os,E	be strong	Os
be empty	L,Os	be sure	E,Os
be exhilarating	Os,E	be tall	Os
be faint	Os	be there	Os,L
be fearful	E,Os	be thick	Os
be fearless (A)	A=E,O	be true	Os
be flat	Os	be where	Os,L
be fond of	E,Os	be with	Os,L
be frightened	E,Os	be wrapped	Os,L
be frightening	Os,E	become + adj	O
be gone	Os,L	become + noun	O,O
be good	Os	become + poss	O,B
be good for	Os,B	begin,iv	O
be gutted	L,Os	begin,tv	A,O
be happy	E,Os	believe in	E,Os
be here	Os,L	belong to	Os,B
be home	Os,L	blame	A,B,O
be hooked	L,Os	blame (=put blame)	A,B,*O/O-lex
be hot (w)	Os	bleed	L,O
be human	Os	bore (−agt)	O,E
be in	Os,L	bottle	A,O,*L/L-lex
be in bad shape	Os	break,iv	O
be interested	E,Os	break,tv	A,O
be interesting	Os,E	bribe (=give bribe)	A,B,*O/O-lex
be joined	Os,L	bring,tv	A,O,L
be kind	Os	buy	A,B,O
be kind (A)	A=O		
be light	Os	**C (32)**	
be like	Os,Os	call	A,O,O

can =be able	A,O	drop,tv	A,O,L
can =be permitted	A,B,O/(P)		
can =be possible	Os	**E (11)**	
carry,tv	A,O,L		
catch	A=B,O	eat	A,O
cease,iv	O	elect	A,O,O
cease,tv	A,O	empty (place) (−agt)	O,L
clean,tv	A,O	empty (place) (+agt)	A,L,O
clear (place)	A,L,O	empty of	L,O
climb (+agt)	A=O,L	enjoy	E,O
cloud over	L,O	enter (−agt)	O,L
come (−agt)	O,L	enter (+agt)	A=O,L
come (+agt)	A=O,L	err,iv	O
come (=extend)	Os,L	exist	Os
come to (=become)	O,B	extend	Os,L
commence,iv	O		
commence,tv	A,O	**F (26)**	
consider	E,Os		
contain (−agt)	L,Os	fall	O,L
contain (+agt)	A=L,O	fall (=decrease)	O
continue,iv	O	fascinate (−agt)	O,E
continue,tv	A,O	fasten,tv	A,O,L
cost	Os,Os	feel + adj	Os,E
cough (−agt)	O	feel	E,O
cough (+agt)	A=O	feel (+agt)	A=E,O
could =was able to	A,O	feel (body)	O,E
could =was permitted	A,B,O/(P)	feel that (=believe)	E,Os
could =was possible	Os	fill (−agt)	L,O
cover	Os,L	fill (place)	A,L,O
cross (+agt)	A=O,L	find (−agt)	B,O
cut (away)	A,O,L	find (+agt)	A=B,O
		finish,iv	O
D (14)		finish,tv	A,O
		fix,tv	A,O,L
dance,iv	A,*O/O-lex	float (=go)	O,L
dance,tv	A,O	fly	A=O,L
deafen,tv	A,O	follow	A=O,L
die,iv	O	forget (−agt)	E,Os
do good for	O,B	forget (+agt)	A=E,O
do,tv	A,O	formalize	A,O
dream	E,O	free,tv	A,O,L
drift (−agt)	O,L	frighten (−agt)	O,E
drift (+agt)	A,O,L	frighten (+agt)	A=O,E
drink	A,O	furl	A,O,*L/L-lex
drip from	O,L		
drip,tv	L,O	**G (8)**	
drive,iv	A,*O/O-lex		
		get (=become)	O

get (do)	A,B,O	keep,tv	A,O
get (self)	A=B,O	keep (from)	A,B,O
give	A,B,O	kill,tv	A,O
go (−agt)	O,L	know (−agt)	E,Os
go (+agt)	A=O,L	know (+agt)	A=E,O
go (=extend)	Os,L		
gut	A,*O,L/O-lex		

L (23)

H (21)

		lack	B,Os
		lash,tv	A,O,L
hammer,tv	A,O	lay,tv	A,O,L
hang	Os,L	leak	L,O
happen	Os	leak from	O,L
happen (=occur)	O	lean (+agt)	A=O,L
have	B,Os	learn	E,O
have (=cause)	A,O	leave,iv	A=O,L
have (=exp)	E,Os	leave,tv	A,O,L
have in	L,Os	let (do)	A,B,O
have on	L,Os	let (happen)	A,O
have to = be necessary	Os	lie	Os,L
have to = be obliged	A,B,O/(P)	lie (=remain)	A=O,L
have with	L,Os	lie (down)	A=O,L
hear	E,Os	lie (tell)	A,E,*O
hear that (=learn)	E,Os	lift	A,O,*L
heat,iv	O	listen to	A=E,O
help (do)	A,B,O	live	Os,L
hoist,tv	A,O,L	live (temp)	O,L
hold	L,Os	load (place)	A,L,O
hook	A,*O,L/O-lex	look + adj	Os,E
howl,iv	O	look at	A=E,O
hurt (+agt)	A=O,E	love	E,Os

I (6)

M (19)

impress	Os,E	make (−agt cause)	O,O
inhabit	Os,L	make (=cause)	A,O
inhabit (temp)	O,L	make (=do)	A,O
interest (−agt)	O,E	make (=earn)	A=B,O
issue,tv	L,O	make (=form)	Os,Os
issue from	O,L	make (do)	A,B,O
		make (happen)	A,O
		march,iv	A=O,L

J (1)

jail	A,O,*L/L-lex	march,tv	A + A=O,L
		matter	Os,E
		may = be permitted	A,B,O/(P)

K (6)

		may = be possible	Os
keep,iv	O	mean	Os,Os

might = was permitted	A,B,O/(P)	regard	E,Os
move (−agt)	O,L	remain,iv	O
move,iv (+agt)	A=O,L	remember (−agt)	E,Os
move,tv (+agt)	A,O,L	remember (+agt)	A=E,O
must = be necessary	Os	remind (−agt)	Os,Os,E
must = be obliged	A,B,O/(P)	remind (+agt)	A,E,O
		remove,tv	A,O,L
N (1)		require	B,Os
		rest	Os,L
need	B,Os	rest (=come to)	O,L
		rest (=remain)	O,L
O (5)		rest (+agt)	A=O,L
		ride,tv	A,O
open,iv	O	rise (−agt)	O,L
open,tv	A,O	rise (=extend)	Os,L
ought to =be obliged	A,B,O/(P)	roar,iv	A,*O/O-lex
ought to =be probable	Os	rob	A,B,O
own	B,Os	roll (−agt)	O,L
		roll (+agt)	A=O,L
P (16)		ruin (=bring ruin)	A,B,*O/O-lex
		run (−agt)	O,L
pass (−agt)	O,L	run (+agt)	A=O,L
pay	A,B,O	run (=extend)	Os,L
peel	A,*O,L/O-lex	run (in)	O,L
plant (place)	A,L,O	run (with)	L,O
play	A,O	run,iv (=move)	O
please (+agt)	A=O,E		
please (−agt)	O,E	**S (62)**	
possess	B,Os		
pour	A,O,L	sail (−agt)	O,L
powder	A,*O,L/O-lex	say	A,E,O
pray (=say prayer)	A,E,*O/O-lex	scream,iv	A,*O/O-lex
project	Os,L	seat	L,Os
pull,tv	A,O,L	see	E,Os
push,tv	A,O,L	see that (=notice)	E,Os
put on	A,O,*L/L-lex	seem	Os,E
put,tv	A,O,L	sell	A,B,O
		serve (=give service)	A,B,*O/O-lex
Q (3)		set (sun)	O,L
		set,tv	A,O,L
question (=ask)	A,E,*O/O-lex	shine (=appear)	Os
quit,iv	O	shine,iv	O
quit,tv	A,O	ship (oars)	A,O,*L/L-lex
		shiver,iv	O
R (29)		should =be obliged	A,B,O/(P)
		should =be probable	Os
rain,iv	O	show (=appear)	Os,E
read,tv	A,O		
refuse	A,O		

show (+agt)	A,E,O
sing	A,O
sink	O,L
sit	Os,L
sit (=remain) (−agt)	O,L
sit (=remain) (+agt)	A=O,L
sit (down)	A=O,L
skin	A,*O,L/O-lex
slam,iv	O
sleep (−agt)	O
sleep (+agt)	A=O
slip	O,L
smear (place)	A,L,O
smell + adj	Os,E
smell (−agt)	E,Os
smell (+agt)	A=E,O
smoke,tv	A,O
sound + adj	Os,E
speak	A,E,O
spray (place)	A,L,O
spurt	O,L
stand	Os,L
stand (=remain)	A=O,L
stand,iv (+agt)	A=O,L
stand,tv (+agt)	A,O,L
start,iv	O
start,tv	A,O
stay,iv	O
stay,tv	A,O
stay (out)	A=O,L
steal	A,B,O
step (mast)	A,O,*L/L-lex
stop,iv	O
stop,tv	A,O
store,tv	A,O,L
stretch	Os,L
strew (place)	A,L,O
strike	Os,E
surround	Os,L
swarm in	O,L
swarm with	L,O
sweep,tv	A,O
swim (=go)	A=O,L
swing (−agt)	O,L

T (18)

take (course)	A,O
take (self)	A=B,O
take (strain)	L,O
take off	A,O,*L/L-lex
take,tv	A,O,L
taste (+agt)	A=E,O
taste (−agt)	E,Os
taste + adj	Os,E
teach	A,E,O
tear off,tv	A,O,L
tell	A,E,O
thank (=say)	A,E,*O/O-lex
thicken,iv	O
think (−agt)	E,Os
think (+agt)	A=E,O
tie,tv	A,O,L
try,tv	A,O
turn into + noun	O,O

U (4)

understand (−agt)	E,Os
understand (come to)	E,O
untie,tv	A,O,L
use	A,O

W (14)

walk,iv	A=O
walk,tv	A + A=O
walk (= go)	A=O,L
want	E,Os
wash,iv	O
watch	A=E,O
water	A,*O,L/O-lex
weigh	Os,Os
widen,iv	O
win (−agt)	B,O
win (+agt)	A=B,O
work,iv	A,*O/O-lex
worry	E,O
write,tv	A,O

Case Lexicon

The case lexicon is a list of predicates illustrated in the text, separated into verb types. Within each type the predicates are listed in alphabetical order together with the pages where the predicate is found.

A. Basic domain (139)

    A.1. State (48)

        With single Os (39)

be (= exist)	63, 66, 200
be bad	115
be blue	77
be broken	61
be calm	73
be certain	59
be clean	86
be cold	94
be cold (w)	58, 188
be dangerous	205
be dead	62, 97
be faint	115
be flat	87
be good	65
be hot (w)	59
be human	58
be in bad shape	65
be kind	79

be light	78
be mistaken	205
be patched	62
be polite	60
be possible	199
be sick	190
be silver	66
be strong	65
be tall	58
be thick	76
be true	59
can = be possible	199
could = was possible	205
exist	63
have to = be certain	200
happen	64
may = be possible	199
must = be certain	200
ought to = be probable	200
shine (=appear)	66
should = be probable	200

With double Os (9)

be + noun	66, 205
be + clause	67
be better than	67, 68
be called	88, 89
be like	67
cost	68, 140
make (=form)	68
mean	68
weigh	68

A.2. Process (36)

With single O (33)

be (=occur)	64, 69, 205
be (=remain)	64
become + adj	76, 77
begin,iv	71
break,iv	59
cease,iv	74
commence,iv	72
continue,iv	74
cough (=agt)	80
die,iv	70
err,iv	58
fall (=decrease)	68
finish,iv	74
get (=become)	78
happen (=occur)	64, 69
heat,iv	75
howl,iv	70
keep,iv	73
open,iv	75
quit,iv	74
rain,iv	72, 74
remain,iv	73
run,iv (=move)	74
shine,iv	70
shiver,iv	96
slam,iv	70
sleep,iv	70
start,iv	72
stay,iv	73
stop,iv	74
thicken,iv	76
wash,iv	76, 87

widen,iv	75

With double O (3)

become + noun	77
make (=−agt cause)	78
turn into + noun	77

A.3. Action (55)

With A=O (6)

be cautious (A)	80, 85
be kind (A)	80
be polite (A)	60
cough (+agt)	80–81
sleep (+agt)	70
walk,iv	89

With O-lex (5)

dance,iv	83
drive,iv	82
roar,iv	96
scream,iv	78
work,iv	81, 84

With both roles overt (41)

avoid	205
be careful with	80, 83
begin,tv	71–72, 84
break,tv	59, 61, 87
can = be able to	203
cease,iv	74
clean,tv	73
commence,tv	72
continue,tv	73
could = was able to	207
dance,tv	83
deafen,tv	75
do,tv	81, 85, 97
drink	184
eat	192, 213
finish,iv	74
formalize	87
hammer,tv	86
have (=cause)	100
keep,tv	84
kill,tv	84
let (happen)	85, 141

make (=cause)	89	be sad (E)	104, 119
make (happen)	86, 141	be sure	101, 105
open,tv	85	believe in	195
play,tv	215	consider	104
quit,iv	74	feel that (=believe)	97
read,tv	72, 83	forget (−agt)	121
refuse	203	have (=exp)	99–100
ride,tv	111	hear	96
sing	196	hear that (=learn)	98
smoke,tv	201–202, 206	know (−agt)	102, 105
start,tv	73	love	99
stay,tv	84	regard	103
stop,tv	85	remember (−agt)	121
sweep,tv	86	see	95–97, 99,
take (course)	206		105, 119
try,tv	85	see that (=notice)	98
use,tv	206	smell (−agt)	120
walk,iv	89	taste (−agt)	120
write,tv	83	think (−agt)	103
		understand (−agt)	114

With double O (2)

		want	100, 105
call	89		
elect	88		

With Os-subject (20)

With double Agent (1)

		be amusing	106
walk,tv	89	be annoying	117
		be boring	110, 117
		be comfortable	111

B. Experiential domain (97)

	be difficult	107, 111
	be easy for	107–108

B.1. State Experiential (56)

	be exhilarating	111
	be frightening	110

With E-subject (35)

		be interesting	110
be afraid	98–99, 105	be pleasant	106, 111
be amused	116–17	feel + adj	106
be annoyed	116–17	impress	104
be appreciative	98	look + adj	95, 111
be aware	101	matter	112
be bored	101	seem	110
be cold (E)	94, 104	show (=appear)	112
be desirous	99	smell + adj	95
be eager	107, 108	sound + adj	106
be fearful	98	strike	104, 113
be fond of	98	taste + adj	106
be frightened	116–17		

With double Os (1)

be happy	60, 99		
be interested	101, 110	remind (−agt)	113
be pleased	118		

B.2. Process Experiential (15)

With E-subject (6)

dream	118
enjoy	114
feel	96, 114–15, 120
learn	114
understand (come to)	114
worry	118

With O-subject (9)

amuse (−agt)	117
annoy (−agt)	117
attract (−agt)	119
bore (−agt)	101, 110
fascinate (−agt)	119
feel (body)	115
frighten (−agt)	121
interest (−agt)	101, 110
please (−agt)	118

B.3. Action Experiential (26)

With A=E (11)

be fearless (A)	124
feel (+agt)	120, 124
forget (+agt)	121, 124
know (+agt)	102
listen to	95
look at	95
remember (+agt)	121, 215
smell (+agt)	120
taste (+agt)	120
think (+agt)	102
watch	96, 106, 119, 186

With A=O (4)

amuse (+agt)	106
frighten (+agt)	121
hurt (+agt)	125
please (+agt)	107, 117

With O-lex (4)

lie (tell)	199–200, 209
pray (=say prayer)	125

question (=ask)	123
thank (=say thanks)	122

With all roles overt (7)

ask	123
remind (+agt)	113
say	103, 124
show	123
speak	124
teach	123, 125, 197
tell	123–24

C. Benefactive domain (49)

C.1. State Benefactive (13)

With B-subject (8)

be against	132
be armed	105
have	130, 132–33
lack	131–32
need	131–32
own	129–30
possess	134
require	132

With Os-subject (5)

be + poss	134
be bad for	134
be good for	136
be necessary	134
belong to	134

C.2. Process Benefactive (6)

With B-subject (3)

attain (−agt)	135
find (−agt)	135
win (−agt)	135

With O-subject (3)

become + poss	136
come to (=become)	137
do good for	137

C.3. Action Benefactive (30)

With A=B (6)

catch	137
find (+agt)	135, 138
get (self)	138
make (=earn)	138
take (self)	138
win (+agt)	99, 101, 135

With O-lex (4)

blame (=put blame)	138
bribe (=give bribe)	138–39
ruin (=bring ruin)	138–39
serve (=give service)	138–39

With all roles overt (12)

blame	140
buy	140
give	215
get (do)	142
help (do)	97, 142
keep (from)	142
let (do)	85, 141
make (do)	86, 142
pay	140, 202
rob	107, 140
sell	140
steal	140

Passives (8)

can = be permitted	201
could = was permitted	206
have to = be obliged	203
may = be permitted	202
might = was permitted	205
must = be obliged	203
ought to = be obliged	202
should = be obliged	202

D. Locative domain (165)

D.1. State Locative (52)

With Os-subject (36)

abound in	157–58
band	155
be abundant in	157–58
be alone	148
be anchored	149
be at	65, 147
be by himself	148
be gone	150
be here	147–48
be home	200
be in	147
be joined	151
be on	64, 147, 158
be situated	63
be somewhere	148
be strewn on	157–58
be there	148
be where	148–49
be with	149, 157
be wrapped	150
come (=extend)	154
cover	155
extend	154–55
go (=extend)	154–55
hang	152–53
inhabit	156
lie	150–53
live	156
project	152–53
rest	152–53
rise (=extend)	155
run (=extend)	155
sit	150, 169
stand	150–52
stretch	154–55
surround	154

With L-subject (16)

abound with	157
be abundant with	158
be barred	158
be covered	159
be drained	159
be empty of	158, 189
be gutted	159
be hooked	159
be painted	159
be strewn with	158, 180

contain (−agt)	156, 170
have with	157–58
have on	157
have in	157–58
hold	157–58
seat	157

D.2. Process Locative (39)

With O-subject (29)

arrive (−agt)	192, 195
come (−agt)	161
drift (−agt)	162
drip,iv	163
empty (place) (−agt)	181
enter (−agt)	160, 167
fall	162, 213
float (=go)	160
go (−agt)	160–61, 167
inhabit (temp)	156
issue from	163
leak from	163
live (temp)	156
move (−agt)	161
pass (−agt)	162
rest (=remain)	153
rest (=come to)	153
rise (−agt)	161–62
roll (−agt)	165
run (−agt)	86, 162
run (in)	163
sail (−agt)	162
set (sun)	161
sink	161
sit (=remain) (−agt)	169
slip	162
spurt	96
swarm in	163
swing (−agt)	162

With L-subject (10)

bleed	164
cloud over	164
drip from	163
empty of	181
fill (−agt)	164
issue (−agt)	163

leak (−agt)	163
run (with)	164
swarm with	163
take (strain)	164

D.3. Action Locative (74)

With A=O (23)

climb	168
come (+agt)	123, 154, 189, 199
cross (+agt)	97
enter (+agt)	167, 188, 191
follow	168
fly	199, 208
go (+agt)	166–67, 203
lean (+agt)	169
leave	100, 123, 188, 202, 207
lie (down)	169
lie (=remain)	170
march,iv	90
move,iv (+agt)	167
rest (+agt)	170
roll (+agt)	165
sit (down)	170
sit (=remain) (+agt)	170
stand (up)	170
stand (=remain)	169
stay (out)	206
swim (=go)	166
walk (=go)	194–95

With A=L (1)

| contain (+agt) | 170 |

With O-lex (7)

bait	171
gut	172
hook	172, 176
peel	172
powder	171
skin	172
water	171

With L-lex (8)

| bottle | 173 |

furl   173
jail   173
lift   207
put on   174
ship (oars)   173
step (mast)   173
take off   173

With all roles overt (26)

anchor   149
bring,tv   175–76
carry,tv   174–75
cut (away)   100, 178
drift (+agt)   176
drop,tv   78, 176
fasten,tv   178
fix,tv   177
free,tv   177
hoist,tv   176
lash,tv   178
lay,tv   177
leave,tv   176
move,tv (+agt)   174
pour   180–81
pull,tv   176

push,tv   174
put,tv   176
remove,tv   165
set,tv   177
stand,tv   177
store,tv   176
take,tv   174–75
tear off,tv   178
tie,tv   178
untie,tv   178

With A-L-O order (8)

clear (place)   180
empty (place) (+agt)   180–81
fill (place)   180–81
load (place)   178
plant (place)   180
smear (place)   179
spray (place)   178, 180
strew (place)   180–81

With double Agent (1)

march,tv   182

References

Abraham, Werner. 1978. Valence, semantic case, and grammatical relations. Amsterdam: John Benjamins.

Allen, James. 1987. Natural language understanding. Menlo Park, Calif.: Benjamin/Cummings.

Allwood, Andersson, and Dahl. 1977. Logic in linguistics. Cambridge: Cambridge University Press.

Anderson, John M. 1971. The grammar of case: Towards a localistic theory. Cambridge: Cambridge University Press.

———. 1976. On case grammar. London: Croom Helm.

———. 1977. Phonological structure and the history of English. New York: North-Holland.

Austin, J. L. 1962. How to do things with words. Oxford: Clarendon Press.

Bach, Emmon, and R. Harms, eds. 1968. Universals in linguistic theory. New York: Holt, Rinehart, and Winston.

Becker, Alton. 1967. Conjoining in a tagmemic grammar of English. Georgetown University Round Table on Languages and Linguistics 1967, 109–21. Washington, D.C.: Georgetown University Press.

Binnick, Robert. 1968. On the nature of the lexical item. Chicago Linguistic Society 4:1–11.

Bolinger, Dwight. 1975. Aspects of language. 2nd edition. New York: Harcourt, Brace, Jovanovich.

261

Carlson, Greg and Michael Tanenhaus. 1988. Thematic roles and language comprehension. In Wendy Wilkins (ed.), Thematic relations. Syntax and semantics 21. San Diego: Academic Press.

Chafe, Wallace L. 1970. Meaning and the structure of language. Chicago: Chicago University Press.

Chomsky, Noam. 1957. Semantic structures. The Hague: Mouton.

──. 1964. Current issues in linguistic theory. The Hague: Mouton.

──. 1965. Aspects of the theory of syntax. Cambridge: MIT Press.

──. 1981. Lectures on government and binding. Dordrecht: Foris.

Comrie, Bernard. 1976. Aspect. Cambridge: Cambridge University Press.

Cook, Walter A., S.J. 1978. Semantic structure of the English modals. TESOL Quarterly 12(1):5–15 (March, 1978).

──. 1979. Case grammar: Development of the matrix model (1970–1978). Washington, D.C.: Georgetown University Press.

──. 1985. Case grammar applied to the teaching of English. In Kurt Jankowsky (ed.), Scientific and humanistic dimensions of language: Festschrift for Robert Lado. Amsterdam: John Benjamins.

──. 1989. Case grammar theory. Washington, D.C.: Georgetown University Press.

──. 1990. Passive semantics: Ambiguity of the short passive. Georgetown Journal of Languages and Linguistics 1(1):25–30.

──. 1991. Case Grammar: What? Whence? Whither? Georgetown Journal of Languages and Linguistics 2(3):234–42.

──. 1992. Conceptual graphs: The new semantics? Georgetown Journal of Languages and Linguistics 3(1):23–33.

Dowty, David R. 1972. Studies in the logic of verb aspect and time reference in English. Austin: University of Texas.

Fillmore, Charles J. 1968. The case for case. In Emmon Bach and Robert Harms (eds.), Universals in linguistic theory, 1–88. New York: Holt, Rinehart, and Winston.

──. 1969. Towards a modern theory of case. In David Reibel and Sanford Shane (eds.), Modern studies in English, 361–75. Englewood Cliffs, N.J.: Prentice-Hall.

──. 1970. Lexical entries for verbs. Foundations of Language 4:373–93.

──. 1971a. Types of Lexical information. In Danny D. Steinberg and Leon A. Jakobovits (eds.), Semantics: An interdisciplinary reader, 370–92. Cambridge: Cambridge University Press.

──. 1971b. Some problems for Case Grammar. Georgetown University Round Table on Languages and Linguistics 1971, 35–56. Washington, D.C.: Georgetown University Press.

————. 1975. Principles of Case Grammar: The structure of language and meaning. Translated by Tanaka and Funaki. Tokyo: Sanseido Publishing Company.

————. 1977. The case for case reopened. In Cole and Jerrold M. Sadock (eds.), Syntax and semantics 8:59–81. New York: Academic Press.

Fodor, J. D. 1977. Semantics: Theories of meaning in generative grammar. New York: Thomas Y. Crowell.

Francis, Winthrop Nelson and Henry Kucera. 1967. Computational analysis of present-day American English. Providence, R.I.: Brown University Press.

Green, Georgia M. 1969. On the notion 'related lexical entry'. Chicago Linguistics Society 5:76–87.

————. 1972. Some observations on the syntax and semantics of instrumental verbs. Chicago Linguistic Society 8:83–92.

————. 1974. Semantics and syntactic regularity. Bloomington: Indiana University Press.

Grimshaw, Jane. 1990. Argument structure. In Samuel Jay Keyser (ed.), Linguistic inquiry monographs 18. Cambridge: MIT Press.

Gruber, Jeffrey S. 1976. Lexical structures in syntax and semantics. Amsterdam: North Holland.

Hale, Austin. 1974. On the systematization of box 4. In Ruth Brend (ed.), Advances in tagmemics, 55–74. Amsterdam: North Holland.

Harris, Mary Dee. 1985. Introduction to natural language processing. Reston, Va.: Reston Publishing Company.

Helbig, Gerhard. 1971. Beitrage zur Valenztheorie. The Hague: Mouton.

Hoffman, Ronald. 1966. Past tense replacement and the modal system. In A. Ottinger (ed.), Mathematical linguistics and automatic translation. Cambridge: Harvard University Press.

Ikegami, Yoshihiko. 1969. The semological structure of English verbs of motion. New Haven, Conn.: Yale University Press.

Inoue, K. 1974. Experiencer. Studies in descriptive and applied linguistics, 139–62. Tokyo: International Christian University.

Jackendoff, Ray S. 1972. Semantic interpretation in generative grammar. Cambridge: MIT Press.

————. 1976. Toward an explanatory semantic representation. Linguistic Inquiry 7(1):89–150.

————. 1983. Semantics and cognition. Cambridge: MIT Press.

————. 1987. The status of thematic relations in linguistic theory. Linguistic Inquiry 18(3):369–411.

————. 1990. Semantic structures. In Samuel Jay Keyser (ed.), Current studies in linguistics 18. Cambridge: MIT Press.

Jankowsky, Kurt. 1985. Scientific and humanistic dimensions of language: Festschrift for Robert Lado. Amsterdam: John Benjamins.

Lakoff, George. 1966. Stative adjectives and verbs in English. In A. G. Ottinger (ed.), Mathematical linguistics and automatic translation. Cambridge, Mass.: Harvard University Press.

———. 1970. Irregularity in Syntax. New York: Holt, Rinehart, and Winston.

———. 1972. Linguistics and natural logic. In Donald Davidson and Gilbert Harmon (eds.), Semantics of natural language, 545–665. Dordrecht: Reidel.

———. 1976. Toward generative semantics. Syntax and semantics 7:43–61. New York: Academic Press.

Langacker, Ronald. 1975. Functional stratigraphy. Papers from the parasession on functionalism, 351–59. Chicago Linguistic Society.

Leech, Geoffrey N. 1969. Towards a semantic description of English. Bloomington: Indiana University Press.

———. 1971. Meaning and the English verb. London: Longmans.

———. 1974. Semantics. Baltimore, Md.: Penguin Books.

———. 1981. Semantics. Second edition. Middlesex, England: Penguin Books.

Levin, Beth. 1993. English verb classes and alternations. Chicago: University of Chicago Press.

Longacre, Robert E. 1964. Grammar discovery procedures. The Hague: Mouton.

———. 1976. An anatomy of speech notions. Lisse: Peter DeRitter.

Lyons, John. 1968. Introduction to theoretical linguistics. Cambridge: Cambridge University Press.

———. 1977. Semantics. Cambridge: Cambridge University Press.

McCawley, James D. 1971. Prelexical syntax. Georgetown University Round Table on Languages and Linguistics 1971, 19–34. Washington, D.C.: Georgetown University Press.

———. 1973. Grammar and meaning. Tokyo: Taishukan. (Republished 1976. New York: Academic Press.)

Mellema, Paul. 1974. A brief against case grammar. Foundations of Language 11:39–76.

Morgan, Jerry L. 1969. On arguing about semantics. Papers in Linguistics 1:49–70.

Newmeyer, Frederick J. 1975. English aspectual verbs. The Hague: Mouton.

———. 1980. Linguistic theory in America. New York: Academic Press.

Nilsen, Don Lee Fred. 1972. Toward a semantic specification of deep case. The Hague: Mouton.

————. 1973. The instrumental case in English. The Hague: Mouton.

Peirce, Charles S. 1931. Collected papers of Charles Sanders Peirce. Existential graphs 4(2):293–470. Cambridge: Harvard University Press.

Pepinsky, Harold B. 1974. A metalanguage for systematic research on human communication via natural language. Journal of the American Society for Information Science 25(1):59–69.

Perlmutter, David M. 1970. The two verbs 'begin'. In Roderick A. Jacobs and Peter S. Rosenbaum (eds.), Readings in English Transformational Grammar, 107–19. Waltham, Mass.: Ginn.

Pike, Kenneth L. 1967. Language in relation to a unified theory of the structure of human behavior. The Hague: Mouton.

————. 1971. Crucial issues in the development of tagmemics, Georgetown Round Table on Languages and Linguistics 1971, 79–98. Washington, D.C.: Georgetown University Press.

———— and Evelyn Pike. 1977. Grammatical analysis. Summer Institute of Linguistics and the University of Texas at Arlington Publications in Linguistics 53. Dallas.

Platt, John T. 1971. Grammatical form and grammatical meaning: A tagmemic view of Fillmore's deep structure case concepts. Amsterdam: North Holland.

Postal, Paul M. 1971a. Crossover phenomena. New York: Holt, Rinehart, and Winston.

————. 1971b. On the surface verb 'remind'. In Fillmore and Langendoen (eds.), Studies in linguistic semantics, 181–270. New York: Holt, Rinehart, and Winston.

————. 1974. On raising. Cambridge: MIT Press.

Quirk, Randolph, Sidney Greenbaum, Geoffrey Leech, and Jan Svartvik. 1985. A comprehensive grammar of the English language. New York: Longmans.

Radford, Andrew. 1988. Transformational grammar. New York: Cambridge University Press.

Rappaport, Malka and Beth Levin. 1988. What to do with Theta roles. In Wendy Wilkins (ed.), Thematic relations. Syntax and semantics 21. San Diego: Academic Press.

Rogers, Andy. 1971. Three kinds of physical perception verbs. Chicago Linguistic Society 7:206–22.

Ross, John R. 1969. Auxiliaries as main verbs. Journal of Philosophical Linguistics 1(1):77–102.

————. 1970. On declarative sentences. In Roderick A. Jacobs and Peter S. Rosenbaum (eds.), Readings in English transformational grammar, 222–72. Waltham, Mass.: Ginn.

———. 1972. Act. In Donald Davidson and Gilbert Harmon (eds.), Semantics of natural language, 70–126. Dordrecht: Reidel.

Rudanko, Juhani. 1989. Complementation and case grammar. Albany: State University of New York Press.

———. 1993. Pragmatic approaches to Shakespeare. Lanham, Md.: University Press of America.

Sapir, Edward. 1921. Language. New York: Harcourt, Brace, and World.

Shank, Roger and Kenneth Colby. 1973. Computer models of thought and language. San Francisco: W. H. Freeman and Company.

Somers, Harold. 1982. The use of verb features in arriving at a meaning representation. Linguistics 20:237–65.

———. 1987. Valency and case in computational linguistics. Edinburgh: Edinburgh University Press.

Sowa, John F. 1984. Conceptual structures: Information processing in mind and machine. Reading, Mass.: Addison-Wesley.

———. 1988. Using a lexicon of canonical graphs in a semantic interpreter. In Martha Evans (ed)., Relational models of the lexicon, 113–37. Cambridge: Cambridge University Press.

———. 1991. Toward the expressive power of natural language. Principles of semantic networks, 157–89. San Mateo, Calif.: Morgan Kaufman.

———. 1992. Conceptual graphs as a universal knowledge representation. Computers Mathematical Applications 23(2–5):75–93.

——— and E. C. Way. 1986. Implementing a semantic interpreter using conceptual graphs. IBM Journal of Research and Development 32(2):251–67.

Stockwell, Robert P., Paul Schacter, and Barbara Hall Partee. 1973. The major syntactic structures of English. New York: Holt, Rinehart, and Winston.

Tesniere, Lucian. 1958. Elements de syntaxe structurale. Paris: Klincksieck.

Ullman, Stephen. 1957. The principles of semantics. Oxford: Basil Blackwell and Mott.

Van Riemsdijk, Henk and Edwin Williams. 1986. Introduction to the theory of grammar. Cambridge: MIT Press.

von Wright, Georg Henrik. 1963. Norm and action. New York: Humanities Press.

———. 1971. Explanation and understanding. Ithaca, N.Y.: Cornell University Press.

Wierzbicka, Anna and Cliff Goddard. 1994. Semantic and lexical universals. Amsterdam: John Benjamins.

Winograd, Terry. 1983. Language as a cognitive process. Reading, Mass: Addison-Wesley.

Index

A

A,*E,O /A=E 120, 121
A,O,B 129
A=E,O 120
action adjectives 79
  transitive 82
action verbs 21, 22
  with complements 140
adjectives, comparative 67
agent
  causative agent 141
  permissive agent 141
agent (A) 12
agentive reinterpretation 60
Allen, James 21
Anderson, John 4, 7, 9, 14, 21, 24, 26, 38,
  40, 41, 45, 57, 58, 61, 66, 80, 81,
  82, 87, 89, 94, 152, 157, 165, 180
animate process 69, 70
apparent passives 61
argument 9
aspectual verbs 71
  intransitive 71
attachment verbs 177
Austin, J.L. 211
auxiliaries as main verbs 183

B

basic action 56, 78, 226
  derived action 86
  with A=O coreference 78, 80, 226
  with both roles overt 82, 228
  with complement 84
  with double agent 88
  with double object 87, 88, 228
  with O-lexicalized 227
basic domain 55
basic procedures 48
basic process 56, 69, 225
  with double O 226
  with single O 225
basic state 57, 63, 65, 223
  transitive verbs 83
  with double Os 66, 224
  with single Os 65, 224
be + adjective 149
be + locative 147
be + participle 149
become + adjective 76, 77
become + noun 77
Benefactive (B) 15
benefactive action 128, 137, 236
  with A,O,B order 237
  with A=B coreference 137, 236
  with all roles overt 139, 237
  with O-lexicalized 138, 139, 237
  with reversible roles 140

benefactive process 128, 135, 235
  with B-subject 135
  with O-subject 136
benefactive state 127, 129, 234
  with B-subject 129, 132, 234, 235
  with Os-subject 133, 235
  with O-subject 236

C

can = be able to 203
can = be permitted 201
can = be possible 199
Carlson, Greg 39
case frame
  matrix 26
case frames 20
  assignment 20, 24
  matrix 23, 24
  revised matrix 27
Case Grammar theory 1, 3, 5, 7, 9, 11, 13,
    15, 17, 19, 21, 23, 25, 27, 29, 31,
    33, 35, 37, 39, 41, 43, 45, 47, 49,
    51, 53
  case systems 3, 4
  goals 1
  lexicon 2
  structure 1
case roles 10
  coreferential 26
  covert 37, 38
  inventory 12
  lexicalized 26
  nature of 10
causative
  causative predicates 77
  causative-durative paradigm 35
  causative-inchoative paradigm 31
  causative-inchoative structure 32
  defined 34
causative-durative-state 36
Chafe, Wallace 4, 7, 12, 20, 21, 23, 25, 28,
    29, 34, 44, 58, 66, 68, 74, 82, 86,
    147, 165
Chafe, Wallace 13
Chomsky, Noam 5, 21, 103, 107, 183, 197,
    208
cognition 100, 101, 102, 108, 120
  cognitive action 120
  cognitive adjectives 101
  cognitive predicates 101
  cognitive process 114

cognitive states 100, 108
cognitive verbs 101, 102, 114, 120
Comrie, Bernard 185, 193, 195, 197, 219
conceptual graphs 46, 47, 51
coreferential roles 40, 44, 50
could = be/was permitted 206
could = be/was possible 204

D

deletable object verbs 44, 82
deletable roles 38
derivation 27, 28
derived process 74
domain 22, 53, 221
domain, basic 22, 221, 223, 245
domain, benefactive 22, 127, 222, 234,
    245
domain, experiential 22, 91, 221, 223, 229,
    245
domain, locative 23, 143, 222, 238
domain, physical location 245
domain, time 27, 222
domain, verbal 246
domains, semantic 245
double Object (Os,Os) 57
double-O frames 25
Dowty, David 33, 34, 37, 74, 76, 152
durative 35
  durative-state structure 36
durative-state 35

E

E,Os 117
emotion 98, 105
  emotive adjectives 98, 105
  emotive process 114
  emotive state 98, 105, 106
  emotive verbs 99, 114
Experiencer (E) 15
experiential action 92, 119, 232
  with A=E coreference 119, 232
  with A=O coreference 121, 232
  with all roles overt 122, 233
  with O-lexicalized 122, 233
experiential process 92, 113, 231
  with E-subject 113, 231
  with O-subject 115, 231
experiential state 91, 92, 93, 229
  with double Os 112
  with E-subject 93, 229

with Os-subject 105, 111, 230
extension verbs 154
    text analysis 155

F

features 2, 3
    semantic 2, 3
    syntactic 2
feel 114, 115
feel + noun 115
Fillmore, Charles 2, 3, 4, 8, 9, 10, 11, 12,
    14, 15, 16, 17, 18, 19, 23, 24, 38,
    40, 44, 58, 66, 81, 82, 131, 139,
    145, 157, 160, 162, 165, 179, 180
Fraser, Bruce 179

G

Green, Georgia 86
Grimshaw, Jane 116
Gruber, Jeffrey 4, 8, 13, 14, 23, 24, 34, 40,
    41, 140, 165

H

habitation verbs 155
have 130
    have (located) 131, 156
    have + complement 131
    have + NP 130
    have, other uses 130
    have to = *be certain* 200
    have to = *be obliged* 203
Hoffman, Ronald 184

I

Ikegami, Yoshiko 160
impression verbs 103
inanimate process 70
inchoative 33
    inchoative structure 32
indirect discourse 102
infinitives, unmarked 96
intransitive 63
intransitive predicates 78

J

Jackendoff, Ray 4, 5, 8, 13, 19, 23, 24, 30,
    35, 40, 141, 165

K

kernel sentence 5

L

Lakoff, George 8, 9, 21, 31, 33, 34, 56, 57,
    74, 79, 86
Langacker, Ronald 211, 219
Leech, Geoffrey 152, 187, 188, 189, 190,
    191, 193, 194, 195, 196, 219
Levin, Beth 20, 178, 179
lexical decomposition 31
lexicalized prepositions 160
lexicalized roles 41, 44, 51
liquid verbs 163
Locative (L) 16
locative action 144, 164, 241
    verbs with the A,*O,L /A=O frame 144
    verbs with the A,*O,L /O-lex frame 145
    verbs with the A,O,*L /A=L frame 144
    verbs with the A,O,*L /L-lex frame 145
    with A,O,L order 243
    with A=L coreference 170, 242
    with A=O coreference 165, 167, 241
    with all roles overt 174, 243
    with double agent 181
    with L-lexicalized 173, 243
    with O-lexicalized 170, 172, 242
locative alternation 178, 181
locative expressions 145
locative process 144, 159, 160, 240
    verbs with the O,L frame 144
    with L-subject 162, 240
    with O-subject 159, 161, 240
locative state 144, 238
    reversible states 157
    verbs with the L,Os frame 144
    with L-subject 156, 158, 239
    with Os-subject 238
    with O-subject 146
logical structure 5, 211
Lyons, John 30, 87, 88

M

matrix 26, 27

may = *be permitted* 202
may = *be possible* 199
McCawley, James 12, 33, 34, 35, 36, 86,
    183, 184, 185, 186, 208, 219
Mellema, Paul 179
methodology 45
might = *be /was permitted* 206
might = *be/was possible* 205
modal cases 17
    modal locative 18
modal verbs 197
modal, ability 203
    with negation 211
    with tense 207
modal, epistemic 198
    with negation 209
    with tense 204
modal, root 201
    with negation 210
    with tense 205
modality 183
motion verbs 174
    intransitive 160
    transitive 174
must = *be certain* 200
must = *be obliged* 203

N

need 131
negation 208
    propositions 208
    with modals 208
neutralization of the perfect 184
Newmeyer, Frederick 71
noun phrase modification 214

O

O,B 128
O,E 117
Object (O) 13
obligatory O hypothesis 4, 13, 14, 24
occurrence verbs 69
Os,E 117
ought to = *be obliged* 202
ought to = *be probable* 200

P

parse, sample 214
performative layer 211

Perlmutter, David 71
placement verbs 176, 177
position verbs 150
    active position 168
Postal, Paul 8, 9, 101, 107, 110, 112, 116
predicate 7
    related predicates 29
predicate adjectives 58
predicate adverbs 64
predicate nouns 66
process verbs 21, 22
process with double O 77
process with single O 69
proposition 5
propositional layer 213
psych movement adjectives 110
psych movement verbs 117, 231
put-on verbs 171

Q

Quirk, Randolph 61

R

Radford, Andrew 96
Radford, Andrew 2
rank shift 19, 25
Rappaport, Malka 20, 178, 179
reflexivization 41
roles overt 82
Ross, John 45, 81, 183, 212, 219
Rudanko, Juhani 60, 79

S

Sapir, Edward 9
seem 110
self-movement verbs 165
sensation 94
    sensation adjectives 94
    sensation state 94, 105
    sensation verbs 94
should = *be obliged* 202
should = *be probable* 200
single Object (Os) 57
Somers, Harold 5, 9
Sowa, John 11, 21, 46, 48, 50, 186, 198,
    201, 208
state locative 146
state verb 23
    defined 21, 22

subject choice hierarchy 18
syntactic environment 246

T

take-off verbs 171, 173
Talmy, Leonard 160
Tanenhaus, Michael 39
tense system 186
tense-aspect-modal layer 212
tenses, habitual 193
    past habitual 194
    past perfect habitual 196
    present habitual 194
    present perfect habitual 195
tenses, nonprogressive 186
    future 188
    future perfect 189
    past 187
    past perfect 189
    present 187
    present perfect 188
tenses, progressive 190
    future perfect progressive 193
    future progressive 191
    past perfect progressive 192
    past progressive 191
    present perfect progressive 192
    present progressive 190
text analysis of verbs
    A,*O verbs 81
    A,*O,L /A=O verbs 165, 166, 169
    A,*O,L verbs 171, 172
    A,B,*O /O-lex verbs 138
    A,B,O verbs 140, 141, 142
    A,E,*O /O-lex verbs 122
    A,E,O verbs 112, 123, 124
    A,L,O verbs 178, 179, 180, 181
    A,O verbs 85, 87, 141
    A,O,*L /A=L verbs 170
    A,O,B verbs 140
    A,O,L /(P) verbs 149
    A,O,L /A=O verbs 168
    A,O,L verbs 165, 174, 177, 178, 179,
        180, 181
    A,O,O verbs 88

A+A=O,L verbs 182
A=B,O verbs 135, 137, 138
A=O verbs 80
B,O verbs 135
B,Os verbs 130, 131, 132, 134
E,O verbs 115
E,Os verbs 105, 107, 108, 120, 121,
    130
E,Os,Os verbs 113
L,O verbs 163
L,Os verbs 131, 156, 157, 158, 170,
    181
O verbs 160
O,*L verbs 161
O,B verbs 136
O,E verbs 110, 115, 121
O,L verbs 151, 156, 160, 163, 165, 166,
    169, 181
Os,B verbs 134, 136
Os,E verbs 107, 108, 109, 110, 111,
    113
Os,L verbs 131, 147, 149, 150, 151,
    152, 154, 156, 157, 158, 169,
    180
Os,Os verbs 140
text analysis procedures 45
text reduction 6
that-complements 97
theme, where? 43
time predicates 26
tough movement 107
transitive predicates 68
transitive stative verbs 67

V

Van Riemsdijk, Henk 12
verb adicity 20, 23
verb hierarchy 221, 245
verb type hierarchy 22
verb type, defined 21
verbs with A=O coreference 80
verbs with single O 78
verbs with the B,Os frame 128
von Wright, Georg Henrik 33

Summer Institute of Linguistics and
The University of Texas at Arlington
Publications in Linguistics

Recent Publications

127. Case grammar applied, by Walter A. Cook, S.J. 1998

126. The Dong language in Guizhou Province, China, by Long Yaohong and Zheng Guoqiao, translated from Chinese by D. Norman Geary. 1998.

125. Vietnamese classifiers in narrative texts, by Karen Ann Daley. 1998.

124. Comparative Kadai: The Tai branch, ed. by Jerold A. Edmondson and David B. Solnit. 1997.

123. Why there are no clitics: An alternative perspective on pronominal allomorphy, by Daniel L. Everett. 1996.

122. Mamaindé stress: The need for strata, by David Eberhard. 1995.

121. The Doyayo language: Selected studies, by Elisabeth Wiering and Marinus Wiering. 1994.

120. A discourse analysis of First Corinthians, by Ralph Bruce Terry. 1995

119. Discourse features of ten languages of West-Central Africa, ed. by Stephen H. Levensohn. 1994.

118. Epena Pedee syntax: Studies in the languages of Colombia 4, by Phillip Lee Harms. 1994.

117. Beyond the bilingual classroom: Literacy acquisition among Peruvian Amazon communities, by Barbara Trudell. 1993.

116. The French imparfait and passé simple in discourse, by Sharon Rebecca Rand. 1993.

115. The function of verb prefixes in Southwestern Otomí, by Henrietta Andrews. 1993.

114. Proto Witotoan, by Richard P. Aschmann. 1993.

113. A pragmatic analysis of Norwegian modal particles, by Erik E. Andvik. 1992.

112. Retuarã syntax: Studies in the languages of Colombia 3, by Clay Strom. 1992.

111. Studies in the syntax of Mixtecan Languages 4, ed. by C. Henry Bradley and Barbara E. Hollenbach. 1992.

110. Windows on bilingualism, by Eugene Casad. 1992.

109. Switch reference in Koasati discourse, by David Rising. 1992.

108. Phonological studies in four languages of Maluku, ed. by Donald A. Burquest and Wyn D. Laidig. 1992.

107. Language in context: Essays for Robert E. Longacre, ed. by Shin Ja J. Hwang and William R. Merrifield. 1992.

106. Tepetotutla Chinantec syntax: Studies in Chinantec languages 5, by David Westley. 1991.

105. Studies in the syntax of Mixtecan languages 3, ed. by C. Henry Bradley and Barbara E. Hollenbach. 1991.

104. Sentence repetition testing for studies of community bilingualism, by Carla F. Radloff. 1991.

103. An autosegmental approach to Shilluk phonology, by Leoma G. Gilley. 1992.

102. Tone in five languages of Cameroon, ed. by Stephen C. Anderson. 1991.

101. Barasano syntax: Studies in the languages of Colombia 2, by Wendell Jones and Paula Jones. 1991.

100. A reference grammar of Southeastern Tepehuan, by Thomas L. Willett. 1991.

99. Tense and aspect in eight languages of Cameroon, ed. by Stephen C. Anderson and Bernard Comrie. 1991.

98. The structure of Thai narrative, by Somsonge Burusphat. 1991.

97. Can literacy lead to development? A case study in literacy, adult education, and economic development in India, by Uwe Gustafsson. 1991.

96. Survey on a shoestring: A manual for small-scale language surveys, by Frank Blair. 1990.

95. Syllables, tone, and verb paradigms: Studies in Chinantec languages 4, ed. by William R. Merrifield and Calvin R. Rensch. 1990.

94. Ika syntax: Studies in the languages of Colombia 1, by Paul S. Frank. 1990.

93. Development and diversity: Language variation across time and space (A Festschrift for Charles-James N. Bailey), ed. by Jerold A. Edmondson, Crawford Feagin, and Peter Mühlhäusler. 1990.

92. Comanche dictionary and grammar, ed. by Lila W. Robinson and James Armagost. 1990.

91. Language maintenance in Melanesia: Sociolinguistics and social networks in New Caledonia, by Stephen J. Schooling. 1990.

90. Studies in the syntax of Mixtecan languages 2, ed. by C. Henry Bradley and Barbara E. Hollenbach. 1990.

89. Comaltepec Chinantec syntax: Studies in Chinantec languages 3, by Judi Lynn Anderson. 1989.

88. Lealao Chinantec syntax: Studies in Chinantec languages 2, by James E. Rupp. 1989.

87. An etymological dictionary of the Chinantec languages: Studies in Chinantec languages 1, by Calvin R. Rensch. 1989.

86. Comparative Kadai: Linguistic studies beyond Tai, ed. by Jerold A. Edmondson and David B. Solnit. 1988.

85. The verbal piece in Ebira, by John R. Adive. 1989.

84. Insights into Tagalog: Reduplication, infixation, and stress from nonlinear phonology, by Koleen M. French. 1988.

83. **Studies in the syntax of Mixtecan languages 1,** ed. by C. Henry Bradley and Barbara E. Hollenbach. 1988.

82. **Dinka vowel system,** by Job Malou. 1988.

81. **Aspects of Western Subanon formal speech,** by William C. Hall. 1987.

80. **Current trends and issues in Hispanic linguistics,** ed. by Lenard Studerus. 1987.

79. **Modes in Dényá discourse,** by Samson Negbo Abangma. 1987.

78. **Tense/aspect and the development of auxiliaries in Kru languages,** by Lynelle Marchese. 1986.

77. **Discourse features of Korean narration,** by Shin Ja Joo Hwang. 1987.

76. **Hixkaryana and linguistic typology,** by Desmond C. Derbyshire. 1985.

75. **Sentence initial devices,** ed. by Joseph E. Grimes. 1986.

74. **English phonetic transcription,** by Charles-James N. Bailey. 1985.

73. **Pragmatics in non-Western perspective,** ed. by George Huttar and Kenneth J. Gregerson. 1986.

72. **Senoufo phonology, discourse to syllable (a prosodic approach),** by Elizabeth Mills. 1984.

71. **Workbook for historical linguistics,** by Winfred P. Lehmann. 1984.

70. **Babine & Carrier phonology: A historically oriented study,** by Gillian L. Story. 1984.

69. **Affix positions and cooccurrences: The PARADIGM program,** by Joseph E. Grimes. 1983.

68. **Syntactic change and syntactic reconstruction: A tagmemic approach,** by John R. Costello. 1983.

67. **Pragmatic aspects of English text structure,** by Larry B. Jones. 1983.

66. **Phonology and morphology of Axininca Campa,** by David L. Payne. 1981.

65. **A generative grammar of Afar,** by Loren F. Bliese. 1981.

64. **A framework for discourse analysis,** by Wilbur N. Pickering. 1980.

63. **Discourse grammar in Gaªdang,** by Michael R. Walrod. 1979.

62. **Nung grammar,** by Janice E. Saul and Nancy F. Wilson. 1980.

61. **Predicate and argument in Rengao grammar,** by Kenneth J. Gregerson. 1979.

60. **A grammatical description of the Engenni language,** by Elaine Thomas. 1978.

59. **The functions of reported speech in discourse,** by Mildred L. Larson. 1978.

58.2. **Discourse studies in Mesoamerican languages 2: Texts,** ed. by Linda K. Jones. 1979.

58.1. **Discourse studies in Mesoamerican languages 1: Discussion,** ed. by Linda K. Jones. 1979.

57. **The deep structure of the sentence in Sara-Ngambay dialogues, including a description of phrase, clause, and paragraph,** by James Edward Thayer. 1978.

56.4. **Southern Uto-Aztecan grammatical sketches: Studies in Uto-Aztecan grammar 4,** ed. by Ronald W. Langacker. 1984.

56.3. **Uto-Aztecan grammatical sketches: Studies in Uto-Aztecan grammar 3,** ed. by Ronald W. Langacker. 1982.

56.2. **Modern Aztec grammatical sketches: Studies in Uto-Aztecan grammar 2,** ed. by Ronald W. Langacker. 1979.

56.1. **An overview of Uto-Aztecan grammar: Studies in Uto-Aztecan grammar 1,** by Ronald W. Langacker. 1977.

55. **Two studies in Middle American comparative linguistics,** by David Oltrogge and Calvin R. Rensch. 1977.

54. **Studies in Otomanguean phonology,** ed. by William R. Merrifield. 1977.

53. **Grammatical analysis,** by Kenneth L. Pike and Evelyn G. Pike. 1977.

52.3. **Discourse grammar: Studies in indigenous languages of Colombia, Panama, and Ecuador 3,** ed. by Robert E. Longacre and Frances Woods. 1977.

52.2. **Discourse grammar: Studies in indigenous languages of Colombia, Panama, and Ecuador 2,** ed. by Robert E. Longacre and Frances Woods. 1977.

52.1. **Discourse grammar: Studies in indigenous languages of Colombia, Panama, and Ecuador 1,** ed. by Robert E. Longacre and Frances Woods. 1976.

51. **Papers on discourse,** ed. by Joseph E. Grimes. 1978.

For further information or a full listing of SIL publications contact:

International Academic Bookstore
Summer Institute of Linguistics
7500 W. Camp Wisdom Road
Dallas, TX 75236-5699

Voice: 972-708-7404
Fax: 972-708-7433
Email: academic.books@sil.org
Internet: http://www.sil.org